"Unsuitable" Books

ALSO BY CAREN J. TOWN

*The New Southern Girl: Female Adolescence
in the Works of 12 Women Authors* (McFarland, 2004)

"Unsuitable" Books
Young Adult Fiction and Censorship

CAREN J. TOWN

McFarland & Company, Inc., Publishers
Jefferson, North Carolina

LIBRARY OF CONGRESS CATALOGUING-IN-PUBLICATION DATA

Town, Caren J., 1957–
 "Unsuitable" books : young adult fiction and censorship / Caren J. Town.
     p.   cm.
 Includes bibliographical references and index.

 ISBN 978-0-7864-7419-6 (softcover : acid free paper) ∞
 ISBN 978-1-4766-1682-7 (ebook)

 1. Challenged books—United States. 2. Young adult fiction, American—Censorship. 3. Young adults libraries—Censorship—United States. 4. School libraries—Censorship—United States. 5. Teenagers—Books and reading—United States. I. Title.
 Z1019.T69 2014
 098'.10973—dc23   2014022562

BRITISH LIBRARY CATALOGUING DATA ARE AVAILABLE

© 2014 Caren J. Town. All rights reserved

No part of this book may be reproduced or transmitted in any form or by any means, electronic or mechanical, including photocopying or recording, or by any information storage and retrieval system, without permission in writing from the publisher.

Cover images © iStock/Thinkstock

Printed in the United States of America

McFarland & Company, Inc., Publishers
 Box 611, Jefferson, North Carolina 28640
 www.mcfarlandpub.com

To the memory of
Frank Robert "Rickey" Black (1951–2009).
I do know how lucky I am.

Table of Contents

Acknowledgments — ix
Preface — 1

One. Dangerous Words: Censorship in the Public Schools — 5

Two. "Someone should tell them": S. E. Hinton's *The Outsiders* (1967) — 15

Three. The Great Adventure: Judy Blume's Resilient Young Narrators (1970–1981) — 24

Four. "When fear seizes": Jean Craighead George's *Julie of the Wolves* (1972) — 38

Five. Censorship 70s Style: Robert Cormier's *The Chocolate War* (1974) — 47

Six. "No clouds of glory": Katherine Paterson's Prodigal Children (1977–1980) — 57

Seven. Chris Crutcher's Painful Honesty (1983–2001) — 80

Eight. "A stronger weapon": Cassie Logan on *The Road to Memphis* (1990) — 100

Nine. "Simple moments of exquisite happiness": Lois Lowry's *The Giver* (1993) — 115

Ten. "Don't you two be strangers!" M.E. Kerr's *Deliver Us from Evie* (1994) — 125

Eleven. "Be the tree": Trauma, Recovery and Voice in Laurie Halse Anderson's *Speak* (1999) — 138

Twelve. "A beautiful and ugly thing": Sherman Alexie's *Absolutely True Diary* (2007) — 150

Table of Contents

Conclusion—Challenges Ahead   167
Chapter Notes   173
Bibliography   179
Index   189

Acknowledgments

I owe a profound debt of gratitude to Georgia Southern University, which has been my intellectual home for almost thirty years now and which has given me concrete support in the form of an academic leave to write this book and emotional support in the form of a job that I have loved since I first stepped into a classroom in graduate school. In particular, I want to express my heartfelt thanks to my boss, David Dudley, who has been in my corner through thick and thin (and there were many times that were very thin indeed). I also want to thank my students, who have challenged me over the years to think hard about adolescent literature and the role that teachers play in making this work available and championing it in the face of numerous obstacles. I also want to praise librarians—both those I count as friends and those I don't even know—for their front-line defense of the First Amendment. You are my heroes. On a personal note, I'd like to thank my husband, Patrick J. Perkins, for all the grocery shopping, yard work, meals, proofreading, patient listening, and kisses, which made the final stages of this book possible, and even pleasurable.

Preface

This study should help give teachers and media specialists some of the ammunition they need in the fight against censorship, both by focusing on young adult (YA) books that have frequently been challenged and by offering theoretical and critical justifications for their value. The first chapter establishes the legal background to censorship cases in libraries and public schools and suggests ways in which teachers and community members can effectively respond to book challenges. The subsequent chapters are organized in rough chronological order (although several of the chapters treat more than one work by the same author, which complicates the timeline a bit). The organization is simply convenient; I don't attempt to show chronological changes in either themes or subject matter nor, for that matter, changes in the censorship battle.

Although writers are taking even more chances with language and subject matter since the 1960s, not much has changed, unfortunately, in the arena of book challenges. Would-be censors challenge YA books today for much the same reasons they challenged them four decades ago: "adult" themes/subjects (such as death, infidelity, and sexuality), language they consider to be inappropriate especially for middle grades (and sometimes even high school) students, and questioning of religion or authority figures (such as parents, teachers, or school administrators). Sadly, book banners have about the same rate of success as they have had in previous decades.

After the legal and historical groundwork has been laid, the second chapter concentrates on a relatively early and frequently challenged YA book, S.E. Hinton's *The Outsiders*, which appeared in 1967. Chapter Three deals with perennially challenged (and wildly popular) novels of Judy Blume, starting with her first work for young adults, *Are You There God? It's Me, Margaret* (1970), and continuing through *Tiger Eyes* (1981). Chapter Four focuses on Jean Craighead George's *Julie of the Wolves*

(1972), which won her the Newbery Award[1] and, thirty years after its publication, is still in the top 100 challenged books for 2000–2007. Robert Cormier's *The Chocolate War*, which was number two on the American Library Association's (ALA's) list of most frequently challenged books of 2007 (and which has made the list of challenged books nearly every year since its publication in 1974), is the subject of Chapter Five. Katherine Paterson's long career as a writer for children and young adults—and in particular her novels *Bridge to Terabithia* (1977), *The Great Gilly Hopkins* (1978), and *Jacob Have I Loved* (1980)—makes up Chapter Six.

Moving on to the 1980s and 90s, Chris Crutcher's controversial novels are the subject of Chapter Seven, beginning with his first YA novel, *Running Loose* (1983). Crutcher is nearly always included on any list of banned books; *Athletic Shorts* (1991), his collection of short stories, and his novels, *Staying Fat for Sarah Byrnes* (1993), *Ironman* (1995), and *Whale Talk* (2001) all made the ALA's 2000–2007 list of challenged books. Chapter Eight concentrates on the feisty (and hence controversial) female main character, Cassie Logan, whose story begins in Mildred Taylor's *Roll of Thunder, Hear My Cry* (1976) and ends (so far, at least) with *The Road to Memphis* (1990). Lois Lowry's Newbery Award–winning *The Giver*, a perennial favorite on challenged books lists since its publication in 1993, is the focus of Chapter Nine, and M.E. Kerr's *Deliver Us from Evie* (1994), a story about a young lesbian's first love, is discussed in Chapter Ten. Chapter Eleven concentrates on Laurie Anderson's *Speak* (1999), which also made the 2000–2007 list of challenged books, in large part because of its subject matter (date rape). Bringing the book discussion to a close, Chapter Twelve focuses on Sherman Alexie's 2007 novel *The Absolutely True Diary of a Part-Time Indian*, which has been shocking adults and delighting young readers since it came out. The conclusion examines the possible ideological bases underlying many of these book challenges and considers what the future holds for writers and readers.

Of course this is by no means an exhaustive survey of the wonderful and controversial works for young adults. Harry Potter and his friends at Hogwarts have risen to the top of the list of challenged books every year since the publication of *The Sorcerer's Stone* in 1998, but I have decided to limit the focus to realistic novels (except perhaps for Lowry's dystopian vision), and so I have also not included the always-controversial Phillip

Pullman. In addition, I have not chosen "adult" titles that frequently make banned books lists, such as Maya Angelou's *I Know Why the Caged Bird Sings*, Mark Twain's *The Adventures of Huckleberry Finn*, John Steinbeck's *Of Mice and Men*, Alice Walker's *The Color Purple*, and Harper Lee's *To Kill a Mockingbird*, among many, many others. These books, it seems to me, offer a more ready defense on the basis of established literary reputation than the young adult novels discussed here and are (these days, at least) rarely removed from classrooms and libraries. The purpose of this study is to provide educators with the ammunition to argue for works with less obvious (but still very much present) artistic and thematic merit.

So, then, these are my challenging and challenged authors. Their novels tackle racism, sexuality, religion, abuse (among the many subjects they treat), and they are frequently discomfiting, sometimes shocking, and often profane. More importantly, they are *good* books, although in an aesthetic and ethical, if not in a conventionally moral sense, and they are worth reading and teaching. These authors' novels teach kids about value of perseverance, tolerance, kindness, generosity, honesty, and stubbornness. They allow young people of all races, religions, and sexualities to experience love and acceptance. They paint an honest picture of the difficulties and degradations and joys young adults actually experience in their lives. Most importantly, they tell the truth. As Sheila Schwartz says in *Teaching Adolescent Literature*, "Good literature tells the truth, mainly. Bad adolescent literature pretends to tell the truth but confuses sentimentality with sentiment, panders to the cheap triumph, and sacrifices the universal for the topical" (11). Above all, these books tell the truth. I think I have chosen well, and I hope that the discussions that follow will provide more detailed justification for their value. Ultimately, though, it will be up to those who teach these books to show their students, their parents, and their neighbors *why* they are teaching them. I give this book to them as ammunition in that fight.

CHAPTER ONE

Dangerous Words
Censorship in the Public Schools

> We cannot protect our children from this world, which is a scary place. The only thing we can do is help them develop an inner strength to meet the inevitable challenges they will face.—YA author Katherine Paterson, Foerstel interview, 168–9

> The most effective antidote to the poison of mindless orthodoxy is ready access to a broad sweep of ideas and philosophies.—Judge Joseph L. Tauro, qtd. in Foerstel, 84

To begin thinking about book censorship, it is important to visualize the participants in a representative book challenge. First, picture a new ninth-grade language arts teacher, fresh out of college, filled with new ideas and inspired by the large number and wide variety of books available today for young adults, who assigns his class a novel by, say, Chris Crutcher. Students appear to like the book, class discussions are lively, and the teacher is certain that he is teaching them about reading, interpretation, and argument. Best of all, students actually seem to be *enjoying* themselves. Then the principal calls the teacher into his office, closes the door, and tells him there's been a complaint by one of the parents.

Now imagine that parent, trying to teach her daughter by precept and example how to live what she considers to be a good and honest life. Her child has just started high school, and she is worried about the wider range of influences—both good and bad—on her. She's tried to keep her as innocent as possible in today's world, limiting television and movie access, monitoring computer time, paying attention to her friends. One day, that daughter comes home with a book she's reading for class, and the mother casually picks it up and glances at a couple of pages. What she sees concerns her—profanity, lack of respect for authority figures, explicit sexuality—and she picks up the phone to call the principal.

Envision the principal of that high school. She's spent all day managing crises—fights in the lunch room, a possible teachers' strike, mold in the gym—and she is exhausted. In general, she is happy with her teachers; they are hardworking, innovative, committed to the welfare of the students, and she believes in letting them have as much freedom in the classroom as possible. Still, her salary is paid by the taxpayers of her community, and she must be sensitive to their concerns. School is nearly over for the day when the phone rings.

These are some of the main actors in a book challenge—others include the student's classmates, their extended families (grandparents often raise challenges), unrelated community members, school boards, and, if things go very badly, the courts. Usually by the time a book challenge reaches the legal system, a number of things have gone wrong: most importantly, those concerned about book content feel that their positions haven't been heard or respected, and/or those providing the books haven't provided adequate or widely-accessible rationales for their choices. Each side believes itself to be right: they are defending classroom, school, or school board autonomy, intellectual freedom, community values, and, ultimately, the Constitution. The history of the case law on book challenges is complex: in some cases the courts have ruled that school boards have the right to enforce community standards by removing books from classrooms and libraries; in others, that local officials cannot remove them strictly on the basis of particular religious values. Teachers and librarians have responded to this somewhat murky legal climate in a number of ways, from strenuously resisting book challenges, to trying to accommodate community concerns without removing books, to self-censoring even the most unlikely (and inoffensive) works out of fear for their jobs.

In this climate, those on the front lines defending books (and their right to provide them to young people) are usually teachers and school librarians, and therefore it is vital that they have clear, written, public justifications for the books in their classrooms and libraries. It is equally important that they are certain of the literary, social, and moral value of the works they teach and provide to children. Teachers and librarians must always ask why they should purchase or teach a particular novel, short story, play, or poem. They should also consider the bigger question:

One. Dangerous Words

Why teach literature at all or make it available in school libraries, especially when parents, administrators, and school boards seem determined to challenge any book (and any teacher) that raises "controversial" issues?

Through a close look at a number of challenged books and authors, this study may help educators find some answers to these questions. Certainly, the authors discussed here raise these issues through their frank and open treatment of subjects that are often painful and upsetting, and they do so in language that is sometimes irreverent and frequently profane. They challenge teachers, librarians, and students to look closely at difficult issues, to confront racism, sexism, and homophobia, to face up to religious fanaticism, to accept the realities of adolescent sexuality and profanity, and, most importantly, to consider the consequences of *not* taking up such issues.

As James Davis says in his article on censorship and the young adult novel, "What is *not censorable*? Probably almost nothing. Certainly all of the plots themes, characters, values, and words of which young adult literature is made are possibly objectionable to someone at some time for some reason" (170). By its very nature, young adult literature is controversial; that is, if it looks at the complex (and frequently troubled) lives of young people honestly. Joan DelFattore, in her landmark book on censorship, says that literature is easier to challenge than scientific concepts like evolution (problematic, unfortunately, in its own way) because "the ideas it contains are often ambiguous or abstract, opening the door to a wide range of justifications for declaring particular literary works unsuitable for certain age groups" (100). The multitude of possibilities for interpretation and wide variety of responses invoked by literature are, of course, its greatest asset, while at the same time creating its greatest vulnerability to censorship.

Most of the books chosen for this study—as well far too many others—have appeared on the American Library Association's list of frequently challenged books, and the problems raised by book challenges show no sign of diminishing. Probably from now on, certain books will be raising the eyebrows of parents, causing trouble for teachers, librarians, administrators, and school boards and, mostly likely, becoming the subject of court cases. The legal aspect is of concern because, as DelFattore shows, an examination of the court record shows that "no matter how little sense a school board's decision seems to make, the board has the authority to determine curriculum unless protesters can prove the establishment of a religious or political orthodoxy" (118). In other words, as long as the religious or political biases of school boards aren't transparently obvious, they will continue to succeed, with the apparent permission of the court system, in removing, banning, or restricting access to literary works that fail to meet their standards.

This potential for book challenges should raise concerns, but it should not cause language arts teachers and librarians in middle and high schools to give up hope. Books potentially open to challenges *need* to be taught, studied by middle and high school students, made available in school libraries, and discussed by English departments, principals, school boards, families, and communities. The truth is that these books are beneficial to students (and their teachers and parents), and that with a clear sense of mission and well-thought-out rationales, teachers and librarians can defend, teach, and make these novels available to young people.

It does take some careful thought and preparation, though. As the authors of *Teaching Literature to Adolescents* say, "The Literature classroom is a delicate ecosystem of texts, teaching strategies, human circumstances, choice, and constraint" (241). Within this "ecosystem," they continue, teachers should consider how they can make their English classrooms "a site of transformation" (244). Teachers can change how students view the world, but only if they are willing to stand up to the censors, who often seem determined to keep any challenging ideas and controversial topics off the radar of young people.

Jim Burke, award-winning high school English teacher and author of *The English Teacher's Companion*, expresses the moral imperative well:

> [I]t is the discussion of what it is right and wrong, the growth of moral intelligence that counts. We cannot make our students act "better," but we can put them at the center of such essential conversations and, by allowing students to occupy the lives of others—through literature—help them develop the habit of asking themselves such questions [qtd. in Beach 244].

It is an obligation of teachers to engage students in "essential conversations" about big issues—life, love, betrayal, sexuality, religion, hatred—all subjects that literature takes as its bread and butter. They are not obligated (and indeed shouldn't) indoctrinate students in particular political or religious dogmas but instead teach them how to ask the right sort of questions about those subjects. To do otherwise is to inadequately prepare them for the world they are about to enter.

One. Dangerous Words

Equally important, they should trust their students with these ideas and questions. As the National Council of Teachers of English (NCTE) says in their landmark "The Students' Right to Read":

> The right of any individual not just to read but to read whatever he or she wants to read is basic to a democratic society. This right is based on an assumption that the educated possess judgment and understanding and can be trusted with the determination of their own actions. In effect, the reader is freed from the bonds of chance [qtd. in Beach 249].

Educated people, *even* adolescents, they assert, "can be trusted with the determination of their own actions." In other words, young people, who are in the process of becoming educated citizens of a democracy, should have the freedom to read what they choose. They should not be subject to the "bonds of chance" or the whims of a parent, a teacher, a principal, or an outraged member of the community. In fact, as Schwartz says, "exposure to a problem through literature enables the reader to express himself in relation to the literature and thus to escape possible embarrassment and vulnerability" (9). The more students know about how others have handled difficult issues, Schwartz implies, the better able they will be able to handle them themselves.

It is also important to emphasize that adolescents are experiencing all of the things—and more—that these works describe; teachers do kids a valuable service when they validate their experiences, strengthen their confidence, and give them a sense of belonging to a larger human community. James Davis strongly suggests this: "[P]ublic schools and libraries in a free society have an obligation not only to provide," he says, "but also to encourage such diversity of opinions and points of view, thereby developing what tests show contemporary students lack so much—critical thinking ability" (171). Not only can students feel their particular burdens shared when they read about teens like themselves, they can also learn to deal with the inherent diversity of a complex society and learn to evaluate critically their own (and others') judgments.

It may be an obligation as well to create inclusive and tolerant English classrooms. As Richard Beach says, "A fundamental responsibility in creating an ethical classroom is selecting texts that represent this vast and rich heritage [in the United States] for all students regardless of the cultural, ethnic, and racial makeup of the schools in which we teach" (248). Contemporary classrooms have become increasingly diverse, with students of different races, ethnicities, religious (or non-religious) perspectives, and sexual orientations, and therefore teachers must, he says, "consider the cost of not confronting such issues [racism, sexism, and homophobia] head-on as part of our teaching" (250). To put it another way, it may be an "ethical responsibility to bring issues of hatred and bias to the foreground of [the] curriculum so that no student is ever forced to suffer for being outside the norm of social stereotypes" (251). Novels, plays, poems, and short stories about a wide range of people and issues can help teachers help students to do this.

However, defending students' rights to read and to be exposed to a variety of ideas and positions is no easy task. Challenges arise frequently, in part because, as John Bushman and Kay Haas say, "many parents, for whatever reason, are often frustrated about their relationships with the schools.... As a result, they strike out at something very specific—what is taught in the classroom, especially if they believe that it is incongruous with their values" (249). When parents don't feel they are being heard by teachers or politicians (either at the local or national level) when it comes to school curriculum, they frequently take it out on the books taught in classrooms and found in libraries.

Teachers often self-censor as well, avoiding books that raise controversial subjects and therefore might be subject to challenges. Davis reports that "[m]any teachers, librarians, and administrators are so intimidated by a single call or the fear of a single complaint that materials are never ordered or are removed after any criticism, even in a nearby school" (171). He notes that this "is the most unfortunate kind of censorship, done, not under pressure, but in fear that the pressure might come" (172). The inherent isolation of the classroom teacher is also a contributing factor. In "The Ripple Effect of Censorship," Elizabeth Noll says that "a significant difference in the teachers' responses to the threat of censorship lies in the extent to which they did or did not involve others—colleagues, administrators, parents, and students—in their decisions" (62). Clearly, there is a need for teachers and administrators to find common ground in talking about book challenges, as a single teacher may find it very difficult to stand up to them.

Even though teachers and administrators often self-censor, fearing job losses or lawsuits, the case law concerning school book challenges is complicated and inconclusive. As Herbert Foerstel points out in his *Banned in the USA*, "the overwhelming majority of book banning is local, not federal" (xxv), but the issues have often been brought to the federal courts. It is important to note, though, that "most of the case law on such book banning [in public schools] does not deal directly with books at all, concentrating more generally on the authority of school officials to control the curriculum and the libraries as part of the process of inculcating and socializing students" (Foerstel 73). The bottom line, Foerstel says, is that "the courts have usually held that a student's right to receive information is subject to a school board's authority to determine the curriculum, including the library's collections" (81). The debate centers most often on the autonomy of local school boards to make community-appropriate decisions.[1]

Although the courts take the First Amendment very seriously, they also reserve the right of local schools and communities to oversee textbook and library selection. As Foerstel puts it, landmark cases have "established that teachers, principals, and school boards may take action within the school's educational mission that might otherwise be unconstitutional" (98). What this means, then, is that "the best defense against book banning ... [is] enlightened school boards and supportive courts" (108). Since school boards and administrations do have the right to limit students' access to reading material, provided they can claim legitimate educational reasons, these groups must be educated about the very books they want to censor.

Thus it falls to educators to be their own best advocates for literature. Teachers and librarians must know why they are teaching or providing certain books, as well as what their literary and educational values are, and they must be able to articulate those values in their schools and in public. Written rationales, especially for potentially controversial books, are important, as are written permissions from parents, but, most importantly, educators must be able to give voice to these books and the values that they teach. Works that are honest about the lives of adolescents are likely to have words and concepts that may shock some parents (although it isn't likely that most students would even be *surprised*). With that in mind, educators have to be able to explain why these works—for all their mature and controversial subject matter—are worth teaching and reading. As Seventh District Judge Richard Posner said in *American Machine Association et al. v. Teri Kendrick et al.* (2001), "People are unlikely to become well-functioning, independent-minded adults and responsible citizens if they are raised in an intellectual bubble" (qtd. in Doyle 203). Teachers have an obligation to burst the intellectual bubble created by (usually) well-intentioned parents and communities and, more importantly, to offer worthwhile and satisfying reading material to fill the vacuum.

They also need to find innovative approaches to teaching and think critically about the existing curriculum. Arthur N. Applebee, who has been studying high school curricula for more than 20 years, noted in 1989 that two decades of strategies to broaden the curriculum haven't worked:

> The factors that shape the curriculum have been too strong to be offset by the consciousness-raising and resource development activities that have taken place so far. New strategies are obviously needed, perhaps strategies that focus on asking teachers to read and discuss specific titles during preservice coursework, inservice workshops, and department discussion groups, so that teachers can gain the familiarity with alternative texts that they now have with the texts that dominate the lists [18].

Teachers needed to break out of old patterns and become familiar with new (and perhaps more challenging) works. When he looked at high school curricula again in 1993, however, Applebee noted that "the overall impression of literature instruction that emerges from the present series of studies is one less of confusion than of complacency. During the past two decades, goals for and approaches to the teaching of literature have been taken for granted rather than closely examined" (192). He continues: "The most prevalent approach at present seems to be treating the curriculum as a kind of mosaic, but it is a mosaic within which works from alternative traditions continue to be poorly integrated rather than well-assimilated into an overall pattern" (193). Between 1989 and 1993, teachers were teaching a more diverse selection of literary works, but with no comprehensive program for teaching them. Appleby concluded that

> what is lacking is a well-articulated overall theory of the teaching and learning of literature, one that will give a degree of order and coherence to the daily decisions that teachers make about what and how to teach. Such a theory is needed to place the various critical traditions into perspective, highlighting the ways in which they can usefully complement one another in the classroom, as well as the ways they are contradictory [202].

Teachers need to operate in less of a vacuum; they need to develop coherent theoretical justifications for the works they choose to enhance curricula and render it more diverse. Almost two decades later, unfortunately, such a comprehensive theory remains unarticulated.

One. Dangerous Words

Curricular reform is part of the picture, but in the meantime, teachers and administrators, especially, need to have plans in place to respond effectively to would-be censors. Davis says:

> Problems tend to be resolved much more quickly and effectively when all involved—parents, students, teachers, administrators—are aware of district policies and procedures and can work within a complaint process which is already in place [176].

If policies concerning book challenges exist at the district level (and often they don't), teachers and others involved need to be aware of and work within that process. Most importantly, he continues,

> in the initial selection of materials, a decision to use a work needs to be justified and supported.... Taking the time and making the effort to prepare effective rationales allows teachers not only to preclude confrontation but also to become prepared to discuss and defend a book selection intelligently [177].

Rationales are important to the teacher in a book challenge, certainly, but by providing parents with information about the reasons why a book was chosen, they can *prevent* challenges from happening in the first place.

Another option is teaching about censorship directly. "By exposing the issue to scrutiny," Davis says, "teachers can help student learn why books are censored, by whom, and how it affects them and their communities" (177–78). Most importantly, Davis says, "as we prepare for the fight, we need to remember that many of the books that appear on censors' lists affirm life. They are not immoral, and thus teachers and librarians must challenge anyone who interferes with our right to teach them or with readers' right to read them" (179). Throughout the profession, language arts teachers need to be more articulate about why they love the books they love, what they offer to students, what important lessons they teach students about the world.

Returning to the original example, one could imagine a principal responding to that worried parent by telling her that the school has both book review and book challenge policies in place and that, if she so desires, a committee can be formed of parents, teachers, students, and administrators to evaluate the book and decide if can continue to be used in the classroom. This allows all stake holders in the debate to be heard and, one would hope, would end the matter there (with the book returned to the classroom, ideally). If not, the teacher could produce her already-written justification of the book to both the parent and, if need be, to the school board. This is usually brings the conflict to a close, or at least allows enough conversation that a satisfactory compromise can be reached. Written policies and justifications go a long way toward nipping potential censorship challenges in the bud, but, most importantly, administrators must have confidence in their teachers and teachers must have confidence in the books—and the students—they teach. This book should help boost that confidence, and, ideally, prevent more censorships cases ending up in the courtroom and allow more novels such as these to be taught. Now it's time to get to the novels, which is always the best part.

CHAPTER TWO

"Someone should tell them"
S. E. Hinton's The Outsiders *(1967)*

> [With *The Outsiders*] the door was opened for all the honest, fresh, stylistically daring, startling, terrifying, and wonderful fiction that has been our legacy ever since—Patty Campbell, 183

The Outsiders (1967) has recently been reissued in a 40th anniversary edition, which is certainly testimony to its ongoing salability, and perhaps to its contemporary relevance. Critic Frank Tribunella points out that the 2001 *Publisher's Weekly* ranked the novel "second in its list of all-time bestselling children's paperbacks, behind only E.B. White's *Charlotte's Web*" (87), and Jay Daly calls it "the most successful, and the most emulated, young adult book of all time" (preface). The story of social class, gang violence, and family loyalty also remains (although less so in recent years) a subject of controversy. Coming in at number 43 on the ALA's Most Frequently Challenged Books list for 1990–1999, it failed to make the 2000–2009 list. It is possible that the relatively tame violence and even milder language of the novel accounts for its disappearance, but its near-classic status may also explain why censors have turned their attentions elsewhere.[1] Still, the novel retains the capacity to speak to young adults about masculinity, identity, and the economic forces that drive our society. It also continues to move them with its pathos, its idealism, and its dangerously attractive young heroes.

Writing in *Print* magazine, Rebecca Bengal notes that *The Outsiders* was a "model for how YA books were first packaged: as mass-market paperbacks" (NP), and the novel became an model for many adolescent novels to follow. Although there has been some debate about what constitutes the first young adult novel,[2] most critics and historians of the genre agree that *The Outsiders*' publication was a landmark event. Veteran YA librarian Patty Campbell said that although *The Outsiders* struck her "as melodramatic and crudely written" when it came out, she was nevertheless "glad to have a book that kids pounced on as relevant" (180). Much of what we take for granted in fiction today by writers such as David Levithan or Laurie Halse Anderson would not have been possible if the way had not been paved by Hinton and a little later, by Judy Blume. Interestingly, though, Daly says that although the book is often lauded as inaugurating the "New Realism" in young adult fiction, the reason the novel was (and remains) so popular with young readers is that it "captures so well the idealism of that time of life" (16). Indeed, there is much in this novel to encourage hope in the face of desperate conditions.

Although it is praised as a trail blazer, *The Outsiders* (as with most of the young adult novels in this study) has provoked a divided critical response. Readers, especially in the social sciences, applaud the novel's emphasis on the impact of economics on daily life and American youth culture. For example, in a recent essay on "justice consciousness," Sociologist Michelle Inderbitzin comments that Hinton's novel "was one of the first books that really made me consider the importance of social structure and how the environment shapes the choices of individuals" (361). Indeed, she implies that her choice of career was in part based on the awareness she gained from reading this novel. M. Pearlman reaffirms this in *Adolescence,* saying that this novel has much to teach students about the relationship between socioeconomic status and adolescent behavior.

Other critics damn with faint praise. Writing in *The Nation* in 1986, Michael Malone says Hinton's novels are less realism than "romances, mythologizing the tragic beauty of violent youth" (277). Although Daly would agree about the book's idealism, Malone sees it in a more negative light. Hinton's prose, he says, "can be a fervid, mawkish and ornate as any nineteenth-century romance" (277). He continues:

> The lyricism, the lack of novelistic detail, the static iconography of Hinton's books keep the clutter of creation from interfering with the sources of their obviously persistent appeal—their rapid actions (most violent) unfettered by the demands of a plot, their intense emotions (mostly heavy) and their clear-cut moral maps [277].

It seems harsh to say the "clutter of creation" is absent from *The Outsiders,* or that it is "unfettered by the demands of a plot." Still, Malone does admit grudgingly that Hinton's novels operate in a specific tradition: "Like the protagonists of all *Bildungsromans,* Hinton's leather-jacketed young Werthers are lyrical on the subject of their psychic aches and pains" (278). Unlike Blume's problem novels, he would have to admit, Hinton's works are clearly novels of development, showing "lyrical" characters who grow, painfully but determinedly. They do complain of "psychic aches and pains," but these can be seen as necessary to their growth.

The most sustained recent criticism of the novel comes from Eric Tribunella. In an article in *Children's Literature in Education,* he says, "[A]lthough it tantalizes audiences with the relatively rare acknowledgement of social class as a problem, the novel offers a safe and undisruptive palliative for class inequality and the endemic malaise of modernity" (88). The novel, he argues, presents complex problems while offering bland and ineffective solutions. Tribunella concludes that instead of offering a sustained critique, the novel engages in "a kind of slight of hand," and the solutions it offers (Ponyboy's growing awareness of the forces behind and the inevitability of class conflict as well as his decision to write about it) "cannot be seen as constituting adequate or successful responses." Therefore, the novel "is able to be listed safely on school reading lists without raising any serious flags about radical social reform or revolution" (95). I would argue, however, that Ponyboy's growing awareness and apparent refusal to engage in further violence is a more-than-adequate response to the events and circumstances of his difficult life.

As the novel opens, readers learn that Ponyboy lives with his brothers Sodapop and Darry, who both have dropped out of school and are now working to support the family, because their parents have been killed in a car accident. This is, of course, a fairly typical beginning to a young adult novel, the removal of one (or in this case both) of the parents to put the adolescent protagonist alone against his struggles. What makes this novel unique (especially for its time), is its emphasis on (literal and metaphoric) social class warfare. Ponyboy and his brothers live on the wrong side of the tracks and are "greasers" (working class kids) who are in a perpetual war with the "Socs"[3] (their wealthier counterparts). The greasers, depending on their temperaments, live either in a state of continual fear or anger, as the threats from the Socs are constant and often unexpected.

Out of his group of greasers, Ponyboy is the smart one, or at least the one who spends the most time in school and shows enthusiasm for learning. Their gang consists of the three brothers, Two-Bit (the jokester), Johnny (who has been beaten up and permanently traumatized by the Socs, goes on the run after killing a Soc in self defense, and dies trying to save children from a burning church), and Dallas or "Dally" (who is killed by police after a robbery). The gender imbalance is partially remedied by the amusingly-named Cherry Valance, a tough, smart Soc who is drawn to the greasers and tries to help them in their conflicts.

Interestingly, Tribunella says that the conflicts in the novel represent "a clash between conflicting models of youth—on the one hand a nineteenth century and Depression-era model of the child as a necessary economic contributor to the household, and on the other hand the new teenager of the mid-twentieth century whose primary job is going to school and spending money on youth culture" (89). Ponyboy and his brothers symbolize the earlier model; they work in garages, wear their hair long and greasy, sport blue jeans, and drive beaters that they have fixed up themselves. Cherry and her friends represent the later one; the boys wear madras shirts and English Leather cologne, drive Corvairs, and never seem to have much to do but start fights, drive around, and play on the football team. Interestingly, the Soc girls don't do much at all, other than flirt with boys (or resist their advances), and the greaser girls are nearly absent from the story, except for one who gets pregnant and has to leave town. Overall, Tribunella says, the novel represents "the tensions that emerge from overlapping models of youth shaped by economic trends" (90). The stakes are high; these tensions lead to conflict, and eventually to death.

It is true that the novel is concerned with the effect of economics on social conditions and behavior, but the novel begins by focusing on the physical appearance and mental state of Ponyboy, who is a the typical YA first-person narrator (with longer, greasier hair). As the novel opens, Ponyboy is emerging from a movie theater thinking only about "Paul Newman and a ride home." This leads him to wish he looked more like Newman, disparaging his "almost-red hair and greenish-gray eyes" and expressing satisfaction over his hairstyle (9). This attention to his appearance feminizes Ponyboy, while at the same time it defines the masculine model emulated by the greasers. This first description also sets him apart from his gang, though; because no one else likes movies as much as he does, he goes by himself (10). Ponyboy is an update on

Two. "Someone should tell them"

the classic hero of Westerns transplanted to a smallish Oklahoma town—a loner, with artistic leanings, dissatisfied with himself and his life (who also worries about his hair and the color of his eyes). Jay Daly comments in his book-length study of the author that Hinton calls herself a "character writer" who concentrates more on developing both her heroes and secondary characters than on the plot of her novels (18), and from the beginning the emphasis of the novel is on character description/motivation.

Although he defines himself within the context of his social group, Ponyboy does have a fairly clear sense of his place in his larger world. He recognizes early on that he and his fellow greasers can't win against the Socs (19), and he identifies with Pip in *Great Expectations*, "the way he felt marked lousy because he wasn't a gentleman or anything, and the way that girl kept looking down on him" (23). Attempting to figure out why the Socs hate his friends and family, he almost goes "to sleep over [his] homework trying to figure it out" (25). Ponyboy is alienated, puzzled, persecuted, and, most importantly, studious and literary. He is a character in his own story. Still, he insightfully remarks, "I lie to myself all the time. But I never believe me" (26). He may be identifying with fictional characters, both in books and on the screen, but he has enough self-awareness to know that what he is creating, in part, is a fantasy.

His encounters with Cherry Valance and her friend cause him to reflect on gender relations as well as masculine identity and social class. Unlike the boys in *The Chocolate War*, Ponyboy is concerned about the ways in which the greasers objectify women. He wonders why his group tries "to be nice to the girls we see once in a while, like cousins or the girls in class, but we still watch a nice girl go by on a street corner and say all kinds of lousy stuff about her" (34–5), and he is left with no answer. Although Daly perhaps rightly argues that Cherry's "cardboard" characterization is the novel's "major disappointment" (27), I believe she is useful in focusing the reader's attention on both class differences and basic human similarities. Even though Cherry tells Ponyboy that the greasers and Socs have different values, the greasers being more emotional and the Socs "cool to the point of not feeling anything" (46), he still sees that, even though it's "funny," the sunset they both see is the same (49). Daly says that sunsets are a good choice to emphasize this commonality, as they "suggest an unspoiled, untarnished closeness to life, to natural processes, that is a part of the birthright of everyone"

(30). Still, when Ponyboy considers whether Dally and Cherry could fall in love (they are flirting at the drive-in), he thinks that it would be a "miracle," as the "fight for self-preservation had hardened him beyond caring" (67). Girls and boys may see the same sunsets, but they can't fall in love across class boundaries.

When, after much persecution and anxiety, Johnny finally snaps and kills a Soc in a fight, Johnny and Ponyboy hide out in a church while they wait for their gang to help them and try to figure out what to do. Tribunella astutely points out that the abandoned (and later burned to the ground) church is symbolic. It suggests, he says, "the epochal decline of religion as an available and effective source of sanctuary or comfort in the modern age" (91). Unlike Blume's Margaret, who is anguished about her relationship with God, or Cormien's Jerry, who sees religion (or at least religious hypocrisy) as an antagonist, the outsiders in Hinton's novel are outside the influence of religion.

Instead, Ponyboy is going to put his faith in people—and in literature. In fact, while Johnny and Ponyboy hide out, they read *Gone with the Wind* and discuss Robert Frost's poem "Nothing Gold Can Stay," a work which will reappear later in the novel. During their time on the lam, Ponyboy realizes that his brothers and Two-Bit appeal to him because they "were like the heroes in the novels I read." Dally, on the other hand, "was so real he scared me" (84). Johnny remarks that he never "noticed colors and clouds and stuff until you kept reminding me about them." Given his limited experience with such responses, his final conclusion is that Ponyboy's family "sure is funny" (86). In comparison with the other greasers, and the Socs, for that matter, Ponyboy and his family are "funny," in that they care about family more than fighting.

Indeed, one of the major revelations in Ponyboy's life is that his older brother Darry, who has been quite harsh in his role as father figure, actually loves him. When he returns after the church fire (which lands Johnny in the hospital where he eventually dies), Ponyboy realizes that Darry cares for him "and because he cared he was trying too hard to make something of me" (106). He even comes to understand that Darry's "silent fear" was that he was going to lose another family member. This causes Ponyboy to think that although he had "taken the long way around," that he is "finally home" (107). Tribunella says that throughout the novel, the Curtis brothers "experience a sense of the increasingly inescapable force of law" (92), beginning with their justifiable fear that

Two. "Someone should tell them"

their family will be split up, with Ponyboy sent to foster care. The tensions between brothers, he says, are "are aggravated by the problem of guilt and state interference under the critical gaze of the law" (92). The novel, he argues, "documents the culmination of nearly a century of efforts on the part of the law to penetrate the domestic sphere on behalf of children and adolescents" (92). Much of the problem between Darry and Ponyboy arises from the anxiety Darry has about whether or not he will lose him to the state. Daly calls this recurring motif in Hinton's fiction the "Society of Orphans," which is "the world of children, bereft of adult guidance, girding themselves to go it alone" (28). Darry, certainly, has girded his loins to be the tough caretaker of his younger and more vulnerable brother.

After Ponyboy returns, the greasers and Socs have a large scale "rumble," although the pointlessness of their fighting is becoming clearer both to Ponyboy and even some of the Socs. In the lead up to the fight, Randy, whose friend was killed by Johnny, tells Ponyboy that he isn't going to fight, and that Ponyboy shouldn't either: "You can't win, even if you whip us. You'll still be where you were before—at the bottom. And we'll still be the lucky ones with all the breaks" (125). Ponyboy decides that the "Socs were just guys after all" (126). He also decides that he has learned "all the wrong things and seen "all the wrong sights" (130). He even begins to question his look and lifestyle, wondering why he should be proud of "his reputation for being a hood, and greasy hair" (140) and determines "there's no good reason for fighting, except for self-defense" (145).

In spite of his misgivings, Ponyboy and the others go on with the rumble. As he watches Darry square off with the leader of the Socs, Ponyboy thinks that the fight reminds of Jack London "where the wolf pack waits in silence for one or two members to go down in a fight. But it was different here. The moment either one swung a punch, the rumble would be on" (151). Once again, Ponyboy is seeing his life in the light of literature, although the young men aren't nearly as smart as the dogs, when it comes to fighting.

After the fight, Johnny (who has been in the hospital all this time) dies, telling Ponyboy to "stay gold" (157), reminding the reader of their earlier discussion of the poem. Daly says that the novel shifts the emphasis in Frost's poem from "gold" to "stay." He continues: "Rather than agree that Ponyboy's image of perfection cannot exist in this world, the

"Unsuitable" Books

book agrees only that it cannot stay here. By dying, Johnny stays gold in a way he could never have achieved in life" (34). This is an interesting perspective. Critics have thought the message was to Ponyboy—that he should "stay gold"—when actually it may be a final message that goodness, purity isn't possible in this world, although something else may suffice.

As if it's not bad enough that pitiful Johnny dies, Dally is shot by police after a robbery that appears to have been set up as a suicide. Ponyboy decides that Dally wasn't a hero, but he was "gallant" (179), much as Rhett Butler in *Gone with the Wind*. He is a scoundrel, but he stages a Romantic end for himself. Daly says that Dallas has all the necessary qualities for a hero, but because readers "can never be sure of him" he catches their attention throughout the novel (25). This may well be true; certainly Dally is the one unredeemable main character.

Ponyboy (and perhaps the others left alive) do have the possibility of growth and change however. Two-bit admonishes Ponyboy not to "get tough" and to recognize that he is different from the other greasers (179). Ponyboy appears to take this to heart. At the end of the novel, he has this epiphany:

> I could picture hundreds and hundreds of boys living on the wrong sides of cities, boys with black eyes who jumped at their own shadows. Hundreds of boys who may be watched sunsets and looked at stars and ached for something better. I could see boys going down under street lights because they were mean and trough and hated the world, and it was too late to tell them that there was still good in it, and they wouldn't believe you if you did. It was too vast a problem to be just a personal thing. There should be some help, someone should tell them before it was too late [187].

That "someone" will be Ponyboy. Because he can see his fellow greasers so clearly and recognizes that he can do something about their plight, he decides that he will write their story, in part to fulfill an English assignment he has missed while he was running from the law, but also to put the story of the greasers in perspective and to share what he has learned. As Pearlman says, "Ponyboy has learned that self-esteem doesn't have to be based only socio-economic status and that even greasers can be heroes" (NP). Because he now can see their heroic qualities, he can write a novel about them.

Tribunella, not surprisingly, takes a different approach. While writing his story "might help Ponyboy process his traumatic experiences and ground his emotional recovery," he says, "this individual catharsis does not itself address or intervene in the larger social processes at work to produce or sustain the problem of class inequality and alienation" (101). The conclusion, he argues, "involves the transformation of Ponyboy, but not the transformation of the system, as socialization involves transforming people, not social structures or processes" (99). I agree that transformation of society is a noble goal, but it may not be the goal of this *Bildungsroman*. The growing awareness of Ponyboy may be enough. In fact, once might argue that novels are not charged with changing the world (or the people who read them); all *The Outsiders* (and other novels like it) must do is paint a clear enough picture of a world and the people caught in it.

This novel, written by a young woman with considerable sensitivity for the concerns and the impulses of young men, crosses the gender divide handily, offering both pathos and action, introspection and impulse. Ponyboy starts out wishing he were more like Paul Newman (probably in *Cool Hand Luke*) and realizing he's more like Robert Frost or Pip—and that Dally is more like Rhett Butler. Although he couldn't prevent the deaths of Dally or Johnny, it seems that the catharsis of telling his story (and allowing his readers to share in that experience) might be his (and our) best way to "stay gold."

Although *The Outsiders* is now more than 45 years old and clearly entering middle age, it still has the potential to speak to young adults. It may not challenge parents and school administrators as much as it used to (or as it ever did, as some critics suggest), but it still encourages young men and women to "stay gold"—to look beyond social status, and to wonder if sunsets and poetry aren't really better than gang warfare. This message, unfortunately (given the gang violence many teens experience today), has considerable contemporary relevance. Like many of the other works in this study, it may not change the world for every teenager, but it may cause a few to take a moment to reflect before they act—to notice the sunset, read a poem, write something in a journal rather than take out a gun.

CHAPTER THREE

The Great Adventure
Judy Blume's Resilient Young Narrators (1970–1981)

> To her I owe not only the intangible imprint that surely paints my own craft but something even more dear: my health, my self-respect, and my confidence in my own imagination and intelligence—Kenner, 124
>
> It's too hard to worry alone—Judy Blume, on *Blubber*

Author of 27 books for children, young adults, and adults, Judy Blume, who began her career in 1969, has been, to put it mildly, the subject of much conversation, both critical and laudatory. When the American Library Association's Booklist polled thousands of children in 1982 to determine the fifty most popular children's books, Judy Blume's were four out of the top five (Weidt 18). However, she also takes four places on the ALA's Top 100 Banned/Challenged Books for 2000–2009. Would-be censors attack her for her subject matter, language, and what they consider her "lack of moral tone" (Weidt 26), while literary critics sneer at her simplistic style and accuse her of promoting outdated and even damaging images of women. Defenders praise her honesty, her skill in manipulating the first-person narrative voice, her ability to articulate the concerns of young men and women, and what might be called her general warm fuzziness. These conflicting attitudes, which paint Blume as both ethical and prurient, novelist Megan McCafferty rather bluntly says, "are reinforced in the media, which depicts our nation's youth as being equally torn between public purity pledges and private rainbow parties" (9). Clearly, both Blume's fans and her detractors exemplify contemporary cultural tensions about young adults and their relationships to their bodies, their peers, and their parents.

Three. The Great Adventure

What often motivates adults to attempt to ban Blume's books (as well as those of the other writers in this study) is her refusal to provide easy answers to the complex moral questions facing young adults, her expectation that they come up with their own solutions (Weidt 27). As Pat Scales, author of *Teaching Banned Books*, says, "[Censors] are fearful of the educational system, because students who read learn to think. Thinkers learn to see. Those who see often question" (2). Blume's reluctance to preach discomfits censors, but it also forces her young readers to think, to see, and to question.

While they wouldn't try to remove Blume's novels from library shelves, certain literary critics would like to see her removed from the young adult literary canon. These writers are critical of her subject matter, her characterization, and her settings. R. A. Seigel, for example, complains in *The Lion and the Unicorn* about Blume's representation of parents as "usually well-meaning but ineffectual characters whose efforts at communication are often comic failures" (73) and about her "narcissistic" main characters (75). He continues that her books "are impoverished because she fails to establish a vital relationship between place and character" and concludes that they are "poor nourishment for the imaginations of children" (76). Seigel worries that the self-centeredness of Blume's main characters and the absence of complexity in her novels leave children poorer for having read them. Prominent adolescent literature critic Roberta Trites says that Blume's novels, especially *Deenie,* are "reductive in their portraits of mothers" (103), and she uses them as foils for what she sees as more appropriately feminist works for young adults.

Other readers take exactly the opposite view. Novelist Beth Kendrick believes that the mothers in Blume's novels are "fully drawn, actively involved in their daughters' lives, and dealing with flaws and conflicts of their own" (203). Writing in the *Children's Literature Association Quarterly*, Joseph Somers agrees: Blume's work, he says, "is among the finest to specifically address young women's concerns such as the mother/daughter plot in an atmosphere charged with a need for those discussions" (275). For these critics, at least, Blume is both realistic and socially aware.

Author of a critical biography of Blume, Maryann Weidt says that "Blume's heroes and heroines depict the powerlessness of childhood. Decisions are made without their input—decisions about jobs, new babies, and relocation of the family. However, they are not abandoned by their loved ones ..." (118–9). Providing their young protagonists with both challenges and supportive adults is typical of the work of many young adult writers in this study, including Chris Crutcher, Cynthia Voigt, and Mildred Taylor. Weidt includes Blume, saying that although Blume has been criticized for not being overtly moral, "What could be more virtuous than a warm, caring family relationship?" (119). She may not explicitly drive home her moral arguments, but she provides her main characters with the necessary love and care; each of Blume's narrator/protagonists are firmly placed in such comforting families and (eventually) draw their strength from them.

Legions of Blume fans agree. After a study of online literary forums on Blume, Jimmie Manning, Jacqueline McNally, and Stephanie Verst conclude that readers see her books as "sophisticated and profound explorations of issues prevalent in everyday life including sexuality, religion, and sensitive life events." The novels, they continue, "both serve as a pedagogical tool and the site for beginning discussion of serious or awkward issues relevant to everyday living." Finally, they argue that "a feminist view of the books suggests that they are sex positive, affirmative to diverse understanding, and are being constructed by many as useful even if they may present uncomfortable situations" (14). Readers, both teachers and students, may disagree about whether or not these books have value in the classroom, but the consensus seems to be that they present positive and useful treatments of issues that concern young adults and those who care for them.

One way to begin a more nuanced discussion of Blume might be to pay attention to her use of the first person, which Weidt says she has "perfected" (117). Renee Curry's analysis of first-person narration in writers such as Dorothy Allison and Jamaica Kincade is a useful place to start. Although she discusses novels more clearly designed for adults, with therefore more sophisticated narrative structures, her analysis of the first-person young female narrator can effectively be applied to Blume. Curry says that the girl narrators she examines "already know what life has brought and that the language prescribed as suitable for girls will not let them tell what they know." They speak, she argues, "with an always already wisdom that profoundly disturbs adult readers because of reader desire for genuine (or, at least, rhetorical) innocence and optimism on the part of girls—regardless of the girls' fictional or lived lives"

(98). In other words, adolescent narrators, while wise in the ways of the world, must contend with adults (both within and outside of their narratives) who think of young girls as both innocent and optimistic.

Still, they are not entirely symbolic or wise. These young female narrators, she says, "are not merely allegorical figures of wider political issues (and, therefore, permitted to have been endowed with surprising wisdom), they are also ordinary girls with unsurprising wisdom" (100). Like the young narrators in Blume's novels, these kids often rely on clichés and sometimes miss the deeper truths. Still, they provide avenues for readers' discoveries of those truths. Most importantly, these girl narrators are resilient: "They grow into the people they were in their youths. Each knows her 'I' at an early age, and by offering readers her story, each claims the innocent girl 'I' as worthy of trust and of love" (104). Clearly, readers of Judy Blume have come to trust and love her young narrators as well.

Using Curry's article as a starting point, Joseph Sommers praises Judy Blume for having "transformed the texts these young women consumed during the late 1960s and 1970s into a literature that spoke to them about difficult issues when no one else would" (262). Blume's first-person narrators, Sommers says, become "attractive candidates to invoke and discuss otherwise difficult subject matter with young women and encourage them to reach a self-actualization of their own" (268). Unlike in a traditional *Bildungsroman*, however, Blume's problem novels do not show characters who grow up. Instead, she reveals "young women struggling to become better young women and attempting to grow but not necessarily achieving all those ends" (275). Blume's readers identify with the narrators (both male and female) in large part because they are not entirely successful in dealing with the problems presented to them. Like real-life teens, Blume's narrators are often confused, sometimes angry, and frequently incorrect in their initial judgments of people and situations.

Blume's first book for young adults, *Are You There God? It's Me, Margaret* (1970),[1] remains one of her most controversial, and it is also probably her most important. This novel, Weidt says, "was a milestone, not only in Judy Blume's career, but in the history of literature for young people." *Margaret*, she says, "ushered in the age of realism in fiction for young people" (48). Although it is simply told and widely read by very young adolescents, this story of a young girl's longing for breasts, her period, and a sustaining religious tradition has remained popular for more than 40 years. Even though much has changed for women since the 1970s, these concerns continue to resonate with readers.

Still, as always, Blume's novel is not without its detractors: Trites says that, unlike George's *Julie of the Wolves*, for example, *Margaret* "borders on using menstruation to titillate the reader" (19). Michelle Martin disagrees, while still not being completely satisfied with the novel: "Even given its literary mediocrity and somewhat stereotypical image of preteen girls," she says, Blume's novel remains popular "because despite Blume's apparent agenda of offering a unified and positive image of menstruation, the polyphony created through multiple girls' voices in the novel invites many different types of readers to empathize with the variety of perspectives that Blume depicts" (25). She continues: "While some readers contend that Margaret must be deranged for *wanting* to get her period, the young women in the novel, taken as a whole, present a credibly multivocal portrayal of what it is like to be on the cusp of adolescence" (25). Somers agrees:

> [U]sing Margaret as a surrogate for their own associations with similar problems, the audience can use Margaret in the same capacity as she uses them: as a momentary escape from the realities of their particular situation as they mire themselves in the counseling (empathetic and sympathetic) of the other who requires them [272].

Thus, Margaret becomes for her readers another sympathetic friend, with whom she can share worries and distract herself (from those deeper issues she's not yet willing to share) at the same time.

In a provocative essay, June Cummins points out that "Margaret is concerned not just with her changing body but also with the question of where she fits into American society" (352). She says that Blume's novel refutes Reisman's *The Lonely Crowd* (1950), which was popular in the 1960s when Blume became a novelist, as she "develops characters and situations that demonstrate constant negotiations of the tension between individualism and conformity in American identity rather than simply illustrate them" (354). She also shows the ways in which Blume explores the challenges described by Werner Sollars and comes closest to David Hollinger's "postethnicity." Blume, she says,

> does not merely reject implicitly Riesman's claims about conformity, nor does she presciently scoff at Sollars's desire for a consent-driven society. She gently demonstrates the limitations of these theories of national culture and anticipates the postethnicity posited more recently by Hollinger [367].

Three. The Great Adventure

As with her other novels, *Margaret* raises issues about class conflict and hints at the fluidity of economic categories. The novel, more uniquely, questions the fixedness of ethnic divisions.

Another interesting reading of the novel focuses on Margaret's religious identity (or lack of it) and on her position as a Jewish child in a mostly-Protestant suburban environment. Jonathan Krasner and Joellyn Zollman say that Blume "gave voice to the contemporary Jewish child in suburbia, fully integrated into American life, often dealing with generic adolescent issues like puberty, peer pressure, and body image. When Blume dealt with particularly Jewish issues, [her novels] likewise represented the true-to-life experiences of the increasingly affluent and assimilated" (23). *Margaret*, they remind us, remained the only book for young adults on the topic of interfaith marriage for many years (26). A trailblazer, *Margaret* focuses on a previously untapped vein in YA literature—the experience of an adolescent living in a two-faith family.

Early in the novel, Margaret wonders why her grandmother wants to know if her boyfriends are Jewish, and she tells her friend's mother she doesn't go to Sunday school (10). She later tells a friend that she's "not any religion" (34), but she spends a good deal of the novel trying to figure out what her true religion is. This may in part be because much of the tension centers on her Jewish paternal grandmother (who, her mother thinks, has too much influence on Margaret) and her Christian maternal grandparents, who are estranged from Margaret and who disowned her mother for marrying a Jew. Not surprisingly, religion has suddenly become the "big thing" in her life (39), and she sets out on a quest to discover who she is. When she asks to go to temple, her grandmother delightedly says that she's "a Jewish girl at heart" (55), but Margaret is not so sure. Instead, she simply promises to look for God in church *and* at temple (57), keeping her perspective resolutely skeptical and non-sectarian.

Throughout her search, she carries on an ongoing conversation in her diary and her mind with God, a conversation that is filled with doubts and questions. As Krasner and Zollman put it, "From Abraham to Tevye, Jewish literature is replete with examples of individual Jews talking to and arguing with God. Like her historical and literary predecessors, Margaret addresses God with curiosity, anger, confusion, and gratitude. Unlike most of her historical and literary predecessors, Margaret is a girl" (29). Margaret, they say, talks to God as a young woman

"Unsuitable" Books

about particularly female issues, like menstruation and breast development, and they wonder if Margaret is "Young Adult literature's first religious feminist" (30). This may be so, but she is an uncertain one at best.

For example, when she goes to temple, she finds she "expected something else," some sort of "feeling, maybe." She then determines that she may have to go back more than once "to know what it's all about" (59). After the service, the rabbi asks her back to "get to know us and God" (60), and instead, she and her father laugh about "count[ing] feathers on hats" in temple (61), how they both focused more on what people were wearing than what the rabbi was saying. Although she laughs about it with her father, Margaret despairs that she may never find God. She tells him that she "didn't feel you at all" in the houses of worship, not like when she "talk[s] to you at night." She asks, plaintively, "Why do I only feel you when I'm alone?" (120). It appears Margaret's relationship with God is always going to be private and personal, and part of what she must learn is to accept that.

In this midst of her religious exploration, Margaret's evangelical and judgmental maternal grandparents visit, in an attempt to mend fences, and instead make a scene about Margaret not going to church and leave in a huff. In the middle of the argument, Margaret says, "All of you! Just stop it! I can't stand another minute of listening to you. Who needs religion? Who! Not me … I don't need it. I don't even need God!" (134). She tells her readers that she also isn't going to be talking to God again. During this tense time, she tells her Jewish grandmother's boyfriend, who insists that she's a Jewish girl at heart, "I'm nothing, and you know it! I don't even believe in God!" (140). It seems clear to readers, though, that Margaret is probably only temporarily angry at God, and, indeed, she does resume her conversations with him, although she doesn't go back to religious services of any kind.

At the end of the novel, Margaret has reached no conclusions in her study of religion, but she continues to talk to God. When she finally gets her period, she ends the book with this: "Are you still there God? It's me, Margaret. I know you're there God. I know you wouldn't have missed this for anything! Thank you God. Thanks an awful lot…" (149). Based on this passage, Krasner and Zollman conclude that Margaret "finds and honors God in her changing self" (34). Her personal (and explicitly female) interactions with God, they believe, show the novel to be feminist in its approach to religion.

Three. The Great Adventure

In many ways, *Margaret* is a typical young adult problem novel: the main character, speaking in the first person, agonizes about boys, breasts, and her period, and she listens mostly to her friends and sometimes to her parents. What makes the novel unusual, though, is the complex treatment of Margaret's search for a sustaining religious faith. It seems that this, above all, ought to make the book appealing to even its most conservative readers, yet it remains troubling, in part for its frankness, and in part for its refusal to accept conventional answers about religion. Margaret has no conversion experience, she doesn't find the Lord, and she doesn't return to her Jewish roots. Still, she hasn't stopped talking to God at the end of the novel, and the novel seems hopeful about her eventual ability to resolve (or live peacefully with) her religious conundrums.

Coming after *Margaret*, *Then Again, Maybe I Won't* (1971) is one of Blume's few books featuring a male narrator. This novel, Weidt says, "more than any of Blume's other books, deals with the isolation of youth, and not coincidentally, with the isolation of old age" (63). In it, 13-year-old narrator Tony Miglione moves to a wealthy Long Island suburb after his electrician father creates a profitable invention and takes a job as an executive. His grandmother has moved with them, but she isn't coping well with the change in her role (she's no longer wanted as the cook for the family) and stays in her room. In addition, his one new friend, Joel, shoplifts. This, along with the tensions at home, causes anxiety for Tony, and the resulting stomach pains land him in the hospital. In many ways he is a typical teen boy: he plays basketball, has wet dreams, spies on an attractive neighbor girl, and, less typically (especially for the 1970s) sees a therapist to help him with his anxieties. With as much sensitivity as she portrayed teen girls in *Margaret,* she explores the issues that confront and confound young men.

The novel also focuses quite astutely on social class conflict. One of the ongoing tensions in Tony's house stems from his mother trying to keep up with the Jones. She won't let his grandmother cook anymore because she thinks it makes them look too working class, and she lets her neighbors shorten their name so they seem less Italian. The boys, too, are confronted with the realities of working for a living. When Tony and Joel, as a joke, tip a waitress by putting pennies inside a chocolate milkshake glass, she says, "Well, let me tell you something. I need that money. And there's no place you can stick it that I won't reach in to get it! Your crummy forty pennies buys me a loaf of bread. Did you ever think of that!" (144). Tony, if not Joel, is humbled by this experience. He learns a hard lesson about social class and the ways in which those with more money (sometimes inadvertently) belittle those with less.

Missing these complexities entirely, censors seem most bothered by the references to wet dreams and the bad influence of Joel on Tony, failing to see the concern shown by Tony's parents toward his increasing anxiety and the important knowledge Tony gains from his experiences, both good and bad. They also miss the subtle messages about the American Dream and social class conflicts. Tony's family may have risen financially, and moved to a "better" address, but they seem far less happy than before. This seems far more important than whether Tony spies on a neighbor undressing or goes shoplifting with Joel. As is the case with most of the novels in this study, would-be book banners focus on (mostly insignificant) details and miss the larger message.

Blume's next young adult novel, *Blubber* (1974), is viewed by critics "one of Blume's most daring pieces of writing" (Weidt 91), in part because Blume refuses to make her point about bullying tediously obvious. Blume's editor and friend Richard Jackson says, "*Blubber* is, morally speaking, the toughest of all the books. That book is really about an ethical dilemma. I think it's a strong book because she doesn't say 'Cruelty is wrong!' She says, 'Cruelty hurts,' and the reader can draw his or her own conclusions" (qtd. in Weidt 96). Had she done that, of course, this would be a far less censored novel—and a far less interesting one. As Scales says, "Blume's keen ear for dialogue, her understanding of kids and their need to be part of a group, and her desire to raise questions related to the realities of life make *Blubber* one of the most significant novels for middle-grade readers" (28). It is probably her honesty—and her refusal to provide easy answers— a 6 out these issues that has caused the novel to be so often challenged

Fifth-grade narrator Jill Brenner makes fun of her teachers, eggs a neighbor's mailbox, goes to a bar mitzvah in an itchy dress, and, most importantly, participates in the bullying of a classmate, Linda, who becomes known as "Blubber," as the result of a rather unfortunate report she gives on whales, is teased for being fat, for being "smelly," and, generally, for being weak. When Jill asks her mother for advice about the bullying, she tells her daughter that "a person who can laugh at herself will always be respected" (62). Eventually, Jill is able to put that advice into practice when she herself is bullied.

A related subplot concerns a cranky neighbor, Mr. Machinist, whose

Three. The Great Adventure

mailbox Jill and her friend egg on Halloween. When caught, Jill argues that he deserved it. In enforcing her punishment for the vandalism, her father tells her that "maybe this way you'll both learn that it's to up to you to decide who deserves what in this world" (99). He comes to realize that Mr. Machinist is not a nice guy (121), although he won't admit that he deserved to have his mailbox egged. The lesson for Jill here is not that people are always nicer than they seem but that it isn't her place to punish those she doesn't like (even when they are unpleasant). This, of course, is connected to the question of whether or not a person being bullied deserves the bullying.

As the bullying of Linda escalates, the school children decide to hold a "trial" for Linda, and Jill stands up to the ringleader, Wendy, and says if Linda doesn't have a lawyer, she won't have a trial. Then Jill becomes the victim (132). "It's rough to be on the other side," her mother comments (142). Jill finds ways to defeat her tormentor, and she makes friends with a quiet girl, Rochelle, and the novel ends, with no lofty moral pronouncements or blinding insights about bullying. Instead, the last paragraph has Jill going back to her usual routines, trying to stop biting her nails before Christmas, collecting stamps with her best friend, and being annoyed by her younger brother.

Judy Blume tells readers in an afterward to the novel, that she wrote *Blubber* because bullying is often kept a secret by the kids who see it happening, and even by the person who's being bullied." Being bullied is "humiliating ... and frightening," which causes kids to keep it a secret. Blume enjoins her readers not to remain silent: "It's too hard to worry alone," she says ("Judy Blume" NP). Clearly, what Blume appears to be doing in *Blubber* is to bring bullying out into the open, to help alleviate the fear and the secrets. Novelist Meg Cabot says that

> Judy Blume is careful not to give *Blubber* that kind of *After School Special* ending. True to life, the victim and the bully in *Blubber* do not become friends, the bully is never even punished for her crimes, nor is there any obvious lesson learning. While the protagonist, through becoming a target of bullying herself, comes to understand that by tolerating the bullying of others, she did something wrong, this is portrayed subtly, so subtly that the careless—or youthful—reader might miss it entirely [67].

The subtleties are exactly what seem to have escaped the censors, yet Blume's complex treatment of the subject is in part why her novel remains popular 40 years after its publication.

"Unsuitable" Books

About this and other sophisticated young adult novels that refuse to devolve into didacticism (much to the consternation of the critics), Faith Sullivan asks this crucial question:

> Is there a better time or safer way for a person to learn about the sensual delights and lurking dangers of the world than as a child bringing home armloads of books from the classroom or library and poring through them where a parent or other adult is present to oversee, to answer questions, and, when necessary, to calm concerns? [84].

This question, also articulated earlier by Weidt, applies to all of Blume's challenging (and challenged) young adult novels. There is no better place for young adults to learn about difficult adult issues than where they are surrounded by caring adults. This could also be applied to YA novels, which are also provide an excellent stimulus for discussion of these subjects between parents and children.

Although nearly all of Blume's novels have been the target of censors, *Forever* (1975) may be Blume's most controversial. In a study of censorship from 1971 to 1984, Kenneth Donelson reports that the one title constantly under attack in junior and senior high schools was *Forever* (qtd. in Weidt 23). Still, novelist Stacey Ballis speaks for many readers when she says, "What resonated with me the most wasn't the feeling of being in the know or the illicit content but rather the clear and beautifully rendered image of falling in love, and falling back out, and being okay" (102). This is the main strength of the novel that censors, surprisingly, miss: the main character survives, and actually flourishes. Perhaps, though, this is actually the reason why they challenge the book—the female character has sex out of wedlock and is *not* dead at the end of the novel.

Narrator Katherine "Kat" Danziger, a senior in high school, is the daughter of a pharmacist and lives in the suburbs. (In a side plot, her friend, Erica, is dating a closeted gay boy, who tries to kill himself.) Kat meets Michael, they fall in love, go on a ski weekend, have sex, go their separate ways over the summer, and eventually break up. Kat has tolerant and helpful adults in her life, and she sensibly visits a Planned Parenthood clinic when the couple decides to have sex. Although another character in the novel gets pregnant and gives the baby up for adoption, Katherine suffers no lasting emotional or physical consequences from her first romance. She's wistful, certainly, but not depressed—wiser, but not cynical.

The novel begins, somewhat surprisingly (at least for a young adult novel in 1974), like this: "Sybil Davison has a genius I.Q. and has been

Three. The Great Adventure

laid by at least six different guys" (9). Weidt rightly points out that "this opening line from *Forever* is one of the most talked about, most disputed, most controversial sentences in all young adult literature" (37). It has definitely raised the ire of the censors, although so much of the novel is both sensible and sympathetic to the concerns of young adults.

For example, although the novel is fairly straightforward about the lovers' sexual activities, it is filled with good advice and good examples from parents and grandparents. When thinking about marriage, Kat says that she has heard that people who come from happy homes have good marriages and that her parents are "the happiest married couple I know." This isn't an idealized picture of marriage, though. Her parents enjoy being together, she says, "which doesn't mean they agree on everything, because they definitely don't but after an argument they laugh about it and I like that" (40). Kat has seen two generations of loving marriages, and it seems clear that she, too, will eventually have such an enjoyable and considerate marriage.

The novel also shows both the ways in which mores are both changing and remaining the same. In earlier times, Kat says, "girls were divided into two groups—those who did and those who didn't." She's glad those days are over, but she still gets angry "when older people assume that everyone in my generation screws around." Her generation is, she admits, is "more open than our parents but that just means we accept sex and talk about it. It doesn't mean we are all jumping into bed together" (44). Would-be censors would be well advised to look more closely at this passage. Young women of her generation, Kat asserts, don't "screw around," but they also aren't labeled as sluts if they do have sex. The world has changed—and probably for the better. Kids are more open and more thoughtful about the choices they make. In addition, Kat's mother is supportive but not encouraging about her having sex. She advises her that "when you give yourself both mentally and physically ... well, you're completely vulnerable" (93). This advice helps Kat to slow down, but also to keep her reactions in perspective when she and Michael do break up.

Weidt rightly summarizes the message of the novel, which has been overlooked by censors:

> A major point that has been missed by critics who cannot get past "getting laid" is that relationships are more than sex, and that is an important message for kids to hear. Katherine is secure in the support she receives from her

parents, from her grandmother, and even from her younger sister. Katherine's strength is grounded in generations of supportive family ties, and that, after all, is the basis for the love that lasts forever [47].

It is true that Katherine and Michael have sex, but they are surrounded by love that strengthens them and allows them to emerge from their first romance with their egos intact.

Tiger Eyes (1981), Blume's most recent young adult novel, is, according to Weidt, one of her "finest works, yet it has never achieved the popularity that it deserves" (16). In addition, the novel is, she says, "the most political of any of her books; it is also the most serious and the most thoughtful" (104). Perhaps because of this political focus, the novel has been the site of many censorship battles. Or it could be, as Duke says, that "Blume traces the responses of the various family members with candor and often a bluntness that probably causes adult readers to squirm a bit, especially since the adult role models in the story, good intentions included, don't necessarily supply the support or answers that the family needs" (414). This is the one thing that will most quickly attract the attention of censors: parents or other adults who aren't able to solve all the teen's problems. Chris Crutcher, S. E. Hinton, and Robert Cormier, just to name a few, have suffered challenges because of this very issue.

Main character and narrator Davey's father has died, and she and her mother have moved to Los Alamos, New Mexico (where Blume once lived). Davey hates the artificiality and Cold War-inspired fear of her new home (which is shared her by relatives), and since her mother is paralyzed by grief and zonked out on "headache medicine," she has no ally. To make matters worse, her one friend, Jane, has a drinking problem. As is the case in *Blubber*, *Margaret*, and especially *Then Again*, friends are little help to the narrator. Eventually, her mother pulls herself together, getting a job and starting to date. While hiking in nearby canyons, Davey meets the mysterious Wolf and, in a surprising plot twist, helps his father, who is dying of cancer, in the hospital where she works as a candy striper. Davey finally comes to terms with her father's death, and buries the blood-stained clothes from his final moments in the cave she shared with Wolf. She tells her father that she is now "only going to remember the good times" (200). Davey, her mother and brother eventually go back to Atlantic City, as Mom decides that she "can't let safety and security become the focus of [her] life" (210). She learns from Wolf that "*la vida es una buena Aventura*," and she tells her aunt as they leave that she and

Three. The Great Adventure

her family are "going to be alright" (216). The novel ends, as do many of Blume's works, on a quietly optimistic note.

In *Tiger Eyes*, as opposed to *Margaret*, Blume never has "her characters enter into any discussion about the role of religion and faith in facing death and related fears" (Duke 416). Indeed, Davey and eventually her mother learn that they must rely on themselves (and each other) to survive the tragedy that has befallen them. As in all of Blume's novels that have raised the ire of censors, solutions are not offered so much as suggested, and we only see the young protagonists *beginning* their journeys toward adulthood and wholeness, not arriving at them.

From a child dealing with bullying, to a girl on the brink of womanhood and trying to discover God and a boy learning not to swallow his fear, to a young woman on the brink of having sex and one trying to cope with her father's death, Judy Blume has certainly run the gamut of young adult problems. (Some of her other novels, which haven't generated quite as much controversy, such as *Deenie* and *Iggy's House*, deal with disability and racism.) Throughout all of them, the young people are offered advice (sometimes helpful, sometimes not appreciated) by the adults in their lives, who are, for the most part, loving and supportive. Although it is true that these adolescents use language that isn't entirely Sunday School appropriate, think about their developing bodies and sexualities, and sometimes are disrespectful to their teachers and family members, overall, they make sound decisions (eventually). We know as we leave their worlds that they are "going to be alright." They are not always up for the grand adventure that their lives are becoming, but they are gathering the tools that they will need to tackle them. Although many of these novels are more than three decades old, they remain valuable to young readers and have inspired several generations of (now) adults to take chances, listen to the grownups around them, and be considerate of those around them. These novels may appear to lack clear morals and adults who are infinitely wise and always patient (as has been said about Cormier, Crutcher, and George), but they offer something better: realistic examples of young people having problems, moving toward solutions, and not being destroyed in the process. Their young readers learn that they are not alone and that they can tell their own scary secrets and have adventurous and confident lives.

CHAPTER FOUR

"When fear seizes"
Jean Craighead George's
Julie of the Wolves *(1972)*

> Childhood is brief, but its impressions are indelible, and it is little enough to tell a child that the tree by the door is a sycamore, that robins nest in it, pigeons sit on it, starlings sleep in it, and that its roots go into the earth. And then to give him a library card—Jean Craighead George, *Horn Book*, 1959
>
> Perhaps we are, after all, traveling a beautiful road. Perhaps we are evolving toward a mutual aid and not toward killing and destruction. Perhaps the growing attitude—that we must share the earth wisely with plant, beast, and man—is much more deeply rooted than we suspect—Jean Craighead George, Newbery Award speech, 346

Environmentally-conscious and socially-tolerant author Jean Craighead George has delighted readers and teachers of *Julie of the Wolves* for four decades with her factual and moving accounts of wolves, Inuit culture, and the emotional development of its endearing main character. However, would-be book banners have attacked what they believe to be its inappropriate subject matter and frankness about survival in the wild and in "civilization." Her novel is still agitating censors today, making the American Library Association's list of banned or challenged books again in 2009, almost 40 years after its publication in 1972. Why such a powerful and sensitive novel should continue to be the subject of book banners' ire remains a significant question.

The novel tells the story of Julie (also known later in the book by her Inuit name, Miyax), a girl of 13. As Julie/Myax's dual name suggests, she is torn between (at least) two cultures, wanting to embrace the Inuit practices of her father, Kapugen, while living in a tourist-oriented

Four. "When fear seizes"

Alaskan village and longing for the urban existence of her pen pal in San Francisco. As critic Mary Lickteig puts it, Julie/Miyax's journey is from "innocence to experience. [She is] caught between childhood and adulthood, between Inuit culture and the Western culture" (84). Throughout the novel, Julie/Miyax longs for and then rejects various cultural and animal options, moving, eventually, toward a hybrid identity all her own.[1]

Her back-and-forth progress mimics that of readers who are *not* trying to eke out an existence on the tundra or coping with the clash between Inuit and white culture, young people who aren't sure if they want to follow the values and practices of their families or create a new life for themselves. George's novel also provides enough cultural, geographic, and natural history to make it fascinating and enlightening for readers in the Lower 48, and it has the potential to teach them much about the differences between their cultures and environments and Julie/Miyax's. Educator and multi-cultural literacy theorist Patricia Encisco puts it well:

> As children read about racial, ethnic, and class differences in literature, they encounter metaphors of and meanings about difference; these new metaphors and meanings must be negotiated by children as they struggle to understand how they will see themselves, their peers, and their teachers in light of the literature's new possibilities [13].

Literature like *Julie of the Wolves* can open up new ways for young people to see their own worlds and themselves in relation to the conflicts and possibilities presented in these books.

This may, paradoxically, also be why critics find the book so problematic. Children questioning their own cultural values (in particular the values of their parents) are troubling to many parents and community members. Still, Geneva Van Horne rightly calls the challenges to the novel a "travesty." The plot of the novel, she says, is "engaging; its themes are noble; its literary quality and expression, artful; its factual information, accurate; its main character, inspiriting; and its content, eminently appropriate and appealing to middle school students" (338). How can a book, she asks, that is enjoyable, well-written, factually correct, and even inspiring even raise a single eyebrow? As I have been arguing throughout this book, the best weapon against these irrational (but nevertheless heartfelt) objections is more information upon which to base rationales for books and arguments against censorship. From

"Unsuitable" Books

plot, to characterization, to themes, *Julie of the Wolves* offers a number of such arguments.

Early in the novel, readers learn that the main character (known by her Inuit name "Miyax" in this section) believes she has been abandoned by her father after the death of her mother. She knows only that he "paddled his kayak into the Bering Sea to hunt for seal, and he never returned" (5). Mother and fatherless, Julie/Miyax has been forced to live with other family members, where she finds out her father has arranged a marriage for her with the mentally-challenged son of his friend. Her bleak but survivable life in Barrow, Alaska, is threatened when her new husband tries to assert his conjugal rights. Consequently, she runs away from the marriage (and Barrow) and heads onto the tundra, on a long trek to the aptly-named Point Hope, literally and figuratively without a compass (10). Her poorly-prepared-for journey is fueled by a dream to catch a freighter to San Francisco, where she believes she will be welcomed into the home of her pen pal, Amy.

Julie/Miyax quickly discovers that she must learn the ways of the wolves (and also re-learn the survival strategies of the Inuit people) in order to find food and survive. She looks to Amaroq, the wolf pack leader, to be her surrogate father figure. Julie/Miyax says she has chosen him because he "walked like her father, Kapugen, with his head high and his chest out" and "possessed wisdom" (5). As well as drawing on his knowledge, she also discovers that she must appear helpless (in spite of her reluctance) to successfully adapt to the pack mentality of the wolves (43). Julie/Miyax must become Amaroq's daughter, but on *his* terms. This is the first piece of information she gathers in her struggle to build a composite and functional identity—sometimes skill must be combined with humility.

Throughout this section, she also draws on her human father's wisdom. When she realizes that the wolves are soon going to leave their springtime nursery den to take up their nomadic winter life, she knows that she must learn to survive on her own. Her father told her: "Change your ways when fear seizes... for it usually means you are doing something wrong" (49). Rather than bemoaning her fate or looking for something else to blame, Julie/Miyax's father has taught her that she must change herself in order to change her circumstances. She learns to hunt for small birds, to dry meat from moose killed by the wolves, and to find fuel to cook her food. Although she still follows the rules the wolves

Four. "When fear seizes"

teach her about dominance and submission, Julie/Miyax must also retain some part of her human identity. She walks on two feet, instead of crouching as she has done, in front of the wolves. Amaroq and the other wolves come to accept her as their "two-legged pup" (72). In order to survive in challenging circumstances, George seems to be saying, one must be able to draw on a number of identities and skills. Julie/Miyax's time learning from the wolves comes to an end in this first section, when the wolves leave. Fortunately, Julie/Miyax has made a compass (that very human invention) to guide her, once again, to Point Hope. She takes out the battered letter from Amy and continues on her quest to civilization.

The second section of the book, where the main character is referred to by her *gussak* (white) name, Julie, tells readers the back story of her life. Here, the novel recounts Julie/Miyax's early years with her father after her mother's death, when he takes her to a seal camp and teaches her the subsistence hunting techniques of the men of her people. He encourages her to remember that she is Eskimo and emphasizes their particular respect for the land. This section, as Lickteig says, "seems to cry out for the maintenance of old ways and to resist the changes being imposed on it" (83). Unlike the first part, in which Julie/Miyax rediscovers her Inuit roots and uses them in conjunction with what she learns from the wolves, here Julie struggles to hold onto those traditional human and natural ways as civilization encroaches.

As well as schooling her in the male ways of hunting, Kapugen also fills the gaps left by her mother, offering to teach Julie/Miyax not just hunting but also the "women's work" of sewing and preserving skins. Throughout the novel, Julie/Miyax will use both her male and female knives and knowledge, just as she uses both her human and wolf strategies. After a while, though, Kapugen isn't considered an appropriate role model for a young girl, and Julie/Miyax goes to her Aunt Martha's house in Mekoryuk, where she is unhappy about her aunt's nagging, is teased by her friends for her traditional ways, and longs to go to San Francisco to visit Amy's pink room. The skills she has gained from her father, however, won't be useful until she leaves civilization.

Eventually, Julie/Miyax is sent to Barrow for the arranged marriage she is fleeing in the first section. It looks at first as if she will be happy living with Daniel as a sister, going to school, being taken care of by Naka and tutored by his wife in making moose hide masks for tourists. But Naka drinks too much, and eventually, Daniel, in a hapless way, tries to have sex with her. He throws her to the floor, and then "the room spun, and grew blurry" (120). Daniel, who, Julie/Miyax says, is as frightened as she is, "kicked violently and was still" (120). Then he leaves, exulting about his success, although it is never clear whether he has accomplished his goal, or even if he was completely certain about what that goal might have been.

This rather mild, somewhat ambiguous rape scene is what raises the blood pressure of the censors, especially since the victim is only 13. What is important to stress, though, is this is the moment when Julie/Miyax's life begins to evolve, eventually for the better. She invokes her father's message about fear, gets to her feet, and changes what she's doing, making plans to leave Barrow and begins walking across the tundra to Point Hope. At the end of this part, "Julie is gone," the main character reports, "I am Miyax now" (125). Until the very end of the novel, "Julie" doesn't return. It is possible to argue that George presents the assault as a fortunate fall, one that leads the victim to greater strength and wisdom, which is problematic, of course, but I prefer to see it as the realistic depiction of a young woman's justifiable fear and her refusal to be destroyed by it.

Born as it was out of panic, Julie/Miyax's escape plan, as the first section indicates, almost leads to disaster. However, her relationship with the wolves improves significantly over her time in the wilderness, as does her skill in survival. By the time readers get to the third part, Julie/Miyax is self-sufficient, watched over but no longer aided by the wolves. Even the theft of her food supply (and later her tools and clothing) by a (literal) lone wolf are only temporary setbacks. When she finds her knife and matches again, she "marveled at how valuable these simple things were, how beautiful and precious. With them she could make a home, a larder, a sled, and clothes" (140). She also has learned to use the once-hostile environment around her. The cold, she says, is "precious. With it she could, like her father, freeze leather and sinew into sleds, spears, and harpoons" (140). Julie/Miyax has truly become a child of the world of wolves and ice, leaving behind (or so she thinks) both the world of the *gussaks* and the world of her human father. As is the case throughout the novel, she survives because she can adapt and change, incorporating new knowledge into her existing skill set.

Happy in her discovery that she can survive on her own, Julie/Miyax's quest to reach Point Hope becomes less important to her (142).

Four. "When fear seizes"

She likes the "simplicity" of the tundra and fits into its rhythms (152). Challenged by a grizzly bear (but saved by her pack), she eventually finds a new friend in Tornait, an arctic plover. She tries unsuccessfully to save Amaroq and the pack from hunters, but she manages to nurse his son, Kapu, back to health from his wound. Still, the encounter with the hunters has left her shattered: her pen pal's pink room is now red with the blood of the wolves (174), and she can no longer go there. As Stott says,

> Julie, in leaving Barrow, believes herself to be setting out on a long journey to a specific end, San Francisco, to her promised land which offers and escape from her unhappy life as an Eskimo child-bride. However, as her attitudes to the Arctic change, her journey becomes one of withdrawal and return into an ideal world and then, a sadder and wiser person, back to a reality which cannot be escaped [135].

Although this may be stating the obvious, Julie/Miyax's specific journey has changed to a more abstract one. She becomes less concerned with reaching civilization and more concerned with finding what she needs to be content, if not blissfully, happy. This, of course, mirrors the progress from childhood, through adolescence, to adulthood, where the challenges move from learning how to walk, and to read, and to take care of oneself, to fitting in with peers, and, eventually, to finding contentment in the world.

Toward the end of her journey, she meets a traditional Inuit couple subsistence hunting and decides that, like them, she wants to live off the land. Still, when she discovers from the couple that her father is, surprisingly, still alive, she returns to Kagik, hopes for a joyful reunion, and is immediately disappointed to find that he has married a *gussak*. She leaves her father's home, headed, it seems, back to the wilderness, but then at the end "point[s] her boots" back toward her father, declaring that "the hour of the wolf and the Eskimo are over" (201). At the end of the novel, as Lickteig says, "the reader does not know, anymore than Julie does, where she belongs" (85). This ambiguity, I think, may be some of what troubles censors, although it certainly reflects the self-doubt and questioning many young adults have. Stott articulates this uncertainty and offers a solution:

> Is the conclusion of *Julie of the Wolves* one of total defeat and despair, or can the reader salvage any hope from it? To find an answer, we must remember that the dominant tone of the pastoral is elegiac, a lament for the passing of a purer, simpler, more harmonious way of life [138].

If one fits Julie/Miyax's story into both the pastoral tradition and the *Bildungsroman*, in which it clearly resides, one can see the sadness and nostalgia for a lost paradise are a necessary part of the journey to adulthood: longing for the lost paradise of childhood while accepting the somewhat mixed blessings of adult awareness.[2]

So, given the clear benefits to young readers of a book like *Julie of the Wolves*, what would be the best answers to the would-be censors who would remove this book from libraries and classroom reading lists? How can we respond to what some have found to be a repugnant representation of the Inuit cultural practice of juvenile marriage and, more important, the horrifying suggestion of sexual violence to a minor? Or how do we placate those adult readers who have objected also to the "grossness" of the early chapters, where wolves (as wolves do) mark their territory with scent glands and feed their cubs by swallowing and then disgorging meat, which Julie/Miyax also eats? The concerns about the behaviors of the wolves seem relatively minor and easily answered, as they are, after all, what wolves *do*. The novel is, after all, biologically accurate.

The larger challenge comes when one tries to defend human behavior shown in the novel. To begin with, one must look at how Julie/Miyax responds to what happens to her, rather than what has been done. As Stott says, "The greatest courage is found in the character's ability to learn from the past and to accept the reality of the present, unpleasant though it may be" (138). The lives of young adults are not always sweetness and light, and the best we can offer them is not protection from all trouble but examples of the ability to survive (and even triumph) after adversity. As Kapugen says, "Change your ways when fear seizes."

In spite of the novel's potential to teach important lessons to adolescents, some critics aren't completely convinced about the potentially redemptive qualities of the ending—and of the novel as a whole. Their criticisms range from endorsing gender restrictions to validating cultural bias. In her mythic/religious Freudian analysis of the novel, Lois Kuznets comments that "Julie's survival has its negative aspects for those things she has learned to deal with and come to value seem doomed" (103). In other words, Julie/Miyax has learned to survive in the Arctic by returning to her Inuit ways, but that culture seems fated to disappear by the end of the novel, according to Kuznets.

Also, although Julie/Miyax builds on and deviates from traditional female role models and embraces the self-determination and power of males, at the end of the story, Kuznets points out, Julie/Miyax cannot, as a son could, "fight the father and redeem a culture that has degenerated under his rule, but as a daughter to accede to his compromises." She also has to "face the Oedipal conflict embodied by her stepmother, who is a representative of the encroaching culture." While her resourcefulness might be an inspiration to young women, she says, "her sex adds only another level of irony to the fact that she has acquired the male skills and power of a doomed culture" (105). Thus, because she is a girl, Kuznets believes, Julie/Miyax must ultimately submit to her father's will, and she will be forced to compete for his attention with her stepmother. Doubly doomed, Julie/Miyax has embraced the "skills and powers" of men, which she cannot use as a daughter in her father's house, and, to make matters worse, those abilities are also from a dying culture. In spite of all this, Kuznets says, George affirms "the basic belief in the self as the final arbiter of one's destiny..." (108). This is a vital point: Julie/Miyax's acquired skills may seem useless in an increasingly civilized world, but she needed those skills to survive and arrive back home. The novel suggests, it seems to me, that someone who was able to live successfully with the wolves won't, finally, have much trouble with her stepmother.

Other critics are less concerned with Julie/Miyax's gendered limitations and more worried about George's stereotypical representations of Amerind peoples. Opal Moore and Donnarae McCann argue that George's picture of Inuit culture "just barely" avoids stereotyping by "emphasizing that the Amerind's intimate understanding of nature is not inherent or romantic, but a matter of survival." However, they say, "the lyrical appeal of this harmony-in-nature theme is marred by George's prediction of the self-extinction of Indian cultures. She presents an imagined dysfunctional primitiveness alongside images of a technological, progressive, white society" (28). Still, they argue, there is much to be said of the ways in which George depicts the Inuits' "responding intelligence" in relation to their harsh and beautiful world. The bottom line, according to Moore and McCann, is that when George predicts the end of wolf and Eskimo, she "consigns the culture, and hope for preserving the Arctic ecosystem, to dust." For George, they believe, the Inuits are "static primitives" able to survive in the Arctic but unable to preserve their culture (28).[3] However, I believe that there is a suggestion at the end of the novel, and in her sequels to the Julie/Miyax story, that what the culture is doing is not dying but adapting and changing, holding on to much of the traditional wisdom while making necessary accommodations to changing realities.

It is true that students in Southern Georgia, where I live, or Miami, or New York City, for that matter, would find the descriptions of Julie/Miyax's trek through the tundra strange and the encounters with the wolves a bit disgusting, but there is much to be gained by the cross-cultural encounter George creates. Young readers learn to construct their own realities in relation to such a character, as Encisco says: "In the midst of discussions, children borrow and often 'talk back' to constructions of difference found in literature, popular culture, and in the words of their classmates and teachers" (36). Young women can find ways to respond to Julie/Miyax's struggles with her father and stepmother; young men can see the need to adapt typically "masculine" ways of coping with difficulty with more "feminine" ways of adapting to the pack. Young people of either gender can see in Julie/Miyax's journey analogies to their own growth and development.

Most importantly, as critic Anne Sherrill says,

> *Julie of the Wolves* is very much the story of a young girl's growth. She is stronger in character upon her return, not only for what she has learned about her Miyax self but because of what she has learned about love. Her survival on the tundra is linked to a chain of love. There is the love for Kapugen, who taught her the Eskimo traditions and was a loving father; and the love for Amaroq, her adopted father, from whom she learns the love of other creatures for each other and human beings [275].

This, I think, is vital. Julie/Miyax is linked by a "chain of love" to her wolves, to her people, to her family, and, thereby, to all the creatures—human and animal—in her world. This message, which is both environmental and psychological, is not one that we should keep from our children. When George says in her Newbery Award speech that we are "travelling a beautiful road," this is what she has in mind: we are all moving toward increased understanding, both of each other and of our interconnected planet. Julie/Miyax is the embodiment of the struggles and the joys associated with that movement toward shared growth.

CHAPTER FIVE

Censorship 70s Style
Robert Cormier's
The Chocolate War *(1974)*

> Those who dare disturb the universe have many things in common. They refuse to submit to the bullies. They will not tolerate phoniness and sham and pretense. They will not settle for the easy answer. They keep on asking questions–of themselves, of the world, of the universe—long after it is clear the people want answers, not questions; bread and circuses, not justice—YA author Madeline L'Engle

> Toleration is meaningless without tolerance for what some may consider detestable—American Library Association Office for Intellectual Freedom

The young adult novelist Robert Cormier (who died in 2000) said in an interview that young adults "know when you are pandering or writing down to them or patronizing them" (Foerstel 149). Especially in the case of his best known novel, *The Chocolate War* (1974), Cormier refused to talk down to his audience, in his case showing them the heart of darkness in an environment they understand—high school. Although he initially intended the novel for adults, Cormier has a message for younger readers that teachers and librarians have recognized for more than 35 years. Censors, too, have been disturbed by the book, making it one of the most consistently challenged young adult novels. Michael Cart calls *The Chocolate War* "[t]he most important of the titles to appear in the seventies, and arguably the single most important title in the history of young adult literature to date" (84). Regardless of one's judgment about the novel's quality or message, there can be no doubt that this is a significant book in the history of the young adult novel—and in the censorship story.

"Unsuitable" Books

With this novel, Cormier is establishing a tradition of writing for young people that continues to this day: one that challenges adolescents to think long and hard about the world in which they live. As Clare Bradford says, "The language of children's books performs and embodies ideologies of all kinds, since children's texts purposively intervene in children's lives to propose ways of being in the world" (6). Cormier's work performs just such an intervention, suggesting in part that the lives of one's parents (and one's teachers) are not necessarily models to be imitated. The challenge is, as Rebecca Totaro says, to educate readers "through the pains of social and physical metamorphosis while entertaining them" (135). If readers aren't entertained, either by a compelling plot or engaging characters, they aren't going to be receptive to the message. Even though Cormier has managed to do this for generations of adolescents, the debate continues between educators and would-be censors as to whether the novel offers a useful or a damaging message.

In her groundbreaking work of young adult criticism, Roberta Trites uses *The Chocolate War* as an exemplar of the socializing function she sees young adult novels performing. She says:

> Although the primary purpose of the adolescent novel may appear to be a depiction of growth, growth in this genre is inevitably represented as being linked to what the adolescent has learned about power. Without experiencing gradations between power and powerlessness, the adolescent cannot grow [x].

Novels like *The Chocolate War*, she believes, teach adolescents more about their relative powerlessness in adult society—and their need to conform themselves to the structures of power—than it does about growth toward an independent identity. Trites goes further:

> This conflict with authority that is embedded in most texts for adolescents in turn provides the author with opportunities for using ideology to manipulate the adolescent reader. In that sense, authors themselves become authority figures in adolescent literature. The mechanisms by which they manipulate the reader to assume subject positions that are carefully constructed to perpetuate the status quo bear investigation. And because of this, YA novels themselves serve as yet another institution created for the purpose of simultaneously empowering and repressing adolescents [xii].

If one believes, as Trites does, that young adult novels function in part to repress young adults, to teach them about the necessity to bow to the status quo, one could argue that the censors have never really had much to worry about with *The Chocolate War*. Protagonist Jerry Renault's story of refusing to sell chocolates for his school's fund raiser becomes an allegory condemning those who resist authority. Parents and other authority figures can rest easy, knowing that after reading this novel, young people will be far too frightened to "resist the universe."

It is true that Cormier's world is a bleak one. As Anne Scott McLeod put it, Cormier suggests "that the adult world is a dangerous, threatening place with few shelters for the innocent" (203). To make it worse, she argues, adults "have lost confidence in their ability to tell children how to live in the world" (208). This is, of course, why many grown-ups have such a problem with the book. In her 2002 article, Anita Tarr has even stronger objections to the novel. Cormier, she says, "presents only the illusion of moral decision making and the illusion of a rebel hero" (96). She also points out the misogyny in the novel which she says no character effectively resists (97). Even worse, the fact that Jerry seems to have no viable options prevents readers from making vicarious moral choices, leaving them only with "paralysis" (98).

In a relatively early essay on "Readers, Realism, and Robert Cormier," Sylvia Iskander acknowledges the ambiguity of the novel, saying that "the complexity of Cormier's work challenges our notions of the proper relationship between events and their meanings" (10). However, she says,

> when readers complain about Cormier's hopeless pessimism, they mean that the novel's close defies their expectations. It is this deviation from narrative convention that repells some readers, who then protest at school board meetings or forbid their children to read Cormier's books. They prefer censorship to an examination of the social issues at stake in Cormier's novels or a reappraisal of American myth [2].

Still, she argues, while the novel doesn't solve social problems, it shows "how we can gain the moral strength to face them" (12). Zibby Oneal rightly claims there is "very little in the book to please the adult devoted to protecting some notion of youthful innocence" (179). She continues: "Stripped of euphemism and sentimentality, the book asks hard questions and refuses to provide the sorts of answers that, even now, we expect to find in books for the young" (180). This is, she says, both the value and the source of problems for the novel. Ciara Ni Bhroin agrees, saying that "Cormier's world is undoubtedly a flawed one, but its darkness is portrayed with an overriding compassion" (30). Honesty and compassion are both necessary for an accurate (and, perhaps therapeutic) picture of the world.

Other critics note the troubling complexities of the novel but offer equally positive conclusions. Nancy Veglahn says in 1988 that Cormier is "one of the few writers of realistic fiction for young adults who creates genuine evil characters" (12). In fact, his disguising of these characters in seemingly benevolent guises, she says, is what has made him controversial (13). Nevertheless, by insisting on the humanity of his bland villains, Cormier "exposes impulses that all of us would prefer to deny" (17). Finally, she says, "Cormier respects his readers enough to offer them the world as he sees it, in all its savagery and beauty, and this same respect shows in his treatment of the fictional victims in the book. Sugar coated-fables fully of easy victories could never have the power of these frightening tales" (17). *The Chocolate War* is a powerful novel (like the others discussed in this study), and one that shows respect for the sophistication of its (often young) readers.

While in 1988, Cormier's morally bankrupt characters and complex depictions of identity might still have seemed an anomaly, by the 1990s, critics are seeing Cormier as a trailblazer in young adult fiction. In her 1996 article, Patricia Head says that Cormier "subverts the assumption that literature should present a straightforward, schematic view of the world" (29). His representation of life encourages readers to "rethink the possibility [or the impossibility] that any unitary or stable sense of self can exist" (29). While many negative reviews of Cormier's novels come from "an anxiety that the author as adult is absent from his more brutal and disturbing books," nevertheless, "what would seem to be the death of the author and the abandonment of the reader to a sometimes brutal fictional world is actually what liberates the adult author/child reader dynamic, allowing author, reader, and genre to mature into adolescence" (32). In Cormier's novels, then, one can see the possibilities of a more mature young adult fiction, and certainly the novels of Crutcher suggest that moral ambiguity in YA novels has arrived.

Mike Cadden argues in his 2000 article that the "double-voiced discourse" of the novel resists easy categorization of right and wrong, allowing the reader to develop his or her own moral agency, as the young adult reader is not being told what to think from either an adult narrator or the protagonists (151). The result of this is that while Cormier doesn't clarify anything in his novel, he does offer "enough contrast to know that truth is still to be determined by the readers—now, later, and later still" (152). Cormier provides, he says, a model for any young adult author "interested in helping young readers detect and cope with the irony, complexity, and contingency so rich in the world they hope so desperately to know" (153). Young adults are, after all, going to become full-fledged adults, and they are desperate for a complete understanding of the world they will soon be entering. Yoshida Junko adds to this discussion, answering Tarr's objection about the novel's treatment of women, saying that the novel records "changing conceptions of masculinity during the turbulent 1960s and early 1970s" (105). Detailing the ways in which Jerry's story re-writes Percival's quest for masculinity, Yoshida argues that Cormier's "achievement in revolutionizing masculinity as a social construct cannot be overestimated" (119), and she says that he paves the way for other novelists who re-imagine the Percival myth, such as Katherine Paterson and Ursula K. Le Guin.

The novel remains even more popular with young adults than it does with critics, perhaps for the reasons Cart suggests:

> Adolescents seem to be inherently divided. On the one hand they are outer directed and passionately concerned about society's problems, especially when they involve real or perceived injustice.... At the same time adolescents are the perfect solipsists in their inner-directed conviction that they are the center of the universe; hence the popularity of the personal-problem novel [38].

Thus *The Chocolate War* appeals to young people's sense of justice *and* to their self-absorption. Young people come to believe at one and the same time that they are the center of the universe and that they can't disturb it. So, both educators who have taught this book for years and censors who have sought to keep it out of the hands of children are both right: the novel may be dangerous for *and* valuable to young readers.

The plot is fairly straightforward: Jerry Renault, the young protagonist of the story, decides to stand up to what he sees as a corrupt system at his parochial school (Trinity) and to do it by refusing to participate in a school-wide fundraiser. He is also resisting a secret society at the school, the Vigils, whose primary purpose seems to be bullying the younger and weaker boys. For his troubles, Jerry is "rewarded" with getting beaten to a pulp in a rigged boxing match.

The novel opens not with Jerry but with his antagonist Archie, the novel's embodiment of uncontrolled adolescent rebellion, which he hides in a carefully-constructed (and poised) exterior. For example, during an early encounter with temporary headmaster Brother Leon, who is pushing a financially-risky sale of chocolates, Archie characteristically discovers his headmaster's vulnerability. He sees that Leon (and most other adults) "were vulnerable, running scared, open to invasion" (22). From the beginning, readers are reminded of the "dangerous, threatening place with few shelters for the innocent" (203) that MacLeod describes, where "adults have lost confidence in their ability to tell children how to live in the world" (208). Archie's knowledge and sophistication makes him especially dangerous, as he concentrates his power through the Vigils and uses that group to both serve and manipulate these corrupt adults.

This epiphany isn't limited to the "bad" characters. Fairly early in the novel, Jerry expresses a similar sentiment about the vulnerability of adults. Watching his widowed father sleepwalk his way through life, Jerry wonders if that is all there is to life, watching your wife die and then living through "days and nights that seemed to have no sunrises, no dawns and no dusks, nothing but a gray drabness," and he questions if we have a choice in how we live. Jerry isn't clear about the meaning of his father's life, but he seems certain that he doesn't want it for himself. Much of what motivates Jerry seems to be avoiding being "a mirror" of his father: "The thought made him cringe. I want to do something, be somebody. But what? But what?" (53). This is Jerry's dilemma: how to be more alive, more importantly, more *engaged* with the world than his father is. This may mark the essential difference between the hero and his antagonists: For Archie, being aware that adults are vulnerable allows him power over them; for Jerry, he realizes that he must live differently, that he must work for greater self-determination and more meaningful connection to others. This knowledge is what connects Cormier's novel to the others in this study and what argues most strongly against the drive to censor them. The world of *The Chocolate War* is disillusioning, but the insight it provides presents opportunities for growth and change.

This realistic view of adult limitations—the more sinister version embodied by Archie and the more heroic by Jerry—is shared by other students in the novel. Another Trinity boy, Paul, pities his parents' "useless lives" and wonders, "What the hell were they living for?" (73). He even believes that "[t]hey were too old for sex even" (74). Of course, this is in part a 1970s view of the generational divide hanging around after the 1960s, but it is also a fairly typical attitude that young people

Five. Censorship 70s Style

of any generation have had toward the adults in their lives—that they cannot control their destinies and find no joy in their existence (not even having sex!).

This disillusionment continues throughout the novel. David Caroni, a top student at Trinity, wonders about whether teachers are "as corrupt as the villains you read about in books or saw in movies and television" (85) and reconsiders his desire to become a teacher someday. When he is blackmailed by Brother Leon (unfairly threatened with a bad grade if he doesn't tell why Jerry is refusing to sell chocolates), he asks, "If teachers did this kind of things, what kind of world could it be?" (87). Caroni comes to view the world as a place where "life was rotten, that there were no heroes, really, and that you couldn't trust anybody, not even yourself" (87). Given much of the plot, it appears that Caroni might be right; no one is trustworthy, perhaps most of all, yourself.

Trites says that teenagers "are repressed as well as liberated by their own power and by the power of the social forces that surround them" in novels like *The Chocolate War*. Therefore, such adolescent fiction is dedicated to "depicting how potentially out-of-control adolescents can learn to exist within institutional structures" (7). It seems true that David, Paul, Archie, and Jerry are recognizing that they must learn "to exist within institutional structures," as unfair or corrupt [or corrupting] as they might be. It is also true, however, that they may remain, at the end of the novel, more "liberated by their own power" than Trites acknowledges.

For example, in spite of the pressure exerted on him from both adults and his peers, Jerry refuses to sell the chocolates. In the pause that follows his first refusal, "cities fell. Earth opened. Planets titled. Stars plummeted. And the awful silence" (89). Clearly, he feels he has made a catastrophic decision. Still, nothing much actually happens to him at this point, and the silence that surrounds his decision allows Jerry to consider his motivations more carefully, to wonder if he was merely responding to Brother Leon's bullying, or if it is "more than that" (91). Jerry comes to realize that his modest refusal to cooperate could be part of a larger resistance to Brother Leon's tyranny and to the climate of fear and intimidation in the school. He is creating a larger context for his actions, one which will eventually allow him to make moral choices beyond Trinity, and this may be the primary argument for having students read this novel.

This larger context includes a literary one. Jerry is moved "mysteriously" (97) by a poster he has inside his locker, which reads, "Do I dare disturb the universe?" (97). T. S. Eliot's words from "The Love Song of J. Alfred Prufrock" affect him without his quite understanding them. However, after he refuses—once again—to sell the chocolates: "He was swept with sadness, a sadness deep and penetrating, leaving him desolate like someone washed up on a beach, a lone survivor in a world full of strangers" (98). Although Jerry identifies Eliot as the author of "that Waste Land thing they were studying in English" (98), he is actually feeling like Prufrock at the end of his poem, alone and wondering what his purpose is. Unlike Prufrock, though, he is also beginning to see himself as a kind of hero in his own life.

This tragic sadness (and heroic resolution) continues at the Vigils meeting, where Jerry is ordered to accept the chocolate and once again refuses. Jerry feels helpless, "as if somebody had died" (126). The existential angst passes, though, and in spite of the harassment he experiences, Jerry has "the sense that his bridges were burning behind him and for once in his life he didn't care," and, while refusing, "his voice sounded strong and noble" (129). At this point, Jerry seems bolstered by his resistance to bullies young and old.

His confidence wavers soon after, though. When his locker is vandalized, he feels, for some unknown reason, "ashamed" (140). Like many victims of harassment, Jerry feels guilty, almost as if he deserves the abuse, or that his vulnerability has been revealed. In spite of his faltering resolve, however, he begins to more fully understand the Eliot poster: "the solitary man on the beach standing upright and alone and unafraid, poised at the moment of making himself heard and known in the world, the universe" (143). Jerry recognizes that while taking a stand against the universe can leave one feeling alone and embarrassed, there is a dignity and pride in that stance. He is learning that challenging bullies can be difficult but rewarding.

Unfortunately, the relentless harassment takes a toll on this new-found calm. When everyone starts ignoring him at school and people make harassing phone calls to his house at night, Jerry recognizes that his rebellion could have consequences beyond his own life. He starts to think that he "didn't want his father's universe to be disturbed, and he wanted his own to be put in order again" (164). Disturbing the universe, he is learning, means disturbing the world of those who share your universe as well. As Roberta Trites says:

Five. Censorship 70s Style

> [I]n the adolescent novel, protagonists must learn about the social forces that have made them what they are. They learn to negotiate the levels of power that exist in the myriad social institutions within which they must function, including family; school; the church; government; social constructions of sexuality, gender, race, class; and cultural mores surrounding death [3].

Clearly, Jerry is learning all about the "levels of power" and the "myriad social institutions" of which he is part, not the least of which is his small family. However, he hasn't fully learned to "negotiate the levels of power" nor, more importantly, to acquiesce to that power.

The novel culminates in a boxing match, which is deceptively represented to Jerry as a chance to clear his slate, but which is in fact a way to humiliate him in front of the school. Jerry is not only badly beaten up, he loses self-respect, which is about all that has kept him going through this difficult period. When he hits his opponent, he feels "the sickness of knowing what he had become, another animal, another beast, another violent person in a violent world, inflicting damage, not disturbing the universe but damaging it" (183). Jerry realizes that he has become part of the corrupt world in which he moves, "damaging" the universe rather than standing up to it.

After the fight, Jerry tries to tell his best friend, Goober: "Don't disturb the universe, Goober, no matter what the posters say.... Otherwise, they murder you" (187). It appears that the final message of the novel is that one shouldn't resist authority, that standing up to the universe is laughable. According to Trites, the young adult novel "came into being as a genre precisely because it is a genre predicated on demonstrating characters' ability to grow into an acceptance of their environment" (19). Certainly, Jerry appears to have learned the hard way to accept his environment: the chocolate sale, Brother Leon's power, the Vigils, Trinity, and by implication the Catholic Church.[1]

So, if this is a novel that teaches young people how to live within the boundaries adults set for them, the censors ought to have nothing to worry about. However, they have been and remain stuck on the negative portrayal of adults and the harshness of the reality Cormier presents. It seems as if it's not enough to show young people that they must conform to the system; books for adolescents must do so in a way that disguises or sugarcoats this reality. Cormier, they believe, gets too close to the ugly truth.

Cormier himself has a possible solution for such concerns:

> If a book is controversial, perhaps the best place for it is the classroom where, under the guidance of a teacher, the book can be discussed and evaluated, where each student will be free to proclaim how he or she feels about the book and, in fact, can even refuse to read the book. The point is that free choice must be involved [qtd. in Foerstel 156].

Although *The Chocolate War* may end with Jerry being defeated in his attempt to resist authority, Cormier is clear that young adults should have some control over what they read and what they "proclaim" about it.

Perhaps the best way to think about the issue of adolescent reading and controversial works such as *The Chocolate War* is to remember, as J.A. Appleyard puts it, "adolescents are, at the very least, passionately principled about the world and its meaning" (118). We need to be careful, he argues, not to "fail to do justice to the adolescents' need to find a usable wisdom in the books they read and study" (118). The "usable wisdom" in *The Chocolate War* is not that life demands conformity and that those, like Jerry, who resist are "murdered," nor is it that adolescents should buckle down and do what adults tell them, even if those adults are misguided or corrupt. With the right guidance, young readers can come to see that the message of the novel is that individuals must struggle against bullying and injustice, even if they *know* they are going to be defeated.

Jerry Renault is being taken to the hospital at the end of *The Chocolate War*, advising his friend to do whatever needs to be done to avoid disturbing the universe. The benevolent adults appear to have been unable to stop the catastrophe, and the wicked ones are watching gleefully from the sidelines. The story isn't over, however. Brother Leon has been caught, his machinations have been stopped, and boys like Archie, even though they haven't been punished, have brought their deeds into the open, where the consequences can be seen. Jerry has disturbed the universe [and gotten beaten up for it], but the disruption has had a salutary effect. As Oneal says, Cormier "forces us to re-examine our comfortable assumptions about who we are and what we believe and what a book for young people ought to be about" (183). Like the other novelists in this study, Cormier knows that this lesson is not one that can be taught in novels that shy away from difficult truths or pander to adults' notions that children need to be protected from these harsh realities.

CHAPTER SIX

"No clouds of glory"
Katherine Paterson's Prodigal Children (1977–1980)

> We cannot surrender to those who fear the power of books—who know that a true democracy of the intellect threatens demagoguery, breaks open the narrowness of the spirit, and challenges the selfish interests of the privileged few—Katherine Paterson, "Still Summoned by Books," IC 105
>
> To be a spy [for hope], to encourage hope for a young reader, Paterson tells stories. Stories of lost souls and found souls, stories of lonely souls and comforting souls, souls of those who have given themselves away and souls who have been given the gift of themselves—Schmidt 2

Katherine Paterson has been writing books for children and young adults since the 1977 publication *of Bridge to Terabithia*, and she has been the focus of censorship challenges since that first book appeared. *Bridge* and *The Great Gilly Hopkins* (1978), for example, made the ALA's Most Frequently Challenged Books lists for *both* 1990–2000 and 2000–2009. However, she was also awarded the Newbery Award for *Bridge* and for *Jacob Have I Loved* (1980), as well as the Newbery Honor for *Gilly*. A practicing Christian, daughter of missionaries, and wife of a minister, Paterson has raised the hackles of censors for the colorful language of her feisty characters, as well as her frank treatment of death and sexuality. She has also given generations of young readers, who are "summoned" (as she phrases it) by her books' celebration of children's strength, and wisdom, and compassion for others. As she says in her Newbery Award speech for *Bridge*, "I discovered gradually and not without a little pain that you don't put together a bridge for a child. You become one—you lay yourself across the chasm" (IC 245). Indeed, this

"Unsuitable" Books

is what Paterson has done in the four decades she's been writing novels and writing about them—put herself "across the chasm" between the pain and fear children experience and the understanding and faith adults can offer them.

In "The Child in the Attic," Patterson says that "a book can give a child a way to learn to value herself, which is at the start of the process of growing a great soul" (IC 32). This is the reason, she says, that she doesn't set out to create characters who serve as role models for children. Role models, she says, "didn't inspire any child that I ever was. They only discouraged me" (IC 32). She adds in her essay entitled "Hope and Happy Endings" that children go to novels for a variety of reasons, but not to find role models. When they go to a serious novel, she says, "they expect to find truth, and everyone knows that role models are ideals, not realities. They want hope rooted in reality, not wishful thinking" (IC 139–40). This commitment to reality over wishful thinking connects Paterson to other young adult writers such as Chris Crutcher, Mildred Taylor, and Robert Cormier and makes her a target for those well-meaning but often deluded adults who think children should only be presented with views of the sunnier sides of life.

This doesn't mean that Paterson's novels are short of her particular kind of hope. In "Story of My Lives," she says she presents "the hope of yearning. It is always incomplete, as all true hope must be. It is always in tension, rooted in this fallen earth but growing, yearning, stretching toward the new creation" (IC 146). This is the hope of a dedicated Christian, who believes we are fallen but that we always have the opportunity for grace. In keeping with her mission to present this incomplete and yearning hope to young people, she challenges those who want to censor her work. She insists that while she doesn't "put words or scenes in my books just to make life harder for teachers and librarians," she is simply "trying to tell a true story about real people." The fact that she is a Christian, she says, "does not make people who wish to ban my books very happy," but she believes she would be "untrue to the gift that God has given me" (IC 158) if she watered down the reality of her plots and characters. Of course, this is ironic, given that many who consider themselves Christians are the first to argue for censorship.

Along with telling the truth as she sees it, Paterson has another purpose. In "Fighting the Long Defeat," she says that her novels are "filled with heroes of the most unlikely sort." Her desire, she says, is to "make common cause with the losers—to show the heroism in those the world tends to despise" (21). In doing this, she says that writers for children must not "surrender to despair or cynicism," but instead must stare "into the very face of overweening power, of sinful greed and criminal indifference" and "join hands to become the unlikely, dancing heroes of the long defeat" (24). Given that life is in a sense one "long defeat" ending in death, and that children in particular but all of us, ultimately, are often defenseless against what life throws at us, she thinks the best thing that she can do is have her characters, who are often judged as "losers" by society, stand up to unjust power and selfishness. Her foster children, her children who feel unloved or unwanted, her prodigals, eventually are welcomed back into homes that they have rejected (or have rejected them), but her endings are often more bitter (or at least wistful) than sweet.

Critics concur with Paterson's astute analysis of her own work, believing her to be a writer who respects children and sees their lives clearly. Karen Patricia Smith says that Patterson's work "demonstrates the respect she holds for the young, their emotions, and the challenges they encounter" (6). Her main characters, Smith says, are "children who have endured certain forms of isolation, but they are also children who triumph and ultimately grow in the face of trial" (6). As Paterson puts it, they are "unlikely" heroes and dance in the face of defeat. Sarah Smedman says that although Paterson is "distinguished by the clarity with which she confronts the evidence leading modern children to despair, each of her novels succeeds in powerfully reminding readers that indeed there is room for hope" (102). Clarity and hope seem to be the twin principles of all of Paterson's fiction.

In his book-length study of Paterson, Gary Schmidt says readers must first turn to Paterson's life to understand her work. She spent much of her childhood in the South, he points out, and she has also been influenced by her experience as a child of missionaries, reading the Bible, moving frequently, and being born in China (3). Consequently, she grew up feeling slightly outside the mainstream, somewhat isolated and certainly different from many of her peers. Schmidt says this may explain "why so few of Paterson's characters have strong friends," as well as "why so many adults figure hugely in her novels, in a field where adult characters are often subordinated" (7). More often than not, Paterson had to turn to her parents for comfort and wisdom. Schmidt adds that her characters are "pilgrims along a narrow path; again and again she would use this archetypal journey in ways not dissimilar of those of John Bunyan. In addition, though, these characters are prodigal children, desperate to find a home but beleaguered by their own fear" (53-4). Her Christian background and her itinerate childhood clearly informs her treatment of her characters as prodigals, never sure where home is—or even if they really want to find it.

Paterson's first novel, *Bridge to Terabithia*, creates two versions of that child in the story of Jess Aarons and his friend Leslie Burke. Paterson says in several of her essays that the story is based on her son David's loss of his childhood friend Lisa Hill (who was killed when struck by lightning), and the book, which treats the tragic death of young Leslie and Jess' resultant grief, is dedicated to them both. In an interview with Heather Quarles and Suzanne Wolfe, Paterson says that real-life events motivated her to write about parents' desires to protect their children and they ways they cannot always do this. "Terrible things happen to children," she says. "Perhaps what we as adults ought to do is prepare children for the world as it is without scaring the life out of them. Books are a way of rehearsing ahead of time for what life is going to bring you" (57). This book is her way of preparing for or rehearsing tragedy.

The novel is more complicated than just a way to help young readers cope with death, however. Joel Chaston, perceptively argues that, in fact, *Bridge* "can be read as an argument against attempting to solve children's problems through literature." The novel reveals that regardless of how much Jess reads, "no amount of literary exposure to death, for example, can prepare Jess for Leslie Burke's death" ("Other" 239). Chaston argues that Paterson "carefully refrains from turning Jess's own story into a prepackaged set of solutions that would try to cure the problems of yet another grieving child." Nevertheless, he says, Paterson respects Jess's "personal response to Leslie's death, making it clear that Jess's grief is genuine and should not be lightly dismissed" ("Other" 240). Although Jess might have appreciated a book such as this one "it is clear that it would not have provided him with pat solutions or wiped away his grief" ("Other" 241). As with all her novels, Paterson attempts in this book to show a child developing and friendship, grieving the loss of his friend, and eventually reaching out to his family (from which he is estranged) for comfort. The prodigal returns and divisions are healed, but the pain remains, Paterson shows her young readers.

Six. "No clouds of glory"

In spite of the sincerity and skill of Paterson's treatment of this difficult subject, Susan Hirsh reports that there have been challenges to the book in Nebraska, Connecticut, California, Pennsylvania, Texas, and Maine to its allegedly profane language, and challenges in Connecticut and Pennsylvania to "negative views of life, witchcraft, disrespect for adults and confusing fantasy worlds" (102–3). However, as Hirsch rightly points out, "the complex characters and moving story by far transcend the fact the children see those words in print" (105). Those who have sought (and continue to seek) to remove this book from libraries and classrooms seem to have missed its essential point. It is extremely difficult to discuss the death of a child without some "negative views of life," and the fantasy world the two children create seems comforting and creative, not dangerous. It seems more likely that would-be censors are troubled, once again, by children who resist adult authority and adult definitions of what is proper (that is, submissive) behavior.

The novel begins with Jess wanting to be "not one of the fastest, or next to the fastest, but *the* fastest" (2) runner in his fifth-grade class. His need to be the best at something stems, in part, from the aesthetic and emotional poverty of his surroundings, including his school, which "was short of everything, especially athletic equipment" (3). Paterson later mentions that the classrooms at the school are overcrowded (20) and that they have been promised, but haven't received, a lunch room (23). Nancy Huse says that Paterson sees the ugliness and poverty of Jess's life as the result of "a lost continuity with spiritual and cultural values now preserved only in religion and the intellectual life" (100). Much of what happens in the novel is centered around Jess's restoring that "lost continuity" with art and imagination, but also with family.

Jess wants to be fast and athletic, not only because he wants to rise above his relatively bleak surroundings, but because his truest talent—in drawing—isn't appreciated (or even respected) by his family or classmates. Ever since he'd been in first grade Jess has been known as that "crazy little kid that draws all the time" (4). In his world, anyone who creates art is seen as odd. His drawing is a release from his sense of estrangement from his family and community. Jess, the narrator says, "drew the way some people drink whiskey. The peace would start at the top of his muddled brain and seep down through this tired and tensed-up body" (10). However, because this talent (and the relief it provides) is discounted at school and at home, he has to keep it "buried inside himself like a pirate treasure" (12). His ability is also suspect because it isn't a typically masculine pursuit. Jess's father, for example, is less than pleased when Jess tells him he wants to be an artist: "'Bunch of old ladies turning my only son into some kind of a—' He had stopped at the word, but Jess had gotten the message. It was one you didn't forget, even after four years" (12). Readers have little trouble filling in the word his father didn't say. The message is clearly that Jess is feminized by his drawing (or perhaps even worse, might be seen as not resolutely heterosexual). Thus, running becomes a sure-fire way of establishing his masculine identity and connecting, perhaps, with his father. Real boys play sports—they don't draw pictures.

Probably because he doesn't fit the expectations rural Virginians have for boys, Jess lives a fairly solitary life before Leslie. He even feels alone among his sisters and mother (without even a rooster in the barnyard filled with hens) and with his father gone all day (15). As Schmidt puts it, "Jess is responsible for many of the chores, which he does alone. In fact, he does almost everything alone" (55). He is even lonely when his father is there, aching to be hugged as his dad hugs the girls. His father believes Jess was "too big for that since the day he was born" (16), and Jess misses that tangible proof of his father's love. A boy in a house full of women, who likes to draw but feels guilty about it, who goes to a school where only athletic ability is prized, is in dire need of a friend who can nurture the artistic and emotional aspects of his personality.

Interestingly, upon first meeting Leslie, Jess can't tell if she's a girl or boy (18), and both his and her names are gender neutral. Paterson appears to be experimenting with gender roles and expectations, showing Jess as the dreamy artist and Leslie as the aggressive athlete, although those roles will shift as the novel goes on. For example, Leslie beats Jess at the race (28), and Jess is later afraid that she might sit by him on the bus, thinking "the girl had no notions of what you did and didn't do" (28). Although he thinks that Leslie's running might be "beautiful," he shakes the thought away and goes into the house (28), thinking that Leslie has taken the fun out of running. As Sue Misheff puts it, "Jess's one hope of gaining social stature by being the school's fastest runner is dashed when Leslie appears. But his relationship with her becomes the catalyst for his artistic growth" (133). She has taken some of the fun out of running, but she offers him the chance to expand his horizons artistically. As Jess is becoming more open to artistic growth, he is helped

Six. "No clouds of glory"

along with way by the new music teacher, Miss Edmunds, and upon meeting her, Jess feels "that it was the beginning of a new season in his life, and he chose deliberately to make it so" (31). Jess has added even more women to his life, but they are committed to helping him branch out rather than follow the norm.

Introducing Leslie into Jess's life, however, is not without conflicts and confusions, the first of which is social and economic. Leslie tells Jess that her family came to the farm to get away from their materialistic lifestyle and to "think about what's important," but Jess comments, and Leslie agrees, that she is the one who has to "pay" for their attempts at self-discovery (33) by being forced to leave her friends and school and move to the country. Leslie also tells him that for her family money is not a problem, and Jess thinks that he didn't know anyone for whom money was not a problem and decides not to talk about money with her again (33). Jess and Leslie come from very different social classes. In school, Leslie tells the class about her hobby, which is scuba diving, a sport of the more leisured class, which none of the other children have experienced. Jess talks about football, which he doesn't really like but thinks it is appropriate for a boy, and it is one with which his classmates are familiar. He doesn't mention his real hobby, drawing, for the reasons discussed earlier. Leslie is slowly leading him out of his familiar world, but this will also mean recognizing the ways in which he will never fit in there.

The second thing that Leslie brings into his life is a sharper awareness of his fear. For example, Jess is scared by Leslie's description of being underwater while scuba diving but thinks that his dad "expected him to be a man" and therefore not afraid (34). This desire to be less afraid of life leads to Jess's participation in the creation of their imaginary land, Terabithia. When Leslie suggests that they make up a place in which to play, where they rule as king and queen, Jess thinks that he would "like to be a ruler of something. Even something that wasn't real" (39), and he also thinks that there are parts of the woods that scare him. Even in their imaginary kingdom, Jess is not free from anxiety. However, when Jess finds he can't draw Terabithia, because he can't "get the poetry of the trees," Leslie tells him that he will someday. Jess believes her because "there in the shadowy light of the stronghold everything seemed possible" (40). Although Jess feels "taller and stronger and wiser in that mysterious land," his mother tells him that his father is worried about

"Unsuitable" Books

him playing only with girls and "what would become of it" (46). Again, his family voices suspicions about Jess engaging in typically female behaviors. What "would become of it" is most likely that Jess would be drawn to Leslie's creative and more leisured world and away from the more traditional values of his family.

Mischeff explains it this way: "The imaginations of the female characters serve to bring the safe places into being, and these places serve to change the lives of the male characters who must also use their imaginations to carry on with life after the deaths of the saviors" (132). Leslie is able to create a safe world for Jess (perhaps because as a girl born to parents with the money and time to indulge her imagination) and also foster the resilience he will need after she is gone. Terabithia becomes a place of play and of personal growth. Paterson says that Terabithia "starts out as a place outside ourselves—a tree, a hideout in the woods, a corner of our backyards, the springhouse on our uncle's farm. As we grow older, however, it becomes a place inside ourselves into which we may go" ("Where?" 156). For Jess and Leslie, it is a place outside their worlds but also becomes a place that at least Jess can take with him anywhere he goes.

Not surprisingly, as a result of his experiences with Leslie and her family, Jess begins to think that he might be a "foundling" (58), that the family with whom he lives could not actually be related to him biologically, given the emotional and aesthetic gulf between them. Christmas seems to reinforce this belief, when Jess receives a racing-car set from his family, which he plays with only to please his father (63). Cars are appropriate pastimes for boys, not drawing, his father emphasizes with his gift. Family finances also play a role, as the car set is cheaply made and disappoints both father and son, although for difference reasons. Leslie, on the other hand, gives him watercolors and art paper, which acknowledges Jess's talents and interests and involves significantly more money. Jess gives Leslie Prince Terrien, a puppy, in part because the dog could be gotten for free, but the gift is also a sign of the familial connection Jess feels toward Leslie (it is very much like their furry child). It is also a more intimate and appreciated gift than Jess's biological family gives him.

Unfortunately, though, Jess is *not* a part of Leslie's family, which he finds out when Leslie starts helping her father restore their old farm house and he is excluded from their work. Left alone, Jess tries to go by

Six. "No clouds of glory"

himself to Terabithia, but find he can't "make the magic" without Leslie (64). Leslie says that by working with her father, she is starting to understand him, while Jess has never considered that parents might be understood or that a child would want to (67). Again, social class differences show up, as Jess's working-class family doesn't have the time or the inclination to get to know each other as people. As Jess becomes increasingly jealous over Leslie's father's taking up so much of her time and attention, he offers to help, and his practical skills are much appreciated by the hapless Bill. Jess's family works with their hands; Leslie's with their brains. The Burkes, he realizes, are smart not about "fixing things or growing things, but smart in a way Jess had never known real live people to be" (69). At this point, it appears that Jess has adopted the Burkes as his surrogate parents and also adopted their artistic and somewhat-more-hedonistic values.

Shortly after, however, this peace is destroyed when Jess's sister May Belle finds out about their hiding place, and threatens to tell, Jess threatens her back and thinks that "his life was a delicate as a dandelion. One little puff from any direction, and it was blown to bits" (77). Jess feels the need to keep his imaginary life separate from his family, in large part because they have no understanding of what inspires and enriches his new life. Of course, Paterson is also here reminding readers that all life is "delicate as a dandelion" and potentially vulnerable to being "blown to bits."

When it begins to rain heavily, Jess is afraid and wants to be inside, while Leslie braves the elements. He worries that he might not be "worthy" to be a king of Terabithia (91). In his mind, boy kings shouldn't have any fear. He doesn't mind telling Leslie of his fear; he minds actually being afraid and what it says about him as a male. Jess feels "as though he had been made with a great piece missing" (93). As a boy, Jess thinks that he should be much braver than a mere girl.

The climax of the story begins when Miss Edmunds invites him to go to the National Gallery. He doesn't think about Leslie until he is in the car with his teacher, and then he enjoys the thought of the two of them going alone (98). He likes the company of the attractive and understanding Miss Edmunds and wants to have her all to himself. After he returns, however, he finds out Leslie has died and believes he is partially responsible for leaving her alone (102). Shocked at the news, Jess takes off running. His father follows and picks Jess "up in his arms as though he were a baby" (104). Jess has finally gotten the physical and emotional comfort he seeks from his father. However, his sisters paradoxically criticize him for eating pancakes the next morning (and therefore being callous) and also inform him that boys aren't supposed to cry (108). It appears unclear just how a boy is *supposed* to respond to tragedy. His father, on the other hand, lightly touches his shoulder and doesn't criticize him for not getting to his chores (109). The clearly-defined lines between masculine and feminine behavior are fading, as father reaches out to son and gives him the concrete demonstration of love he's been craving.

In subsequent pages, Jess tries to find an appropriate response to Leslie's death. He visits her family, but he decides that they aren't crying for Leslie but for themselves, and he concludes that they shouldn't have brought her there (114). He seems to be turning his back on the life the Burkes lead, which he had earlier so envied. After this, Jess throws Leslie's gift paper and paints into the water of the creek where she died (115), rejecting both his art and Leslie's support of it. This sacrifice doesn't seem to be enough, though, and he decides to lay a funeral wreath for her in Terabithia. His sister May Belle follows him, panicking on the branch he's laid across the creek. He tells her it's okay to be scared, reassures her, and helps her across. When Prince Terrien simply swims across and May Belle comments that he's not scared, Jessie tells her, "It's like the smarter you are, the more things can scare you" (123), and he admits that he, too, was once scared. Finally, Jess realizes that Leslie "had taken him from the cow pasture into Terabithia and turned him into a king." He also understands that Terabithia was a place he came to grow strong and then leave. Leslie had "tried to push back the walls of his mind and make him see beyond to the shining world—huge and terrible and beautiful and very fragile" (126). The book ends when he brings May Belle to Terabithia and tells her that she is "the queen they've been waiting for" (128).

Schmidt says that when Jess leads May Belle to Terabithia "it is a moment of consummate grace." Jess, he says, "has grown from a rather shy and somewhat lonely child with no close friends to a giver of grace" (56). He adds that Jess is "no longer trying to set himself apart." Instead, he is "building bridges, making a way for others to participate in the imaginative world of Terabithia" (57). Like Katherine Paterson, in this and all her other novels, Jess is laying himself like a bridge across the water and helping his sister to cross over. Freed by Leslie's love and support, he is able not only to indulge his creative talent—he is able to share it. Jess's moment of grace comes when he can return both to Terabithia and, in small but significant ways, to his family.

Coming out a year after *Bridge*, *The Great Gilly Hopkins* (1978) has probably given Paterson the most grief from would-be censors, who object to the sometimes salty language of the main character, a foster child with a heart of gold and a mouth filled with mud. Connie Russell says the book has been "challenged in Virginia for swearing, in Colorado for profanity and disrespect (of God and parents), and in California for witchcraft references. In Connecticut it was challenged because of profanity, blasphemy and obscenities, and negative views of parents" (183). Paterson has acknowledged these complaints and responds with characteristic confidence in her artistic mission. Many teachers and parents, she says, have "taken [her] to task" for creating Gilly, but she says would not reform her because children love her. The worst children love her the most, she says, and she believes that by "loving Gilly, they can bring a little to love themselves, and children who love themselves do not strike out at other people" (IC 32). However, she recognizes that she had to temper Gilly's language, even while trying to let her mouth "reflect the lost child within." If she had "faithfully reproduced the language of the Gillys some of us know all too well," she says, "the weight of obscenity would have totally unbalanced this story. Such, you see, is the power of words, and the writer must be aware of this power and walk gently" (IC 191). In this novel, Paterson is obviously working hard to balance realism (of action and language) with the love she has for this wayward character.

Sue Ann Carnes notes this dichotomy in Gilly's characterization. "Gilly is angry, mean, prejudiced, and manipulative," Carnes says. "She is also vulnerable, capable of generosity, growth, and love. She is, in short, a complex, multi-dimensional character" (10). Carnes also sees that Gilly has the potential to reach all sorts of children, even those whose lives are easier than hers, who "may recognize kinship with a character who feels anger at adult betrayals and rejections, who fantasizes rescue or escape, and who struggles for power with the only means she has at her disposal" (10). All children, even those who are sweeter tempered and more privileged than Gilly, can share her anger and her powerlessness. Connie Russell makes an even stronger case against those who would keep this book out of the hands of children. Ironically, she says, "many of those who object to this book are the same people fighting for the teaching of values in our schools." She adds that there is no better book to teach values. "Without preaching," Russell says, "Paterson extols the virtues of compassion, honesty, integrity, and responsibility" (184–5). Paterson tells Heather Quarles, and Suzanne Wolfe in an interview that Gilly is actually her "most blatantly Christian book" (53), a story about a prodigal daughter who finally learns, with the help of her foster family and biological grandmother, how to "grow up and love other people" (54). Like Jess in Terabithia, Gilly must return to her less-than-perfect biological family, and also like Jess, she is able to do that after being both chastened and strengthened by her self-created family.

As the novel begins, eleven-year-old Gilly is being taken to yet another foster home by her case worker, Miss Ellis, who is not at all sure whether this placement (or any, for that matter) will succeed. When told by Miss Ellis that Mamie Trotter, her new foster mother, is "nice," Gilly thinks that she herself is not nice but "brilliant." "I am famous across this entire county," she thinks. "Nobody wants to tangle with the great Galadriel Hopkins. I am too clever and too hard to manage. Gruesome Gilly, they call me" (3). As will soon become clear, Gilly's confidence hides insecurities born out of years of mistreatment and rejection. Trotter is an unlikely savior, with her (as Gilly says) "'Before' body with an 'After' smile" (5). Fat, ungrammatical, kind and tough, Mamie Trotter will nevertheless rescue Gilly and give her a home that, sadly, she must eventually leave in order to come to terms with her past.

Readers soon learn that Gilly is not quite as confident and tough as she appears, and that her brashness results from a misplaced confidence in a mother who abandoned her at birth, and whose rejection of her Gilly refuses to acknowledge. Looking at her mother's picture, she feels herself "dissolving like hot Jell-O" (9). In order to cope with these feelings, Gilly tells herself that her mother would come and get her if she only knew what a "dump" she was living in (15), and she begins planning her escape to the mother she naively believes is waiting for her.

In her new school, Gilly feels assaulted by the students, the teachers, and the system. Much like Jess, her school environment was not one that encouraged or celebrated difference from the norm. Facing her classmates, Gilly remembers "a picture in an old book of a red fox on a high rock surrounded by snarling dogs …. They had her surrounded,

Six. "No clouds of glory"

and in their stupid ways, they were determined to wear her down" (22). She decides to pay attention, lest the "low-class bunch of idiots" think they are smarter than she is (44). Sue Ann Cairns says that "in order to feel a sense of control, Gilly uses her intelligence, particularly with language, to scan her environment and search out others' weaknesses" (10). Given that she is a newcomer and in many ways unprotected from the world, she has to use her primary strength, her intelligence, to keep herself safe.

She finds her teacher Miss Harris a relief, in that she judges her work by its merits without a "personal opinion of the person doing the work" (54). But other days, her teachers' neutrality "grated" on her. She is used to being "in charge of her education" and finding herself either "courted" or "cursed." Here, Miss Harris "merely melted her into the mass" (55). Gilly hates being normal most of all; she'd rather be in trouble than be ignored. To break through Miss Harris's perceived indifference, she writes a racist poem and gives it to her African-American teacher, who then teaches *her* a lesson on anger. Miss Harris tells her that she and Gilly treat anger differently. She was taught to deny hers, while Gilly's "is still up here on the surface where you can look it in the face, make friends with it if you want to" (59), for which Miss Harris envies her. After this speech, surprisingly, Miss Harris thanks her for the card, telling her it sent her to the teachers' lounge, where she "cursed creatively for twenty minutes" and came out feeling better than she has in years. Cairns comments that Miss Harris "discloses her anger in order to disclose herself as a subject who can be hurt, not as an object to be used for a trickster's entertainment. She also models a way to work through one's rage and pain without harming others" (15). In this way, Miss Harris becomes one of Gilly's many helpful guides on her way toward adulthood, teaching her that controlled (but not repressed anger) is a useful tool to combat prejudice and fear. Such a lesson would be a good one for would-be book banners to learn. Rather than hide uncomfortable truths, one should discuss (or read about) them.

When her mother sends a postcard saying only that she wishes Gilly could be with her, without offering to come get her daughter, Gilly wonders why things have to be so difficult. Other children, even "stupid kids who didn't even like their mothers much" got to be with them every day. She starts to cry, thinking she hasn't seen her mother since she was three, her "beautiful mother who missed her so much and sent her all her love" (29). She keeps these feelings to herself, however, not disclosing to anyone how sad and lost she really is. Cairns points out that it isn't surprising that Gilly keeps silent, or uses language only minimally (or in the case of Miss Harris, as a weapon). Her mother, Cairns says, "has gained magical power over Gilly" through a few words and an indistinct address on a postcard, and Gilly imitates her relative silence. "Not speaking when expected to do so," she says, "is an effective way for children to exercise power by frustrating adults, who can become childish in their rage" (11). Like Melinda in *Speak*, Gilly learns that silence, like judiciously applied anger, might also be a weapon against powerlessness.

The longer she stays with Mrs. Trotter, though, the less clear Gilly is about what she wants to do. Indeed, Gilly moves back and forth between compassionately trying to fit into her new family and ruthlessly planning to leave it. She helps her foster brother William Earnest (W.E.) fly paper airplanes, for example, and Trotter is grateful for her kindness. However, Gilly hurries off afterward "because the look on Trotter's face was the one Gilly had, in some deep part of her, longed to see all her life, but not from someone like Trotter. That was not part of the plan" (52). Her *plan* is to leave Trotter's house, in part so that she doesn't "become like W.E., soft and no good," as life has taught her that "a person must be tough. Otherwise, you were had" (60). To prevent being "had," she takes advantage of someone else, in this case blind neighbor Mr. Randolph, from whom she steals money. Eventually she steals from Trotter as well, trying to accumulate money for a bus ticket to where she believes her mother lives (and is waiting for her). She thinks, "People were so dumb sometimes you almost felt bad to take advantage of them—but not too bad. Not when it was your only way to get where you had to go" (68). Not knowing about the theft, Trotter continues being nice to her, and Gilly assuages her guilt by thinking, "I can't go soft—not as long as I'm nobody's real kid—not while I'm just something to play musical chairs with" (71). She was left behind "like the rest of the trash" when her previous foster family moved to Florida, and she determines this time to leave instead of being left. Gilly's deception is bad, but the behavior of the adults in her life, for the most part, has been much worse.

With the stolen money, Gilly tries to take a bus to California to see her mother, after writing a letter denouncing Mrs. Trotter's home, but she is caught by the police. When Trotter shows up to claim her, she is

Six. "No clouds of glory"

reluctant to go with her, and it looks as if the police will keep her. She relents when William Earnest pleads with her to come home, and "the ice in her frozen brain rumbled and cracked" (92). After this, she decides to teach William Earnest, who is being bullied, to defend himself (101). It appears that Gilly has finally accepted her foster family as her own and decided to stay, in part because they forgive her for her transgressions and don't treat her like yesterday's trash.

Shortly after her aborted departure, her entire family foster family comes down with the flu, and then her grandmother (*not* her mother) shows up, spurred by Gilly's letter. The family reunion is not quite as imagined it, with "Courtney herself ... sweeping in like a goddess queen, reclaiming the long-lost princess." Her dream had no place for the reality of "dumpy old-fashioned ladies with Southern speech, or barefoot fat women in striped pajamas, or blind old black men who recited poetry by heart and snored with their mouths open—or crazy, heart-ripping little guys who went '*pow*' and still wet their stupid beds" (114–5). Her fairy tale is not turning out as she planned—Gilly and her mother living happily ever after. Instead, "like Bluebeard's wife, she'd opened the forbidden door and someday she would have to look inside" (115). Gilly is going to have to acknowledge her real love for this new family and give up her imagined love of a queenly mother.

Cairns says that Gilly has "fortified herself against her very real losses through magical thinking borrowed primarily from fairy tales. This imagined power helps her stitch together disconnected experiences and losses, but it also clouds her view of reality" (11). As Mrs. Ellis says, she doesn't "understand why a smart girl like you goes around booby-trapping yourself" (121). Instead, what Gilly must do is change the story. She considers the fact that Trotter has given her a chance "to be real without any quotation marks. To belong and to possess. To be herself, to be the swan, to be the ugly duckling no longer" (124). Cairns insightfully comments that letting go of the happy ending is "necessarily painful, but the pain of facing truth is also its own salve" (19). To be a real swan, and not a princess, hurts, but it brings its own rewards, in particular a clear-eyed view of her true situation.

In order to see the whole picture, Gilly realizes that she must go back to her grandmother's house, where her mother grew up. When she arrives there, she has to accept that her mother may never come for her (130). She stays in the room of Courtney's brother, who died in Vietnam, and which seems "less haunted" than her mother's (132). Recognizing for the first time that her mother might not be the queen she imagines, she instead approaches a kind of empathy for the "haunted" girl Courtney might have been. When Courtney finally arrives, Gilly is disappointed in her ordinary looks, selfish behavior, and clear unwillingness to take Gilly back with her, and she calls Trotter. Trotter tells her, "Life ain't supposed to be nothing, 'cept maybe tough" and "All that stuff about happy endings is lies. The only happy ending in this world is death" (147). She says also that life is tough, not bad. "Nothing to make you happy like doing good on a tough job, now is there?" and she reminds her that she is "home" with her grandmother. Gilly blows her nose, washes her face, goes out to meet her mother and grandmother, thinking, "No clouds of glory, perhaps, but Trotter would be proud" (148).

As Schmidt puts it "At the end, Gilly's realization of her growth comes as something of a shock to her—but not to the reader" (68). Readers know almost from the beginning that Courtney is not coming to get her and that Trotter's house is a safe refuge not a prison. They also come to realize that Trotter's is not Gilly's final stop, that she must eventually make peace with her fantasies and create a life with her grandmother. Citing Paterson's familiarity with Gerard Manly Hopkins, Schmidt says, "[W]hen one thinks of the image in 'God's Grandeur' of the Holy Ghost brooding over the bent world, it is hard not to think of Gilly and Trotter in a bent world filled with loss and abandonment, where prodigals may fall away but where they may also, against all hope, find themselves in a family" (69). As in *Bridge*, Gilly has been given a second chance to return home, although in her case it is to a home she never dreamed about. In all of Paterson's novels, grace is not denied her young protagonists, but it rarely takes the form they expect, either.

In *Jacob Have I Loved*, (1980), Paterson continues her focus on adolescents' search for connection and meaning. The novel is, as Chris Crowe says, "the best example of Paterson's insight into human nature, her keen understanding of the complexity of human relations, and her remarkable ability to articulate that knowledge" (29). Indeed, it shows a decided growth in Paterson's skill as a writer and continues to demonstrate her compassion for her readers. However, its focus on adolescent sexuality and conflict with adults has made it a target of many book challenges. *Jacob*, Nancy Huse says, is more "directed to a teen-age audience because of its emphasis on the hero's lonely world making," and it

Six. "No clouds of glory"

is "a provocative example of realism dealing with ultimate values" (101). Again, it appears that Paterson's honesty about issues that make parents uncomfortable and her refusal to sugar coat reality for her young readers has caused censors to overlook the positive messages for the more controversial details. In "Metaphors to Live By," Paterson admits that she confronts envy "rather baldly" (IC 127) in the novel, which certainly concerns some of her critics. Ultimately, though, she thinks of *Jacob* as a quest story in which "a wandering nobody must go out from bondage through the wilderness and by the grace of God become truly someone who can give back something of what she has been given" ("The Story of My Lives," IC 161). Like Gilly and Jess, the main character of this novel finds grace, but only after being lost for quite a while.

The "wandering nobody" in this story is Sara Louise Bradshaw, who is thirteen years old when the story begins, and who is living on Rass Island (an imaginary island in Chesapeake Bay) in the rather large shadow of her delicate, beautiful, and musically-talented twin sister Caroline. She grows up in the novel, eventually leaving the island and moving to the mountains as a nurse, marrying and having a child. Most importantly, she comes to terms with her sister (and her jealousy of her) and finds a way both to heal the hurt of her past and to create a life of meaning and beauty for herself.

As if she hasn't had enough trouble with conservative critics, several of those on the left have been concerned with the way Sara Louise appears to capitulate to traditional values at the end of the story, choosing to become a nurse instead of a doctor and marrying a mountain man and having his child. According to Jane Agee, "Louise's ambivalence about her mother's feelings toward twin sister Caroline and her mother's choices in life haunt her own struggle to become a woman" (175). Louise, she says, "abandons all hope of becoming a doctor and settles for marriage and family in an isolated mountain community" (178), therefore "unconsciously repeat[ing] the pattern of her own mother's life" (179). For Agee, Louise is reproducing her mother's life, to borrow from Nancy Chodorow, and therefore sending the wrong message to contemporary girls.

Angela Hubler says, on the other hand, that "it is not Louise's internalization of gender-role socialization that dictates that she will become a nurse rather than a doctor, but the economic realities of the post–World War II U.S. economy" (88). Someone like Louise would be much more likely to find employment as a nurse than as a doctor in that time period, especially in the mountain community in which she lands. Patterson adds to this debate that unhappiness with the apparently traditional ending is "distinctly a postadolescent phenomenon" ("The Story of My Lives," IC 160), as young readers have never complained about it. She also comments that girls in the story are bound, but not completely, by the world in which they live. "The characters from history or fiction that we remember are those who kicked against the walls of their societies," she says. "But the writer cannot pretend for the sake of her own prejudices that those walls were so flimsy that a character could demolish them with a single dramatic gesture. She cannot even assume that her character would see all of those walls as evil" ("Where?" 155). If there are no challenges for Sara Louise, in other words, she wouldn't be a believable or compelling character. In fact, Rass Island, with all of its restrictions for girls and women, is, Paterson says, vital to creating Louise and determining her future ("People I Have Known," IC 163). Until she discovered the island, she says, Sara Louise "never became flesh" ("Where" 154). Sara Louise needs the island (and also to leave it) in order to become whole.

Caroline Goforth continues the discussion of the necessary relationship between Louise and Rass Island. "Stark and treeless, with graves in its front yards, the island is as much a desert as Louise's resentful, angry self," she says. "At the same time, the tightly organized social structure of the island provides a refuge for the inhabitants, just as Louise's withdrawal from others contributes to her developing self-reliance" (176). That is, Louise isolates herself in order to grow. However, Louise also spends her adolescence "desperately clinging to a stagnant, shrinking self, afraid to make human connections that would open her to love and to a new range of experiences and awareness" (176). Paradoxically, Goforth says, she must learn to "love her island self, embracing the very region of danger she fears" (176). For better or for worse, Rass Island, with its gender stereotyping, is part of Louise's identity, even as she struggles to escape it.

Other critics have looked more closely at the novel's narrative style. Gary Schmidt points out that *Jacob* is Paterson's first use of first-person narrative voice, which he says is "precisely the right narrative perspective to use in a novel about a character who can see only one perspective" (77). Maria Nikolajeva says that through the use of the first person, "the

Six. "No clouds of glory"

authoritative narrative agency that is able to comment on the characters' behavior and opinions and manipulate the reader toward proper assessment of the characters disappears, and with it the inherent didacticism of conventional children's literature" (14). Therefore, she argues, the narrative structure "puts a much stronger demand on the readers, who must liberate themselves from the subject position imposed by the text" (15). Thus this is a harder book for young readers than either *Gilly* or *Bridge*, as it challenges them to be both sympathetic with and skeptical of Sara Louise's world view and judgments.

The novel begins with Sara Louise at thirteen, describing herself as "tall and large boned, with delusions of beauty and romance" (4). Joel Chaston says that Louise is a "quixotic reader," who wishes "the world were more like fiction and cast themselves and others in real-life narratives based on their reading" (100). Unfortunately, though, the story she most tells herself is that of Jacob and Esau, the privileged and the benighted twins. When she was the elder twin for a few minutes, she says, it was the only time she was "the center of everyone's attention. From the moment Caroline was born, she snatched it all for herself" (15). While in the process of telling Caroline's harrowing birth story, her grandmother says she can't remember Louise's birth, and Louise feels "as though I was the new born infant a second time, cast aside and forgotten" (15). In an attempt to console her, Louise's mother tells her that she wasn't any worry, unlike her smaller and more delicate twin, and Louise wonders, "Wasn't it all the months of worry that had made Caroline's life so dear to them all?" (16). Looking at a photograph of them as children, Louise sees that Caroline is "tiny and exquisite" and laughing and Louise is "hunched there like a fat dark shadow, my eyes cut sideways toward Caroline, thumb in mouth, the pudgy hand covering most of my face" (16–17). Clearly, the stories Louise tells herself are not therapeutic. She is Esau to Caroline's Jacob, the dark troll to Caroline's shining princess. As with Gilly, Louise is going to have to find another way to tell that story in order to be happy.

Along with believing that she is standing in Caroline's shadow, the other obstacle Louise sees in her life is her gender. Louise, who loves working on the water with her father (not in the house with her mother and grandmother), "would have given anything" to be the son her father needed. As a girl in those days right before the start of World War II, "men's work and women's work were sharply divided, and a waterman's boat was not the place for a girl" (17). Throughout her early teenage years, she tells us, she prayed to turn into a boy (18). Men of Rass loved the water, but women were not supposed to. "Water was the wild, untamed kingdom of our men," she thinks. "It ruled their waking hours, sapped their bodily strength, and from time to tragic time claimed their mortal flesh" (37). Louise knows that there's no future for her on Rass. "How could I face a lifetime of passive waiting?" (37) she asks. Louise knows that if she stays she will be prevented from what she most loves to do (fishing with her father) and will be forced into a life of passivity in the house, a life she sees reflected in her mother and, more importantly, in her grandmother.

To add insult to injury, Louise also feels that her sister is given greater material privileges. Although money is always tight, the family pays for music lessons off the island for Caroline, who is, Louise says, "the kind of person other people sacrifice for as a matter of course" (21), and Louise, who is proud of her sister, says that "something began to rankle" beneath that pride as her sister saps the limited family income. She even goes as far as attempting to run away after she is embarrassed at school. Caroline, ever the practical one, points out that she can't get the ferry that night and might as well come home and eat. Sara Louise sees this as emblematic of the ways in which her Romanticism is countered by Caroline's practicality. "I would hope for tears and pleading," she says, and Caroline would offer facts she "couldn't argue with" (27). Even though she feels she is the one ignored and slighted, she can't even get pity from her sister, who is, annoyingly, right.

Her resentment begins to poison both Sara Louise's relationship with her sister and her connection to her parents. Caroline is "so sure, so present, so easy, so light and gold, while I was all gray and shadow." She actually begins wishing she were a monster, as "monsters always command attention, if only for their freakishness." Her parents, she fantasizes, "would have wrung their hands and tried to make it up to me, as parents will with a handicapped or especially ugly child" (33). Unfortunately, though, Sara Louise is simply normal. She also begins to fantasize about turning herself into Joseph, and having Caroline bow down to her. Even though they share the same room, table, and classroom, Louise and Caroline grow further and further apart. She wonders, though, "why did only Caroline have the power, with a single glance, to slice my flesh clear though to the bone?" (63). She grows to hate her sis-

Six. "No clouds of glory"

ter, even though she acknowledges that she belongs "to a religion which taught that simply to be angry with another made one liable to the judgment of God and that to hate was the equivalent of murder" (64). Cleverly, Paterson shows her readers how jealousy has separated Sara Louise from her sister, her parents, and even her God.

Her only friend on the island is McCall Purnell, known familiarly as Call, who Louise describes at 14 as "pudgy, bespectacled, and [like Caroline] totally unsentimental" (4). When the mysterious Captain Hiram Wallace appears, with his reputation for cowardice in a storm preceding him, Call actually takes a liking to him. Louise thinks that if she were a "more generous person" she'd be glad he'd found a male role model, but she "can't afford to be generous" (62), given that she has no one else on her side. Shortly after, Caroline seems to want to take both Call and the Captain from her. Eccentric neighbor (and cat lady) Auntie Braxton has a stroke, and they round up her cats. They try to drown them but can't bear to do it. Even though she didn't have anything to do with rounding up the cats, Caroline goes door to door and, through her charm and storytelling, gets people to take them. This makes Louise feel "as I always did when someone told the story of my birth" (99), as if Caroline is stealing not only all her glory but also her friends.

Midway through the novel comes a powerful storm. Sara Louise's grandmother is afraid of the storm, but she is not. "I had never seen a mountain, except in a geography text," she thinks. "I was fourteen, and I had never even seen a real mountain. I was going to, though. I was not going to end up like my Grandma, fearful and shriveled" (108). Her grandmother, Goforth says, "is Louise's ever-present reminder that the island of self-obsession is a region dangerous to the point of destruction" (177). Sara Louise rightly recognizes that her grandmother's fear and self-absorption is more lethal than any hurricane. The storm also brings out an emotional storm in Louise. The Captain loses his house because of the wind and water, and, when they go to see the destruction in her boat, Louise hugs him and "went hot all over" (115). Louise, always proud of "keeping the deepest parts of me hidden from view" (119), feels out of control and thinks that she is going crazy (131). Her grandmother senses the change in Louise and begins taunting her. Her parents are shocked by the grandmother's taunts and general craziness, including accusing Louise of poisoning Auntie Braxton so she can get the Captain. Louse says the shock of her grandmother's insanity and her parents'

"Unsuitable" Books

concern "was so enormous that I found my own puny fear of exposure melting into a much larger darker terror that seemed to have no boundaries" (149). This obsession comes to a head shortly after the storm, when the Captain offers to pay for Caroline's music academy tuition, and her grandmother quotes the "Jacob have I loved" passage from Romans 9:13 in a whisper to Louise (156) to spitefully remind her that Caroline is the privileged one. Louise reads the passage and finds out that God is speaking it. "God had chosen to hate me," she thinks. "And if my heart was hard, that was his doing as well" (159). At this point, Sara Louise has completely turned her back on the God she feels has abandoned her.

Time passes, and Louise starts working for her father, because Call—the only other available male—is away fighting in World War II. She never forgets her second-class status, though, saying that she doesn't mind catching the male crabs, but she hates catching females, as males "always have a chance to live no matter how short their lives, but females, ordinary, ungifted ones, just get soft and die" (162). Clearly, Louise sees a metaphor in the lives of the crabs to the opportunities—or lack of opportunities—given to men and women on Rass. However, Louise is happy on the water that winter, "deeply content with what life was giving me" (164). She is also dead tired at night, which prevents her from nursing her grudges (165). Louise was "good oyster in those days," tightly closed but alive. "Not even the presence at Christmastime of a radiant, grown-up Caroline could get under my shell" (166). Eventually, though, she decides she's foolish to resign herself to an isolated life of a spinster like Auntie Braxton. Her scores on college entrance exams have proven her academic abilities. "Without God, or man," she thinks, "I could still conquer a small corner of the world—if I wanted to" (173). The Captain supports her leaving, telling her that she might have been meant to be a man on Rass but not a woman (192). It appears at this point that Sara Louise will survive on her own, without help from friends, family, or even God.

This is not the end of the story, however. Sara Louise feels the need to have a final confrontation with her mother, accusing her of loving Caroline more than her and forcing her to stay on Rass Island. Her mother tells her that Louise never *said* she wanted to leave the island, and Louise realizes that her mother was right, that she refused to act on her dreams "afraid that if I loosened my fingers an iota, I would find

Six. "No clouds of glory"

myself once more cold and clean in a forgotten basket" (201). Leaving the island, which is in many ways a prison for Sara Louise, would make her feel even more abandoned than she already does. Her mother tells her she will miss her more than Caroline, which is exactly what she needs to hear. "I did not press her to explain," she thinks. "I was too grateful for that one word that allowed me at last to have the island and begin to build myself as a soul, separate from the long, long shadow of my twin" (201). The novel ends with her satisfied with her life and work reenacting the circumstances of her birth with her new twins, this time taking time to pay attention to the strong and healthy one, as well as the weaker (214–15). She is even able to reconcile the beauty and talent of her sister into the meaning and warmth of her own life.

Katherine Paterson says that although Sara Louise was clearly intended to be Esau, that each of us is both the "light and the dark" twin. Because of this Sara Louise, "in order to be a whole person, must come to love Caroline, so that she can love both the Jacob and the Esau within herself" ("The Story of My Lives," IC 159–60). Chaston puts it this way: "Freed from the role imposed on her by others' stories, she finally acts out her own story" (104). Pulling these three novels together, Schmidt says that Gilly, Jess, and Louise have in common "a need for a place or, at the very least, hope that a place can be found. Like Gilly and Jess, Louise is a prodigal who at the end discovers that what she needs is within her all along" (72). Louise, he continues, "has been prepared, like Jess and Gilly, to choose hope and joy. And, like Jess and Gilly, she finds it. Slowly and painfully, she finds it" (81). The mood of the final passage of the novel is joyful, and the message for Paterson's readers in general is that grace is possible, that it might not take the form one expects, and that home is always just around the corner once you stop walking away from it. Jess, Gilly, and Louise all find, eventually, ways to live, gracefully, with what life has given them—the good as well as the very, very hard.

CHAPTER SEVEN

Chris Crutcher's Painful Honesty (1983–2001)

> If I am to make characters real, I have to treat them with … respect, and I have to be willing to tell stories about the ruggedness of their lives. Anything less is far more disrespectful than the use of those really meaningless words in print; disrespectful to the character, to the reader, and to the author—Chris Crutcher, *King of the Mild Frontier*, 228
>
> It's risky business letting people have their own lives, particularly if they are our children. It's risky business giving up *ownership*, which, by the way, we never had in the first place—Chris Crutcher, interview with Betty Carter, 44

Nearly every year since the publication of his first young adult novel *Running Loose* in 1983, Chris Crutcher has made the American Library Association's list of challenged authors. His collection of short stories, *Athletic Shorts*, was number 38 on the top 100 challenged books in 2006–2007, his novels *Whale Talk* (at number 46), *Staying Fat for Sarah Byrnes* (77) and *Ironman* (90) also made the list. Challengers object to the language, the sexual situations, and the overall irreverence of the novels, in which authority figures of all kinds (parents, teachers, coaches, and administrators) come under attack. It's true that Crutcher's characters are often crude—in language, thought, and deed—and it is also true that he takes aim at adults who seem hell-bent on making hellish the lives of the children in their care. Crutcher, who worked for many years as an educator and a clinical social worker, has seen the effects of abuse personally, and he feels that trying to cover up, lie about, or sugar coat the bad things that happen to children is nearly as reprehensible as the abuse. He frequently repeats what he says in his autobiography, *King of the Mild Frontier*:

Seven. Chris Crutcher's Painful Honesty (1983–2001)

> If I have any complaints about my youth ... one is that many well-meaning adults lied to me. Not spiteful lies with malicious intent but lies designed to prevent emotional and psychological pain, lies told by the people who cared about me most: my parents, teachers, relatives. They were lies designed to prevent disappointment, lies about the virtues of love, hard work, and any number of terms around which clichés blossom like desert flowers after a flash flood.... And I believed them, and became disillusioned when life turned out to operate by a different set of rules [233–34].

According to Crutcher, we don't protect our children from the harsh realities of life by cushioning the blow—either in life or in literature. In a letter written when *Running Loose* was challenged in Berlin, Pennsylvania, in 1994, he said, "We cannot control what children think—and hooray for that—we can only help them make sense" (Davis, *Presenting* 61). As Terry Davis says in one of the two book-length critical analyses of Crutcher's work: "The way we misname behavior and then teach the lie to our children is a vital theme in Crutcher's work as a writer and as a therapist" (Davis, *Presenting* 108). For Crutcher, all adults (and this includes novelists) have to do is tell the truth when talking to kids—in fact, it's all they *can* do. For his ardent defense of adolescents' right to read, Crutcher has won Intellectual Freedom Awards from the National Council of Teachers of English and the National Coalition Against Censorship (Gillis and Cole 43).

Crutcher's twin goals are, then, to present the unvarnished truth—warts and all—to young people in his novels and then to offer them hope, to help them to "make sense" of what happens to them and others. One way he helps them to do that is to recognize one of his principles of the universe: "There is no Jesus without Judas, no Martin Luther King without the Klan; no Ali without Joe Frazier; no freedom without tyranny. No wisdom exists that does not include perspective. Relativity is the greatest gift" (*Whale Talk* 95). His novels and short stories contain plenty of bad people—child abusers, bullies (young and old), liars, hypocrites—but they are also filled with caring (if sometimes flawed) parents, coaches, teachers, and friends. Recalling a story from Crutcher's childhood (where he worried about the worm in the proverb about the early bird getting it), Bryan Gillis and Pam B. Cole say that Crucher's stories are "populated far more by worms than birds" (3), and it is true that his young characters are often picked on and picked at by aggressive (if not always industrious) birds. Still, with the help of others, they often learn to turn that proverb on its head.

Life, for Crutcher, is never all good or all bad and never, ever, perfect. "[A]s a therapist I do not allow [the word 'perfect'] to be uttered in my office after the first session," he has said, "because I believe the only reason for the existence of that word is to make us feel bad. It's the only word in the language (that I know of) that is defined in common use by what *can't* be" (204). This overriding sense of optimism, in spite of all that life throws at us, is one of the many things that make Crutcher's novels worth reading.

Not all critics agree that Crutcher's work empowers teens, however. Literary critic Roberta Trites insists that while young adult novels appear to feature young protagonists that challenge the system, the ultimate purpose is to incorporate young adults into the larger social and political system. In *Disturbing the Universe,* Trites says:

> [A]dolescent literature seems to delegitimize adolescents, insisting that "adolescentness," especially immaturity, is unacceptable, even though the surface intention of most YA novels is ostensibly to legitimize adolescence. Texts accomplish this delegitimization by conveying frequently to readers the ideological message that they need to grow up, to give up the subject position culturally marked "adolescent" [83].

Rather than creating an adolescent that "must be repressed for the greater good," as Trites claims, it seems instead that Crutcher's novels show adolescents who *refuse* to be repressed, even to the end of their novels. They are aided by adults and they do "murder" the parents and other authority figures who stand in their way, as she says, but they never accept the "often repressive ideological wisdom" offered by even the most well-meaning adults. This, I think, is why the novels have been so often challenged: not simply because of the "foul" language or gritty depictions of the abuse heaped on children, but because these books send the message that young people are often better off if they resist, both psychologically and physically, what adults are telling them to do, to think, and to want. This, then, is the reason that we should teach these novels, discuss them with our students, make them available in classroom and school libraries—because they offer ways out from under the various sorts of oppression that society seems determined to heap upon young people.

Running Loose (1983), Chris Crutcher's first novel, features Louie Banks, a high school senior, indifferent football player, boyfriend of Becky (a smart and tough-minded cheerleader), and an eventual triath-

Seven. Chris Crutcher's Painful Honesty (1983–2001)

lete. It is no accident that he is athletic (nearly all Crutcher's main characters are). As Chris Crowe says about sports novels in general,

> Whether they're helping adolescent readers vicariously release rage and frustration, or understand themselves and their world better, or learn valuable life lessons, good sports stories provide much more than entertainment. The best young adult sports novels offer the same benefits, challenges, and intellectual stimulations as any other well-written novel [Crowe, *More* 9].

Crutcher's novels are entertaining and tension reducing, no doubt. Unlike many writers of sports fiction for young adults, however, Crutcher insists on a sometimes unflattering but also honest portrayal of his sports heroes. Crowe continues:

> As a young man, Crutcher grew up reading Clair Bee's Chip Hilton novels and longed to be an athletic hero like Chip, but as he got older, he realized that Chip Hilton wasn't really heroic because Chip risked nothing. When Crutcher began to write books of his own, he decided he didn't want any Chip Hilton characters in his stories [*More* 40].

"Crutcher's flawed heroes," Crowe says, "discover truth in more subtle ways than Frank Merriwell or Chip Hilton ever did" (*More* 41). For Crutcher, true virtue (and wisdom, for that matter) is virtue tested (usually on the playing field, court, or swimming pool).

The first of many tests that Louie will undergo comes early in the novel, when his bullheaded, racist football coach orders the boys to disable the only black player on the opposing team. Louie refuses, then curses the coach and is kicked out of the game after the player is injured by someone else. As they are about most of what he does, Louie's parents are supportive about his act of resistance, but they don't try to solve his problems for him. Louie says his father is "a good guy to go to when you have a problem. He'll never tell you the answer, but he'll stick with you till you come up with one" (20–21). His father, Louie says, is also "always counseling me to look things over before I do some knee jerk thing I'll be sorry for. There's nothing wrong with making a mistake as long as you think about it first, but it's stupid to make mistakes by closing your eyes and gritting your teeth. Makes sense" (55). Louie's father, like many other Crutcher parents, knows that kids have to make mistakes to learn, but they nevertheless don't have to act blindly—they can get help if they need it. Gillis and Cole say that the parents in Crutcher's novels are placed in the middle of the action, which "feels authentic" because they are integral to the story's development, and this is true right from the

"Unsuitable" Books

beginning of his career (63). They add that his adult characters "meet the requirements" for YA fiction, in that they have imperfections, readers identify with them, and they contribute to the story (86).

In addition to his father, Louie is also advised by Dakota, the tough-talking owner of the bar where Louie works. Louie comments about him:

> Dakota says if we always judged things by how they ended up, life would more than likely seem like one turd sandwich after another, given the ways things have a tendency to end up. He's a good man to listen to, if you don't mind a little rough language, which I don't [10–11].

In general, Crutcher's protagonists (and their advisors) *never* mind a little rough language, but under that tough veneer are important messages. In this case, Louie needs to hear that the final outcome is less important than the thoughtful, and altruistic, act that precedes it. Dakota also tells him, "A man has to plant his feet somewhere an' say, 'This is as far as I go an' anyone tries to push me any farther's gonna have his hands full'" (98). Not only should act with empathy, one should also stick to one's guns once a decision has been made. This stubbornness serves Crutcher's protagonists well, and it has also served Crutcher in his decades-long battle against censorship—he has both the courage of his convictions and the bullheadedness to see them through.

Along with the teachings of Dakota and his father, Louie learns lessons—both on and off the field—from Coach Madison, who encourages him to run track instead of playing football. Coach Madison stands in opposition to the bullying football coach and the scary, controlling principal (and former coach), who considers Louie disloyal for not playing football. Madison tells Louie, "I think everyone probably gets only a few chances in his life to make a stand for something he cares about, and I've blown one chance already. Now I don't want to do this just to go to war, so if you don't want to run, say so. But if you do, I'll go to the wall with it" (172). Madison reminds him, "You can always take one more step" (187). Each of the parental figures in Louie's life try to move him in the same direction—toward perseverance, clear-eyed decision making, and personal responsibility.

In addition, Madison (unlike the football coach and principal) is "bound and determined to coach me in track and leave the rest of my life to me" (205). Like Madison, Crutcher believes that sports shouldn't be loaded down with spurious connections to loyalty, patriotism, and

Seven. Chris Crutcher's Painful Honesty (1983–2001)

duty. Nevertheless, sports can provide young adults with models for determination, self-reliance, and independence. "Run *your* race," Madison tells Louie as he prepares to run in the triathlon. "Run loose like always" (210). The title of his first novel, "running loose" could easily be a motto for all of Crutcher's adolescent heroes and heroines—they are not running their parents' races, they are not pushing themselves to satisfy someone else's agenda; they are calmly moving (and, sometimes, not so calmly) in the direction *they* want to go.

To add to his struggles in athletics, Louie is challenged further by Becky's death as a result of a car accident. He responds by disrupting her funeral with his rage and smashing the principal's self-aggrandizing monument to Becky placed at the school. In Louie's darkest moments, Dakota tells him, "Ya got to understand that the reason some things happen is just because they happen. That ain't a good reason, but that's it.... This life ain't partial, boy" (157). This is clearly a part of Chris Crutcher's code: life isn't "partial"; it doesn't single us out for good or ill. There are other lessons to be learned, though. At the end of the novel, Louie says that he has "learned some about friendship and a whole lot about love and that there's no use being honorable with dishonorable men. There's nothing they can do to you when you don't care anymore" (215–16). Dishonorable people can, sometimes, win over the honorable ones, and it can seem that the only solution is not to care.

This sounds like a grim message from a young adult who has given up hope. However, not caring anymore is a kind of freedom, especially if you no longer care about what people think about you, what adults might do to you, or what happens if you break the rules. As Chris Crowe says, reading about Louie "will help teenagers realize that not all adults deserve their trust. As readers follow Louie through his story, they will learn with him how to distinguish truth from hypocrisy, reasoned actions from irrational actions, and good adults from bad adults." They will also come to realize "that despite the fact that young people lack adult status and authority, teenagers do have the power—and the responsibility—to resist adult hypocrisy and unethical behavior" (Crowe, "Running" 362–63). This seems a long way from Trites' concept of teenage disempowerment; Louie (and all of the main characters who follow him) is on the road to adulthood, not because he has absorbed the values of the adult world or accepted its authority over him, but because he has learned to be skeptical and discerning about the grown-up world. Of course, this kind of young person is just the sort who makes book challengers uneasy.

Stotan! (1986), Crutcher's second novel, is also filled with damaged (and damaging) characters, whose problems are again hashed out athletically. The novel centers around a week of intensive training during Christmas break for members of the swim team. The coach is Max Il Song, a "Korean cowboy" (4), who pushes the boys to their limit, to become "Stotans," which is "a cross between a Stoic and a Spartan" (39). Max tells the boys: "There are lessons in this week that can serve you for the rest of your lives–but there aren't words for those lessons, so I can't *tell* you what they are. You find them for yourselves. Just remember, when it's time to meet the Dragon, that you can't fight him head on; he breathes fire. But you can go *with* him and beat him" (128). Max, like Louie's father and Dakota, advises the boys to work with their "dragons," not against them, and he also adopts the typical Crutcher pose of refusing to tell young people what they should do.

Each of the boys in this novel has an individual "dragon." Lion's parents were killed in a boating accident, and he lives alone above a tavern. Narrator Walker "Walk" Dupree's older brother Long John "still puts drugs into every orifice he can find and preaches love and nonviolence like he was gathering followers for a migration to Woodstock" (13). Nortie is physically abused by his father, and he quits his job at a day-care center when, programmed by years of abuse, he impulsively hits a child. Jeff gets leukemia and is dying at the end of the novel. As Davis says, "[I]n a Crutcher world we are preyed upon by circumstance, and when circumstance is busy tormenting someone else, other human beings get in line to torment us" (*Presenting* 70). None of these young men escapes unscathed.

Coach Max has his own troubles; he is alienated from his young daughter because of an earlier drinking problem. Max says, "[N]o matter how decent you are, no matter how intensely you work toward the light, nothing changes the past. This is a world where you pay for everything you do" (188). Many of the adults in Crutcher's novels are haunted by a past they cannot change. Young people, however, still get the chance to alter their futures, in large part by learning lessons—sometimes intentional, sometimes inadvertent—from those adults. This doesn't mean, of course, that their lives will be perfect (the word Crutcher hates, after all).

Reflecting on life toward the end of the novel, Walk says, "I think

Seven. Chris Crutcher's Painful Honesty (1983–2001)

if I ever make it to adulthood, and if I decide to turn back and help someone grow up, either as a parent or a teacher or a coach, I'm going to spend most of my time dispelling myths, clearing up unreal expectations. For instance, we're brought up to think that the good guys are rewarded and the bad guys are punished; but upon close scrutiny, that assumption vanishes into thin air (259). This is a typical Crutcher wisdom—the best job for an adult is "dispelling myths" about the fundamental goodness of the universe. As Davis asks, "So, how do the damaged make something positive out of all their pain? We accept our new condition and the new view of the world it gives us, and we act on our new perception" (*Presenting* 83). Or as Max puts it (and other characters in later works will say): "we all do the best we can in our time with what we have, and that kids would be a lot more at peace with adults if they could understand that" (133). Crutcher is telling his young audience here and in every novel he writes that one of the greatest gifts adolescents can give themselves is patience with the limitations (and, sometimes, the mistakes) of others.

Clearly, part of Crutcher's mission is to save young adults—both his characters and his readers. "Crutcher is also a lifeguard as a storyteller [as he was in life]," Davis says. "In all his novels and nearly all his short stories, either the life of the body or the life of the spirit, or both, is at stake" (*Presenting* 1). This is certainly the case in Crutcher's third novel, *The Crazy Horse Electric Game* (1987). In this novel, Willie Weaver is a star pitcher, who is injured in a water skiing accident and suffers damage to his motor skills. His parents, who lost a daughter earlier to SIDS, can't cope with his slow rehabilitation. His father, a former college football star, is especially angry at his slow progress—and at himself for perhaps contributing to the accident.

Willie leaves home without telling his parents where he has gone and ends up in Oakland, California, where he hooks up with the benevolent (if sometimes violent) bus driver and pimp Lacey Casteel, and starts attending an alternative school, named the One More Last Chance (OMLC). (This school very much resembles a school where Crutcher once taught.) Willie says about OMLC, "Nobody here preached at me. Nobody told me everything would be okay, or that I should go back home to my parents and work things out when I knew the time for that wasn't here yet. They let me figure it out for myself; *demanded* that I figure it out for myself; but they never deserted me" (266). As is the case in *Running Loose,* Crutcher's most positive adult figures use this approach with teenagers; they don't tell them what to do or sugar coat the truth. They let the young people in their care find out what they need for themselves.

At OMLC, Willie regains his physical and psychological strength, with the help of caring teachers and administrators, in particular his P.E. coach, who helps him find his "center" (168). Her boyfriend tells Willie during the process of rehabilitation that "every moment of your life is part of you" (223). Once again, characters in Crutcher's world grow from both the good and the bad that happens to them. Toward the end of the novel, Willie says about OMLC, "I guess what I'm saying is that my life is more valuable because I got knocked out of my favored spot. I can't believe I'm saying that, but I am and I know it's true. I learned it from the people who picked me up here" (267). In Crutcher's world, one usually has to be knocked down (and, more importantly, helped up) in order to learn.

After graduating from OMLC, Willie returns home to find that his former life no longer exists: his family home has been sold, his parents are divorced, his father is a drunk, and his mother has remarried. He stops long enough to visit with his mother (and his new half-sister) and heads back to California. The tone is sad, but elegiac; Willie is changed by his troubles, but mostly for the better. Davis sums up the message of this novel: "The positive force in Crutcher's vision is the human spirit. Yes, his work is full of ghastly examples of humankind, but it is also peopled with glorious examples" (*Presenting* 38). Both OMLC and this novel are filled with such "glorious examples" of people who triumph in spite of all the "ghastly" that surrounds them.

Crutcher's fourth novel, *Chinese Handcuffs* (1989), explores another set of difficult issues, in particular the sexual abuse of children, and as a result it is one of the most frequently challenged of Crutcher's books. However, as Davis comments,

> in the world Chris Crutcher creates in his stories the fact of human ghastliness doesn't negate the fact of human glory.... There is no divine intervention. The people in Crutcher's world rise and fall, are saved or lost, by the degree to which they are connected to the humanity in themselves and others ["Vision" 39–40].

Like *Crazy Horse,* this novel has both ghastliness and glory. Structured as third-person narration alternating with first-person letters from Dil-

Seven. Chris Crutcher's Painful Honesty (1983–2001)

lon to his dead brother, the novel tells the twin stories of Jennifer Lawless and Dillon Hemingway. Jennifer is a star basketball player who is being sexually abused by her stepfather. Dillon is a triathlete coping unsuccessfully with his brother's suicide, the emotions he feels for his brother's girlfriend, Stacey, and his devastated family. Bad coaches and heroically good coaches fill the novel; monstrous and well-meaning (but troubled) parents exist side by side. Still, as Davis says, "a close look at Crutcher's work reveals that he uses adult wisdom—and makes help available to his characters—*all* the time" (*Presenting* 40). Of course, adults who try to force that wisdom on young people fail, and only those who provide help without coercion can do any good.

Dillon's assistance comes from his coach, whom he eventually tells about Jennifer, yet he still takes on the smart and dangerous stepfather himself. Dillon's coach offers some of that adult wisdom:

> Dillon, all you have in this world, really, are your responses to it. Responses to your feelings and responses to what comes in from outside. You know how adults are always trying to get you to 'take responsibility?' That's all responsibility is, responding to the world, owning your responses [122].

This is a consistent lesson in Crutcher's novels: young people need to learn to own their own responses, to control themselves and stop trying to control others (or wishing someone adult would come along and take charge for them).

Taking up these same issues of responsibility and self-determination, *Athletic Shorts* (1991), makes its way often to the lists of challenged books, mostly for the subject matter. This is Crutcher's only collection of short stories for young adults (although *Angry Management's* three novellas are similar); the book considers racism, homosexuality, heterosexuality, child abuse, the loss of parents, and other serious topics but does it (mostly) in a funny way. As Crutcher says in his autobiography, "For every bit of humor and compassion I put into a story, I put in a equal dose of anger" (*King of the Mild Frontier* 255). In the foreword to this collection he also says, "I like it when my stories are seen by my critics from the same perspective as that in which most human beings are seen by their critics—for doing their best in tough situations, for failure, for excesses, for heart, for the glorious and the ghastly." This combination of "the glorious and the ghastly" is one readers see throughout Crutcher's work.[1]

In the story "A Brief Moment in the Life of Angus Bethune," main character Angus (who reappears later in *Angry*) has two gay parents (once married to each other but now remarried to same-sex partners), and, if that's not enough of a challenge for a teenager in this still-homophobic society, he's an overweight guy who's been elected Winter Ball king as a joke. Angus' stepfather, Alexander, passes on an important message as Angus gets ready for the dance:

> Superman's not brave. He's smart. He's handsome. He's even decent. But he's not brave. He's indestructible.... You can't be brave when you're indestructible. It's guys like you and me that are brave, Angus. Guys who are different and can be crushed—and know it—but go out there anyway [15].

Eventually, Angus wins (briefly) the girl and humiliates the football player who set him up. Angus may not look like Superman but, unlike him, he is brave in spite of his weaknesses.

The next story, "The Pin," features Johnny Rivers, whose father's tough-love approach eventually crosses over into abuse. Father and son have a classically-Oedipal wrestling match, and, after being defeated by his son, the father hits him after the match. Describing that moment, the narrator says, "Every man, woman, and child in the gym recognizes this, whether from their nightmares or their daily lives" (49). As Crutcher says, tellingly, in his autobiography, "I had shamed myself [with his temper] enough times in my life to have considerable empathy for those who had done so at the expense of their mates or kids, which made me a natural to work with the 'bad guys'" (*King of the Mild Frontier* 10). The father eventually turns out not to be one of the "bad guys," and father and son agree that they need outside help with their relationship.

In "Goin' Fishin'," main character Lion has to learn to forgive the young man who killed his family in a drunken boating accident. Lion says to his friend Elaine: "If I ever quit hating him, I—I—I'll die right with them" (104). Elaine points out that, given his behaviors as a typical teenager, he could have killed someone when he was drunk, too. "What you did was no less stupid than what Neal did," she says. "Only thing is, the universe caught him and it didn't catch you" (105). Once again, the line between the "good" and the "bad" characters is often just a matter of circumstance.

"Telephone Man" exposes the dangers and limitations of racism. In the introduction to this story, Crutcher says,

> I have fears in writing a story about racism. In fact, there are a significant number of people who don't understand the simpler truths about bigotry

Seven. Chris Crutcher's *Painful Honesty (1983–2001)*

> ... and who don't believe that basic lessons are best taught by reflecting the truth. Those people believe then I use the word *nigger* or *spic* or *beaner* or any other of a million slurs, I am condoning the use of those words. They think kids should not be exposed in print to what they are exposed in their lives. But I believe what I believe, and so I write my stories [112].

Shying away from offensive language diminishes the power and the honesty of the message, Crutcher believes. While the story does contain some of the harsh language Crutcher mentions, it is put in the mouths of characters whose perspectives are limited. At the end of the story, Jack, the "Telephone Man," comes to question his father's systemic racism (which he, too, has absorbed) when he is aided by African-American boy. "[I]f my dad made a mistake about *them*," he wonders, could he have "made mistakes about the other colors, too" (128). Critics who focus on the words that both Jack and his father use, miss the point of the potential for change.

The final story, "In the Time I Get," continues the message of forgiveness and acceptance and courage in the face of prejudice (and death). Returning from *Running Loose*, Dakota, says this to Louie (who in this story has to deal with a friend who is dying of AIDS):

> You got to understand that the reason some things happen is just because they happen. That ain't a good reason, but that's it. You put enough cars and trucks and motorcycles on the road, and some of 'em gonna run into each other. Not certain ones neither. Just the ones that do. This life ain't partial, boy [142].

This is a sentiment that readers of Chris Crutcher's work should recognize: life is both good and bad, and there is no discernible reason for it. It "ain't partial." Dakota also tells Louie that he thinks "there's only one lesson if you want the truth. I think we're just supposed to see how far we can go in whatever time we get" (159). Throughout his work, Crutcher makes this point: all we can do is the best we can in the time we're allotted. For Louie, doing the best means standing up the homophobia and being there for his dying friend. The day Louie resists the prevailing fear and hatred is the day that Louie "quietly turned and stood my ground" (161).

In all of these stories, Crutcher stresses that human beings "are a trial-and-error species; we learn from our mistakes, not just our physical mistakes but our emotional and spiritual mistakes as well." Heroes, he says, are "defined so much by what they do 'right,' as by how they respond to what they do 'wrong'" (*King of the Mild Frontier* 233). Louie responds to what he did wrong in the beginning of this story, standing his ground and doing what he can in the time he has been given. This is all that can be asked of anyone, Crutcher believes. His message to those who would censor this story because it deals with "controversial" topics is that, regardless of the subject matter, the lesson is a valuable one.

In *Staying Fat for Sarah Byrnes* (1993), Crutcher's fifth novel, Eric "Moby" Calhoun, is a much-larger-than-average swimmer and childhood friends with Sarah Byrnes, who was severely burned and disfigured at three when her father abused her to punish her mother. (Sarah resurfaces again in *Angry*.) The title refers to Moby's attempt to stay fat (even though he's losing weight from being on the swim team) so he and Sarah can remain outsiders together, but they end up drifting apart. At the beginning of the novel, Sarah has stopped speaking or responding to speech and is in the psychiatric ward of the local hospital. Moby tries to bring her back to life.

Moby is aided in his quest by Ms. Lemry, his English teacher and swimming coach. Lemry is a "thinking man's coach" (4), tough, strong, and caring. Trites says that she "communicates indirectly but explicitly a key ideology in this novel of ideas [that] adults are responsible for protecting children" (81). However, Lemry falls into the pattern of most of Crutcher's benevolent adults, who are available to offer suggestions but don't "protect children." Instead, they suggest that no one can really take responsibility for anyone else. Lemry tells Moby that "one of the worst things schools do is give you the idea that they can take responsibility for other people." The sooner you learn, she says that "you're your own life's accountant, the sooner you'll have the tools to hammer out a decent life" (217). Giving students "the tools to hammer out a decent life" motivates Lemry's teaching as well as her coaching. Her Contemporary American Thought class, for example, raises difficult issues and exposes various "scandals," including a secret abortion by the girlfriend of one of the Christian moralists in the class. (This student, Matt Miller, is fleshed out and more sympathetically treated in *Angry*.) Throughout it all, Lemry doesn't tell students what to do; she helps them find the necessary tools to solve their own problems.

Moby isn't listening all that well to this message, though, and continues in his quest to save Sarah from her father. At the end of the novel, however, Moby has figured things out. He says, "Part of me wishes life

Seven. Chris Crutcher's Painful Honesty (1983–2001)

were more predictable and part of me is excited that it's not. I think it's impossible to tell the good things from the bad things while they're happening" (295). This uncertainty is part of what constitutes maturity in Crutcher's world. Still, the ending of *Sarah Byrnes* is, as Davis says, "a powerful example of a soul saved–or a longer stay in this world, at least– by human intervention and human love" (*Presenting* 43). Again, Crutcher tackles what some might consider inappropriate for young adults—child abuse, violence, religious fanaticism, abortion—but he uses these very realistic situations to show the potential for goodness in (most of) us.

As in *Chinese Handcuffs, Ironman* (1995), Crutcher's sixth novel, alternates between third-person and first-person narration. The main character is Beauregard "Bo" Brewster, who, as with Louie in *Running Loose*, is engaged in a battle of wills with a football coach (one has little trouble imagining Crutcher as a young man after reading several of his novels). Bo's aggressive behavior keeps getting him suspended, and he winds up in anger management class with Mr. Nak, another of Crutcher's Asian cowboys, who "talks like Slim Pickens and dresses like this fashion guru is the Marlboro Man" (26). (Mr. Nak is also the frame narrator— and counselor—of *Angry*. He and Max are based on one of Crutcher's friends, Ron Nakatani, according to Gillis and Cole [27], who embodied the image of the Asian cowboy.) At one point, he tells Bo: "If what's comin' from others don't make you feel better about yourself in the world, then it probably ain't good for you …. An' if it ain't good for you, it ain't love" (129). Once again, the surrogate parent figures in Crutcher's novels help young people distinguish between what is good for them and what isn't, but they don't force them into adopting any particular position.

In contrast, Roberta Trites argues that when Mr. Nak "communicates *in loco parentis* with an air of authority about how Bo can manage his anger," he "temporarily displac[es] the adolescent implied reader" (74). He may displace Bo narratively, but he doesn't replace him as the ethical center of the novel. The plan for living he offers him includes a healthy dose of personal judgment and self-determination, and, finally, the decisions being made and actions being taken are Bo's.

These decisions include making judgments about his father. Bo (like Johnny Rivers in "The Pin") is engaged in a power struggle with his dad, who always has to be right and thinks he knows what is best for Bo. Bo lives with his mother, who gleefully divorced her controlling husband years ago. As Bo trains for a triathlon, his father buys a state-of-the-art bicycle for his competitor because he (mistakenly) thinks it will teach Bo a lesson about pride. In spite of this, Bo, supported by his fellow anger management students, does well and, surprisingly, asks his father for counseling sessions as a graduation present. Mr. Nak tells him that mercy "is the only medicine for our anger, it is the only medicine for our hurt, it is the only medicine for our desperation" (179). Although Mr. Nak prescribes mercy it is up to Bo to dispense (and internalize) it. Although Trites suggests that Mr. Nak has taken charge of the story through his speeches, only Bo has the power to forgive his father; his counselor can't do it for him.

At the end of the novel, Mr. Nak reminds Bo that "life has every kind of holy man an' devil. If you're ever gonna beat all the anger an' hurt inside you, you're gonna have to learn to offset the awful with the magnificent" (180). This sentiment should be quite familiar by now: life is good *and* bad, awful and magnificent, and we don't have a great deal of say about it. Or, as Crutcher puts it, "you can't tell the good stuff from the bad stuff when it's happening. In fact, it isn't good or bad. It's just stuff" (*King of the Mild Frontier* 17). This is an important point to make to would-be censors: Nothing is inherently good or bad for young adults; it's all the "stuff" of life. To represent life honestly, a writer (even one who writes for teens) needs to *deal* with all of it.

In Crutcher's seventh novel, *Whale Talk* (2002), The Tao "T.J." Jones puts together a team of extremely unlikely and unconventional swimmers to get back at a football-player bully and an equally bullying coach. T.J. (who has his own issues) wants them to all earn letter jackets and some pride. Racial conflicts, violence against women, and child abuse provide much of the drama, and T.J. is angry about *all* of them.

His parents are consistently supportive (although his father has a tragic past, having inadvertently caused the death of a toddler). His dad tells him that "we take what the universe gives us, and we either get the most out of it or we don't, but in the end we all go out the same way" (20). T.J.'s father tries to tell his son the truth about life, unlike his own parents, who "didn't want me to know what was out there. They didn't want me to know the real skinny on sex or love or boredom or hate or disappointment. They sold me their wishes as if they were fact" (131). Lying to children, even to protect them, is always a bad idea in Crutcher's world.

Seven. Chris Crutcher's Painful Honesty (1983–2001)

The novel shows considerable sympathy, although plenty of good-natured humor as well, for kids on the team who are dealing with mental disability, obesity, abusive parents, socially-crippling intelligence, or physical limitations. The boys spend a lot of time on a bus riding to swim meets, frankly telling their stories to each other. As Davis says,

> Honesty with ourselves about those things that terrorize us is hard enough to come by, but then to summon up the courage to tell the story of what we've done–or what's been done to us–can be almost impossible. For some of us, telling this story is the most heroic thing we'll ever do. But that's the way to freedom [Davis, *Presenting* 92].

As the novel progresses, readers increasingly come to see the heroic nature of such story telling and the therapeutic quality of the boys' bonding. As T.J.'s therapist tells him: "There is very little about humans that doesn't have to do with connection" (120). One imagines that Crutcher the therapist often said these words himself, reminding his clients that all we have is our connection to one other.

T.J. certainly learns this in the novel. Eventually, everyone on the team *but* T.J. (who is the best athlete) earns a letter, in spite of vigorous opposition from the football coach (who suspects a trick). Still, T.J. has met his goal of helping his team win letter jackets—and foiling the coach. Just when he should be celebrating, though, T.J.'s father is killed by a racist former high school sports star, who resents what he sees as T.J.'s family's interference in his life (he is abusing his stepdaughter and wife). In spite of all this, T.J. offers the now-familiar Crutcher wisdom at the end of the novel: "Nothing exists without its opposite. I didn't earn a letter jacket because I could, and all my friends did because they couldn't. Some things really don't get any better" (204). Crutcher's message should be clear—there is a reciprocal movement between bad and good in every life story, and even in the worst of times it is possible to find humor in the ironic juxtaposition of it all.

The Sledding Hill (2005), Crutcher's eighth novel, features a main character and narrator (and ostensible author of the novel) who has died before the story begins. (This story is based, loosely, on the death of one of Crutcher's classmates in elementary school, much like Paterson used a real death of a child as the basis for the crisis in *Bridge* [Gillis and Cole 6].) Billy Bartholomew, killed by a piece of falling Sheetrock, has stayed connected to the world in order to help his friend Eddie cope with both his father's and Billy's death. The two boys—both dead and alive—also have to face a challenge to a book written, ironically, by Chris Crutcher. The amusingly-titled book, *Warren Peece*, is not actually part of Crutcher's collection of novels, but it stands for all the challenges to his books over the years. Thus *The Sledding Hill* can be seen both as Crutcher's foregrounding of the effects of death on young people and his most direct treatment of the censorship issue—at least in his fiction.

The lead challenger is a familiar Crutcher villain, a fundamentalist preacher who thinks it is the job of adults to protect children from what he considers to be "evil" in the world—blasphemy, disrespect to adults, and, perhaps most dangerous of all, homosexuality. As The Reverend Mr. Tarter says, Crutcher's (imaginary) book is "filled with four-letter words, has a gay character as one of the central figures, taunts fundamental Christianity, and promotes defiance of authority, particularly teachers and parents" (95). The librarian and teacher of the book, speaks for Crutcher when she talks to her ninth-grade students about censorship after the book has been removed from her class. Adults will tell students that "it's about family values and Christian values and morality and our need to get control over our educational system," she says, but the issue is really about them. "Decide whether you think your mind is strong enough to hear tough stories, told in their native tongue—and let the censors know" (100–01), she admonishes them. Both explicitly in this novel and implicitly in his other works, Crutcher tells would-be book banners that kids are "strong enough to hear tough stories," and, more importantly, they should have the right to make up their own minds about what they read.

The book is somewhat of a challenge to defend, however. As Eddie puts it, "if there's a problem the Crutcher guy doesn't stick into his books, it must be because he doesn't know about it. You couldn't find this many problems in a zoo" (102). (This is, of course, an accurate—if tongue in cheek—depiction of Crutcher's real novels.) In spite of the novel's menagerie of problems, though, the kids appear to love the book. Billy's dad, who is the school janitor, and who eventually loses his job because he reads *Warren Peece* in secret to students, opines that when he was in school "it was all you could do to get most of us to read a book. They don't want to be banning one most of the kids like" (122). He also tells Eddie: "You have rights. Just because you're not twenty-one doesn't mean you're not an American. You just need to know what rights you have and how to access them" (123). This is true, but as court cases have indi-

Seven. Chris Crutcher's Painful Honesty (1983–2001)

cated, young people don't have all that many rights inside the schoolroom doors.

Of course, the Reverend Mr. Tarter and the other book banners aren't simplistic embodiments of evil. Tarter wouldn't be in a Crutcher novel if he didn't have a back story of abuse over which he has, in his misguided way, triumphed. And the parents and teachers who support (and oppose) the book have their own complicated stories. Tarter's campaign against the book (as well as the others' defense of it) is based on sincere beliefs. As Billy struggles to create good and bad guys in the story, he decides that "[t]he principal characters here are mad at one another for what they *believe,* so maybe the fact that they look good or bad to *one another* can take the place of good and evil in this story" (135). Once again, we are back to Crutcher's primary message: "Once you understand that nothing exists without its opposite, you understand nothing is good and nothing is evil, that opposites actually hold each other up" (167).

Although the novel ends with a dramatic school board meeting, which includes a cameo appearance by Crutcher himself, the book is *not* returned to the classroom, and several other novels are removed from the library as well. Both the librarian and Billy's father lose their jobs, and it appears that Tarter's forces have "won." Still, the mood of the last pages is optimistic. The librarian has moved to the public library—which has not bowed to community pressure to ban books—and the increased business there provides a job for Billy's father as well. The final point for teens (for everyone, actually) in this novel is, as Billy tells Eddie, "Your job is to tell your truth. That's everybody's job" (161). We cannot control the truths that people like Tarter want to compel us to believe, but we can tell our own stories, as Chris Crutcher continues to do. This novel may also represent a nod to librarians, who are on the front lines of the censorship battle and ardent defenders of students' right to read.

Deadline (2007) continues Crutcher's focus on the complicated effects of death on young adults. The novel has main character Ben Wolf facing the almost unimaginable—a terminal disease at 18. Ben has one school year to live his life as fully as possible, which he does: making the football team (even though he weighs 123 pounds at best), dating the love of his life, and refusing to accept the lies his history teacher passes off as truths. Ben asks that bullying teacher during one classroom confrontation, if students "get educated so we can gather information, right? And so we can discriminate between the kinds of information we get. What other reason is there to get educated?" (290). These are great questions and speak to the heart of Crutcher's message about censorship and education. Education (and this includes the reading of literature) is about getting at the truth and taking that truth out into the world.

All the trademark Crutcher themes are present in this novel: the pure pleasure of athletic contests, the importance of being honest with children, the tendency of life to throw both the good and the bad at us in equal measure, the necessity of doing the very best in the time one has. Ben, who has been keeping his dying a secret, eventually realizes that the "thing that prevents the worst from happening is the truth" (228–29). The familiar Crutcher characters are all here as well: the cocky (and profane) main character, the plucky, damaged female foil, the parents trying (and sometimes failing spectacularly) to help their children each make an appearance, as does Louie Banks, returning from *Running Loose* as the football coach of his old high school. The reasons for challenging this book are also the same—profanity, sexuality, negative depictions of authority figures, irreverence. However, the reasons to read it—and to teach it—also remain. This novel shows teenagers as the really are—rude, horny, often unwise, and frequently funny, brave, and admirable.[2]

Throughout his 30-year career as a novelist for young adults Chris Crutcher has been a champion of the truth as he sees it, and he writes his novels primarily to reach those young people whose lives have been touched by the tragedies he describes—loss of loved ones, mental illness, discrimination, abuse, bullying. He also writes to share the joys of adolescence: the pleasures of being young, and fit, and athletically gifted (or simply enthusiastic), the satisfaction of standing up to abusive power, the thrill of first love (and sex), the fun of mouthing off to parents, teachers, coaches, ministers, and, most of all, the joy of being young and alive. He tells Gillis and Cole that he creates the kinds of characters he looks for when he reads, "characters who have some of my same experiences and perspectives and who give me more articulate ways to say them and who broaden my knowledge and wisdom. A book like that empowers me" (55). We do our young people an extreme disservice when we ban (or simply withhold) these wonderful novels from them because we are offended by the language, annoyed by the disrespect, troubled by the subject matter, or, perhaps most alarmingly, afraid that we will be unable

Seven. Chris Crutcher's Painful Honesty (1983–2001)

to defend our students' rights to books that tell the truth about their lives. As Crutcher puts it, "If a kid comes to me and says, 'God, read this,' we can start talking about that story, but we are just one step away from talking about what's real. It gives kids and adults a place to begin" (Gillis and Cole 132). Crutcher's novels have given both young people and adults that "place to begin" for 40 years.

CHAPTER EIGHT

"A stronger weapon"
Cassie Logan on
The Road to Memphis *(1990)*

> I have been greatly disturbed at the possibility that any child has been hurt by my words. As a parent, I understand not wanting a child to hear painful words. But also as a parent I do not understand trying to prevent a child from learning about a history that is part of America, a history about a family representing millions of families who are strong and loving and who remain united and strong, despite the obstacles they face—Mildred Taylor, interview with Pat Scales, 6

> [W]ell-written, authentic, multiethnic children's literature can provide healing from the damages of living in a racist society—Barker, 122

Mildred D. Taylor has been writing about Cassie Logan and the Logan family in Mississippi for decades now, beginning with a prize-winning novella in 1975 and continuing through six successful and critically-praised novels.[1] Based on her own family's stories (particularly her father's), these works cover a period extending from shortly after slavery to a time still deep in the Jim Crow era. In them, she tells the harsh story of racism and violence, but Taylor also, perhaps more importantly, intersperses that narrative with depictions of a loving family, who respond with (usually) quiet heroism and dignity in the face of brutality. Readers over the decades have been pleased: Taylor has won the Coretta Scott King Award for *Let the Circle Be Unbroken* (1981) and *The Road to Memphis* (1990) and the Newbery in 1977 for *Roll of Thunder, Hear My Cry* (1976), as well as numerous other awards.

Her honest depictions have created controversy as well, however. *Roll of Thunder, Hear My Cry* has the dubious distinction of a place on

Eight. "A stronger weapon"

the ALA's Top 100 Banned/Challenged Books: 2000–2009, and her other novels have been challenged in school systems across the country. Critics have expressed concern about her use of racially-charged epithets, her straightforward representations of white racism, and the mistrust of whites in the black community she describes. As Pat Scales puts it: "Taylor is considered the forerunner in writing books that portray African American history as it really was, not as people wanted it to be" (2). Summarizing an autobiographical essay by Taylor, Chris Crowe (author of the only book-length study of Taylor) says that she came to realize that "there were two Souths: one of racism that alternately terrified and angered her and one of family and community in which she sensed safety and love and from which she developed a sense of history that her feel proud of who she was and where she came from" (11). Taylor has never shied away from showing both sides of her beloved—and hated—South.

To her critics, who think she presents too harsh a picture of the region, Taylor, like Crutcher and Paterson, has a strong response, saying that her father and other family storytellers "told my family's history truly, and it is this history that I have related in my books. When there was humor, my family passed it on. When there was tragedy, they passed it on. When the words hurt, they passed them on" ("Writer" 8). Consequently, she refuses to justify her works to worried (or angry) school boards "because anyone who cannot already understand why does not deserve any answers from me. The books are there; they are the answer" ("Writer" 8). For Taylor, literary honesty speaks louder than any possible objections.

As well as trying to tell her family history unflinchingly, Taylor has a number of other reasons for writing. She explains one strong (and very early) motivation in her Newbery Award acceptance speech. When devouring books at her public library as a child, she was disheartened to discover that "there were no Black heroes or heroines in those books, no beautiful Black ladies, no handsome Black men; no people filled with pride, strength or endurance" (404). In addition to providing a fuller picture of Black life, she also hopes that her novels "will one day be instrumental in teaching children of all colors the tremendous influence that Cassie's generation—my father's generation—had in bringing about the great Civil Rights movement of the fifties and sixties" (407). Perhaps the most important reason emerged from her growing sense of anger at injustice and need to do something about it. At one point she realized "that anger in itself was futile, that to fight discrimination I needed a stronger weapon" (403). Her story of the Logan family, which has now extended to eight works, is that "stronger weapon."

Literary critics of Taylor's work agree that she has done all that—and more. Richard Beach says that Taylor accomplishes the goal of all good multicultural literature, allowing readers to "empathize with characters grappling with racism and then connect that experience to their own real-world perceptions" (83). Indeed, Taylor's sympathetic black (and sometimes white) characters invite empathy from students of all races. Mary Turner Harper agrees, with a slight qualification, saying that Taylor's works enable "young readers to experience a world sometimes alien to them but, at the same time, one that allows them to establish a kinship with characters in their own age group who must confront the challenges of growing up in a less than ideal world" (77). In this less-than-ideal world that victimizes black people, Harper continues, Taylor "presents a positive picture of togetherness where warmth, love, and humor abound" (77).

The ways in which Taylor achieves this balance between empathy and outrage are complex, critics note. While her novels show racism clearly, says Jani Barker in a perceptive article on Taylor's work, they also rhetorically frame readers of all colors to identify with antiracist positions (120). The novels resist "a simple binary of black as good and white as evil" (129), while insisting racism "is not a matter of individual feelings, but institutionalized power structures that create deep-rooted cultural norms highly resistant to change" (132). This may seem like a pessimistic conclusion about novels designed for young readers, but most critics believe that Taylor offers both abstract hope and concrete solutions to these harmful cultural norms and practices. Taylor looks both backward and forward, Karen Patricia Smith says, with adults in her novels training their children "to live life as fully as possible, be a doormat for none, and to function and exist as the discerning protagonists of a cautionary tale: be prudent in what you say or do and never, never forget where you live" (262). Throughout these novels, Cassie Logan, especially, is called to remember the racist realities where she lives and also to discover how to change that reality.

Michelle Martin focuses on Taylor's characterization and message. Agreeing with Barker, Martin says that Taylor offers complex characterizations that force the read reader "to judge characters by their actions and not by their ethnic identities" (6). Novels like Taylor's, she continues, "offer not a simple, dichotomous depiction of racism but a complex portrayal with lots of gray area prevent readers from developing a reductionist view of social problems that take decades of awareness and work to remedy" (6). The problems that Cassie (and her family) face are not easily or quickly remedied, Logan tells her readers, but things can slowly change if one is willing to resist—sometimes directly, sometimes indirectly, but always with integrity—injustice. As Wanda Brooks and Gregory Hampton put it, "Taylor makes no effort to clean up the complicated and too often embarrassing history of race relations in America with mythologies founded on the simple or the simply explainable" (97). Longstanding and institutionalized racism is not easily explained nor quickly solved. Still, as Robert Davis-Undiano says, Mildred Taylor has been a "social-studies teacher," and a large number of her many, many young readers over the decades "attribute their strong sense of the meaning of social inequity and the need for social change to their reading of Taylor's work" (11). Clearly, critics believe that Taylor has accomplished her goals, creating generations of young people who respond empathetically to Cassie's struggles and bring that empathy and resistance to injustice into their own worlds.

The Road to Memphis (1990), Taylor's most recent novel in the series focusing on Cassie Logan (and her one young adult novel), is seen by one critic as "Taylor's angriest book to date" (Smith 255). Certainly, it is different from the other two, in that Cassie is now a young woman in high school, and, as Hamida Bosmajian, one of Taylor's most insightful critics, says, the novel "differs from the first two in that the young people are removed from the central image of the Logan's protective hearth; they are now 'on the road,' with all the dangers and adventures that this quest symbol implies" (155). It is true that Cassie, her brother, and two of their friends are travelling down both literal and metaphorical roads—away from the family home, away from the limited perspective of their small, Mississippi town, and, unfortunately, toward a glimpse of the systemic racism that pervades the United States. In addition, Cassie will have to cope with death, personal danger, and, briefly, romance. The novel also takes up a theme begun in *Let the Circle Be Unbroken* of the sexual harassment and abuse of young black women by white men and the struggles black men have when trying to protect their women from these depredations.[2] Still, at the same time the novel explores the very-real limitations on the freedoms of black women, it also shows Cassie enjoying the pleasures of female adolescence, while she rebels against the (somewhat-more benign) gender stereotyping of her family.

The novel opens with Cassie waiting for her brother Stacey to come home from Jackson, complaining about having to wear a skirt and about the "miseries of ladyhood" (6). From this first page, as critic Angela Hubler says, Taylor "provides an analysis of the way in which racism and sexism are mutually constitutative and mutually interdependent systems" (94). Right from the beginning of this novel, Cassie is limited by both her gender and her race. Hubler continues: "[T]he novel initiates the reader, along with Cassie, into the harsher realities of racial and sexual identity, not only as it is personally experienced, but as it is institutionally structured" (94). The problems that Cassie will face in this novel are taken out of a purely personal context and placed in one that includes the South and the role of black Americans in wider national and international concerns. From the first pages, when Cassie talks about discrimination and harassment at the Wallace store in Strawberry, it becomes clear that racism is pervasive and (perhaps) intractable: "[W]hite folks ruled things, and talking back to them with a smart mouth could only get you into be trouble. Hitting one of them could get you killed. That was the way of things" (11). This reference to hitting them foreshadows the conflict that will propel the young people toward Memphis later in the novel.

Stacey finally arrives, surprising his siblings with his new car, bought from white lawyer (and sympathetic family adviser) Wade Jamison. Echoing their Uncle Hammer's visit in his new car in *Roll of Thunder* and the suspicion raised when a black man has a fancy vehicle, white men ask Stacey almost immediately upon his arrival where he got the money for such a car, and he answers cautiously, taking the position, as the rest of the family has many times, that "the less white folks knew about our business, the better" (24). Again preparing the groundwork for the primary drama that is to come in the novel, she thinks that "there could be no disputing white folks, despite their insults. If a person did, the repercussions could be terrifying" (27). There appears to be no way to win in one's encounters with white folks; evasiveness may lead to more questions, while obvious annoyance could lead to violence.

After their distasteful (but all-too-common) confrontation with their white neighbors, the Logan children reconvene at home, their joy

Eight. "A stronger weapon"

at Stacey's new car only temporarily diminished by white suspicion. As always in Taylor's novels, the Logans home and land offer a refuge from the dangerous world of whites. However, this time Cassie is confronted there with expectations that she capitulate to gender stereotypes. She resists, preferring "scrubbing on the car to standing in the hot kitchen stirring up food on the wood-burning stove" (35). Although she is (relatively) safe from the depredation and deprecations of whites on Logan land, she is not free from gendered restrictions on her activities and her appearance. Cassie must be ladylike and engage in traditionally-female tasks, both to satisfy her relatives' demands and also to avoid, when she is outside of their care, the unwanted attentions of white men. This issue will continue throughout the novel, although Cassie temporarily resists the pressure, spending as much time as she can outside with the car and not inside with the food.

At this point, longtime companion of the Logan children Jeremy Simms shows up. As has always in Taylor's saga, his visits raise concern. Cassie says that he has always been a "puzzlement" to her and that he is unusual in that he is the only white boy they could call by his first name (even though they carefully avoid doing that around other whites, who would see it as a direct insult to Jeremy and an indirect one to themselves) (37). Jeremy's friendship bewilders the young Logans much of the time and concerns their parents, who worry that it will lead to hostilities with other whites (which it does) and will let the children believe (falsely, in their minds) that other whites might have benevolent motives toward them. Cassie's father has also been concerned, throughout the series, that this would lead to a (necessarily doomed and dangerous) romance between Jeremy and Cassie.[3]

Barker says that one of Taylor's strategies for targeting racism is "the depiction of sympathetic antiracist white characters," such as Wade Jamison and Jeremy Simms, "with whom [white] readers can identify, thus rejecting identification with racists" (130). By creating characters like Jeremy, Taylor allows white readers to find a place for themselves in her novels that is not racist, but, unfortunately, Jeremy's place is an uneasy one. (Wade Jamison, although benevolent and sometimes actively helpful to the family, is far more reserved in his social dealings with the Logans, and therefore doesn't present as much of a problem.) The relationship between Jeremy and the Logan children, as it is developed through her earlier novels, is a "cautious" friendship that nevertheless has roots that "ran deep and [were] never spoken" (37). These deep roots, however, may not sustain the friendship through the trials this novel will bring to it. Smith says that Jeremy is viewed carefully by the Logans because of what harm this friendship could bring to them (or, as the novel will prove, to Jeremy). In fact, she says, "Jeremy's presence is a gadfly in the racist inheritance of his family; much of the time they seem angrily perplexed as from where, Jeremy, with his ability to accept people regardless of color, has come" (264). Indeed, Jeremy's family is often more angry than perplexed about his relationship with the Logans, and this anger will erupt later in the novel. Almost everyone, white and black, finds Jeremy a "puzzlement," but Taylor wants to show her readers that although sympathetic white people can emerge from the most unlikely sources, their ability to diminish the effects of racism—on both blacks and whites—is limited.

In general, Jeremy seems not to understand what he's asking of the Logan children when he tries to be their friend. For example, as soon as they arrive with the new car, Jeremy is there asking for a ride, unwittingly causing consternation all around. In the middle of the 20th century in the South, if white people gave black people rides, they sat in the back seat, bed of the truck, or rumble seat, and black people didn't usually have cars to give white people rides. Because of this, Jeremy's request for a ride becomes "an awkward thing" (38). Finally sensing this, Jeremy wishes that he and Stacey could still do things together "and folks wouldn't mind" (40). To Jeremy, strangely, "folks is just folks" (41), which certainly isn't the case for his family, the community around Strawberry, or Mississippi in general, for both the black and white population.

Papa likes Jeremy but nevertheless mistrusts the friendship. He thinks close friendships between whites and blacks could only cause trouble (44). He also worries that Jeremy (now nearly grown) might change, eventually coming to accept his family's white, racist heritage (44). Indeed, it soon appears that he has, when both Jeremy and his cousins and (separately) Cassie and her brothers (and neighbor Harris) go hunting. Jeremy participates, albeit reluctantly, in the white boys' harassment of the overweight Harris, who climbs a tree when they have their dogs chase him. Awkward with physical activity, and scared out of his mind by the dogs, Harris falls and breaks his leg, and Cassie and her brothers never fully forgive Jeremy for his part in the accident (78). It appears for most of this novel that David Logan's predictions for Jeremy have finally come true. Certainly, it seems that Jeremy could have done more than he did to stand up to his cousins.

The hunt also provides a venue for the theme alluded to earlier in the novel, the increasing pressure on Cassie to conform to gender expectations. Accustomed to going everywhere with her brothers, Cassie wants to go hunting too, but matriarch of the family, Big Ma, says, "Boys s'pose t' go huntin', not girls!" (47). Papa reminds his mother that she was a good shot herself, but she says she just did it for the meat, when her husband wasn't home. She adds, to bolster her position, that it is high time for Cassie should start "taking on womanly ways" (48). In Big Ma's mind, a woman going hunting is only acceptable if she needs to feed her family (and, by implication, married women would not as vulnerable to sexual exploitation in the woods alone). Eventually, Cassie is allowed to go, but Big Ma insists that she wear a skirt, which she does but removes it when she out of sight of the house (which is apparently a common practice) (59). It is also during this hunt that Cassie encounters Jeremy's racist cousins, and they taunt her in ways that are implicitly sexual. For the first of several times in the novel, Stacey asks her afterward if they did anything to her (71). This question, a veiled inquiry (which Cassie doesn't fully understand, or perhaps acknowledge) as to whether or not she has been sexually violated, reoccurs with more intensity as the novel progresses.

In addition to Cassie's reluctance to assume "womanly ways" and her family's increasing concern about her safety, other characters weigh in on gender expectations. Some young women in their community still cling to traditional roles, perhaps given their more limited personal expectations. For example, their friend Clarence's pregnant girlfriend Sissy says that while Cassie gets to go to Jackson to finish high school and plans on going to law school, Clarence's is the "only dream" she's got (54). A humorous subplot concerns Sissy's attempts to get Clarence to admit to fathering her child, but the more serious message here is that without education, black women in the South face few choices beyond motherhood and marriage.

In spite of her hatred of being forced to wear skirts and help in the kitchen, Cassie enjoys her increasing attractiveness. When she tries on a dress for church, for example, she decides that she "liked what [she] saw" (55). While trying on clothes, she talks with mother about whether or not she will marry Moe, the neighbor who has shown a romantic interest (not fully reciprocated) in her. Mama refers to Cassie getting married, but Cassie says that she wants to finish law school first, and she reminds her mother that she got her teaching degree before she married Papa (56). In general, Cassie knows she's pretty, but she doesn't "dwell on it" (58); she fully intends to finish high school and college (and eventually law school) before she is ready to marry.

These dreams are threatened by white males in the community, however, who see her coming of age (and thus ripe for sexual exploitation). Walking alone down the road from church, she runs into Leon, Troy, and Statler (Jeremy's cousins from the hunt), and when she responds angrily to their taunts, she realizes that she "couldn't win" with them. If she challenges them, they find her feisty; if she refuses them, they may become angry and attack her. This echoes the confrontation early in the novel at the Wallace store, but this time the emphasis is on sexual as well as racial harassment. Before things get dangerously out of control, her father (increasingly protective of his daughter) comes looking for her and spirits her away from the white boys. He tells her that white men forcing their attentions on black girls has happened many times "and ain't been nothin' them girls' daddies could do 'bout it.... Got no laws t' protect our girls from the likes of him, but I ain't gonna stand for him forcing his attentions on you" (104). He tells her, "Sometimes things happen, and there ain't no way to keep them from happening. Other times things happen 'cause we get to thinking we so smart nothing can go wrong. Don't get so smart, Daughter, you don't use your head" (105). Although these fears will become realities later on in the novel, it is equally troubling that she is more vulnerable because she is smart.

The implication that her desire to use her intelligence may lead to threats on her physical safety may be seen as anti-feminist. However, as Bosmajian says, her submission to her father's authority may stem from "a subtextual acknowledgment on Taylor's part that African American men need to be authoritatively constituted in narratives for the young, because white racism constantly undermines the realization of such constructive authority" (144). It is not men who are keeping Cassie in "her place" but white men, and her father's intervention is necessary to see that she can realize her dreams without physical threat. Hubler notes that Cassie's father, while recognizing their limitations in their world, "also asserts individual agency to resist oppression" (95). Cassie may not

Eight. "A stronger weapon"

be able avoid such confrontations with white men, but she can depend on the strong males in her life (and, one might assume, herself eventually) to keep her safe.

Complicating this issue and the plot, Cassie's friend Moe soon after engages in a violent confrontation at the Wallace store that leads to Moe hitting Jeremy's cousin Statler in the side with a tire iron, Leon in the chest, and Troy in the head, seriously wounding him (124). Apparently, Moe's dangerous aggression is triggered by Statler's insinuation that he might have his way with Cassie. Thus, Cassie's sexuality leads to the blow that causes Moe's exile, suggesting that the protection offered black women by the men in their lives could damage them all. To escape lynching, or, at best, a trial that certainly would lead to a conviction (and possible execution if Troy dies), Moe must leave town immediately. Happening down the road at this very moment, Jeremy allows Moe to get into his truck and hides him in the bed to help him escape. Still uncertain about Jeremy after the hunting incident, the Logans decide that all they can do is "hope that we could trust him still" (136). Jeremy, for his part, sees this as a way to redeem himself with the Logans, although it will precipitate a permanent break with his own family. The bleak assessment of this incident falls to Cassie, who says, "we couldn't win, not against white folks" (118). It certainly appears, at this point in the novel, that no one wins in encounters such as these.

Following Moe's path of escape, Cassie, Little Willie, Clarence, and Stacey leave for Jackson, not being entirely certain that Moe will make it there. There they meet with Mr. Jamison to discuss what Moe should do. He tells them that "the law is an imperfect piece of machinery and not blind to color, not here in Mississippi" and advises Moe to go North (157). The white, aristocratic, educated Wade Jamison, is, according to Harper, "the lost conscience of his community" (77). Although he offers sound advice, he can do very little else to help either Moe or the Logans. Still, he represents a positive alternative (along with Jeremy) to prevailing white racism. (Also in Jackson, Cassie meets the lawyer, newspaper editor, and community organizer Solomon Bradley for the first time, and he sees her reading her law casebook, which impresses him. Bradley will appear with a larger role later in the novel.) Following Mr. Jamison's advice, the young people decide to drive Moe to Memphis so he can catch a train to Chicago to stay with Uncle Hammer, and the road trip (and Cassie's further education in systemic racism) begins.

"Unsuitable" Books

At a gas station along the road, they run into a white attendant who opines that, as African Americans, they of course love "dancing and good-time music places," and Stacey and Cassie are disgusted by those racist assumptions (169). Unfortunately, though, things get much worse very quickly. At that same station, Cassie needs to use the restroom, but she is told that she has to use the woods behind it, as the bathrooms are for white patrons. She knows in this Jim Crow Era South that she would be breaking the law if she uses them, but she "felt such an anger, such a hostility, such a need to defy them that I couldn't just walk right on past" (177). She is caught by a white woman with her hand on the rest room door, and in a confrontation with the attendant, she trips, tearing her stockings and skinning her knees. To complete her humiliation, the attendant kicks her and orders her to leave, making disparaging comments about her anatomy and her race. A suggestion remains that the assault is more than simply humiliating, however. In an echo of her father's response to the Statler boys' harassment and his own question earlier in the novel, Stacey asks if anyone touched her (180), implying a sexual nature to the assault. They leave quickly, fearing that they are being pursued by white men from the station, and they soon pull off the road to hide and sleep, which scratches the car and causes the fraying fan belt to break. During the night, Cassie is sick to her stomach as she recalls what happened to her (188). Bosmajian puts it well; Cassie, he says,

> can no longer stomach a world that denies her even the most natural urges; moreover, she cannot admit to her brothers that she endangered the entire rescue mission by trying to use the segregated restroom. In this existential moment of isolation, she relieves herself from the pain in the depth of her being by vomiting near the bushes in the darkness (the place designated to her by segregation) and thus soils the beautiful and controlled appearance she has acquired for her public persona [157].

Cassie may appreciate her nice clothes and the way they complement her developing figure, but in the eyes of the white world she is simply a black body trying to force itself into unwanted contact with them, while at the same time representing an object of (forbidden) desire to white men. "Ladyhood" and sexual violence cannot be separated in this novel.

Still stranded the next morning, the Logan children argue about the looming war, which becomes increasingly important as the novel progresses. Stacey says that he won't repair the scratch, so that it can

Eight. "A stronger weapon"

continue to remind him "'bout what all Mississippi done for me," which, of course, is very little so far. He admits that if he goes to fight, he will "probably be shooting the wrong white folks" (192).[4] In another conversation that morning, which is related to the ongoing theme of the need to protect women from predatory white men, Cassie teases Moe about his comment that in Strawberry he was protecting his "womenfolks" (197). Cassie acknowledges that Moe feels he protected her with his actions, but she underscores her desire not to be considered his "woman." Here, Cassie asserts her shredded but still-intact belief that she can protect herself (in spite of her father's admonitions and her experiences so far), and her underlying concern that black men aren't capable of preventing what white men might do to her.

This suspicion of white men's actions continues even when they appear to help the young people. They eventually get a fan belt from some benevolent white men, although Cassie and Moe think that "most times it paid to be suspicious of white folks, even in good deeds" (202). Given what they have experienced all their lives, this seems like a reasonable conclusion. In fact, subsequent events prove this to be true. Clarence, who has been suffering with severe headaches throughout the trip, begins to feel even worse, and his friends think about taking him to a hospital, although they know that no white hospital will take him (204). White people, Stacey thinks, "ruled the hospitals like they ruled everything else" (206). Clarence eventually stays with a local healer where he dies shortly afterward, probably of a cerebral hemorrhage. Although the white doctor and nurses at the hospital aren't necessarily responsible for Clarence's death, they certainly abandoned him (and the others) in their hour of need.

In spite of their troubles, the young people finally get to Memphis and stay with Solomon Bradley, who, as a powerful friend of the Logan children's aunt and uncle in Jackson, is best suited to help them in a strange city. Continuing the ongoing conversation about the upcoming war, Cassie argues with one of Bradley's workers about it, wondering what difference it would make if the U.S. won: "If we win," she asks, "are we going to be able to use their restrooms in a gas station or eat in their cafes or sleep in their hotels or go to their hospitals?" (231). She extends the argument with Bradley and also tells him that she doesn't want her brother and friends to know what happened in the gas station (234). She and Solomon talk about the law, and Cassie says, "I was thinking

"Unsuitable" Books

that if I got to know the law as well as they do, then maybe I could get some different interpretation. If we know the law like they do, then we can use it like they do" (245). Since neither force, nor stealth, nor ingenuity seem to be of much help against racist whites, Cassie is coming to realize that she will have to find ways to use laws made by them to fight the injustices they have created. As Bosmajian says, Taylor's novels, and this one in particular, do not "invoke or appeal to divine law, but place the responsibility for justice on laws made by humans" (142). Although the promised sequel to Cassie story has not yet been published, it is possible to imagine Cassie, as a lawyer, doing just that, maybe even someday taking over Mr. Jamison's practice in Strawberry.

At this point, however, the novel takes a romantic turn. After cleaning up in his apartment, Cassie imagines dancing with Bradley, thinking, "I was Cinderella and he was my Memphis Prince" (248). He kisses her shortly after, but decides quickly that he should "know better" about getting involved with a young girl (252). They agree to meet in a year, and he gives her books to read. Critics have mixed feelings about this scene. Donnarae MacCann says that Cassie is "less plausible" in this novel than in the previous ones. The book, she says, "seems obliged to meet the demands of that ambiguous sub-genre, the teenage romance and Taylor seems less ready to deal with the problems this entails" (97). Clearly, MacCann regrets these choices, while halfheartedly acknowledging their necessity. Bosmajian is more qualified in his response. Cassie, he says, "does not interpret Solomon, nor does the authorial control of the narrative create an ironic distance between Cassie the mature narrator and Cassie the teenager infatuated with Solomon Bradley" (154). It is true that there is no irony in the presentation of this rather straightforward (if brief) romantic interlude. However, he adds that we see in the relationship "the beginning of a powerful ambiguity for Cassie, who is far more socialized as a potential student of the law than as a woman." Unfortunately, he points out, there is yet no sequel to show how she resolves this conflict (155). One could argue that this is the joining of the two threads of the novel—Cassie's desire for independence and her desire for love, but, as Bosmajian reminds us, the link is not yet fully developed.

Having deposited Moe safely on the train to Chicago, his friends return to Strawberry to witness Jeremy's violent confrontation with his father when he tells him that Moe snuck into his truck and escaped (he

Eight. "A stronger weapon"

insists) without his knowledge. His father slams his fist into Jeremy's jaw and is only prevented from doing worse by the sheriff. At this point, Charlie Simms disowns Jeremy, telling him that he "ain't white no more" for betraying his kin. "Don' you never again let me see you in this life, boy," he shouts. "Can't stand the sight of ya" (275). Bosmajian says that Jeremy Simms, like T.J. in an earlier novel, functions as a "complex scapegoat figure" (148). He ends up paying a heavy price the price for his desire to cross racial lines. Barker agrees, saying that Jeremy "endangers himself by his attempts to cross the color line and is left isolated" (131). Smith calls this public renunciation a "chilling phenomenon" and points out that, for Jeremy, it appears that death will provide the only resolution (264). Crowe rightly describes the renunciation scene with Jeremy and his father as "one of the most painful in all of Taylor's books" (85). "Charlie Simms is the perfect antithesis to David Logan," he says, "no Logan would ever abuse his own kin the way Charlie Simms does" (113). He concludes that *The Road to Memphis* is Taylor's "most powerful indictment of the dehumanizing effects racism can have on racists" (87), although certainly Mr. Simms (at the time) doesn't realize that he has suffered anything other than shame in his banishment of his son.

Now an outcast in his community, Jeremy shows up one more time at the Logan's house, on his way to join the Army. He says he wishes he could go back to the good old days of their childhood. Cassie comments that they never understood Jeremy and he made them uncomfortable, but, nevertheless, his leaving "tugged at my heart" (288). Cassie recognizes that something important will be lost when Jeremy leaves—her only positive connection with a white person her own age. The novel ends with "We did not see Jeremy Simms again" (290), which implies that Cassie and her family will not experience such a connection across the races again. Jeremy Simms' fate, Smith says, is "to forever witness, internalize the wrongs committed against blacks, and be an outcast among his own people" (260). Unfortunately, he cannot join the Logan family either, and his only response is to join the war effort and, presumably, be killed in the process.

This ending, with its banishment of Jeremy Simms, one of only two white people in the saga who have shown both genuine affection and practical help to the Logan family, is certainly a mixed one. Bosmajian says that at the end, Cassie "senses that great historical struggles may not really eradicate the roots of prejudice" (159). However, even though she has learned that there is little she can do about racism. Crowe perceptively comments that Cassie has also learned how to survive it (128). As Martin puts it in a 2011 essay about the Logan family, true freedom can only be obtained through "owning land; actively fighting injustice, even as children; pursuing an education, which includes acquiring literacy both in the traditional sense and in the sense of cultural literacy; and understanding their own history through family oral traditions" (*Oxford* 372). It is not enough simply to have land and family, Taylor insists, young people must stand up to discrimination while at the same time understanding their personal and familial history, as well as their place in history. In summary, she says, "Taylor succeeds in showing black children a reflection both of who their ancestors might have been and how this legacy contributes to who they may become" (*Oxford* 386). Thus, the Logan family saga directs the gaze of its readers outward and forward toward a time of more racial equality and opportunity.

Given the positive legacy of her novels, it is a wonder that so many people feel the need to prevent children from reading them. It is as if they are so ashamed of America's past history of racism that they would like to keep young people free from the knowledge of it. This is, of course, part of a larger pattern seen again and again with young adult literature, that a certain group of parents and school authorities would rather have children unaware (or at least not exposed in schools and libraries) of the more unsavory aspects of adult life. Still, as Cassie Logan comes to know, being aware of injustices is not enough. One must use one's own wits, one's anger, and, finally, the force of law to change things. Cassie does almost all of these things (although she hasn't yet become the lawyer she wants to be by the end of *The Road to Memphis*), but she is only able to do it through the power of education and her grounding in family stories. Young readers, Taylor shows us again and again, can benefit from the lessons this unofficial social studies teacher wants to teach them, and they can use the "stronger weapon" of literature to fight the injustices that they will undoubtedly encounter in their own lives.

CHAPTER NINE

"Simple moments of exquisite happiness"
Lois Lowry's The Giver (1993)

> I don't hope for young people to "learn" from my books. I hope only that they learn to question—Lois Lowry, Hintz and Ostry, 199
>
> [The idea that] a child can discover the hypocrisy of adult culture is often a lightning rod for those who wish to control the lives of young people—Avi, Karolides, 175

A stark but beautifully written depiction of a utopian community devoted to rationality, equality, and conformity, Lois Lowry's *The Giver*, as with all the novels in this study, has been the object of many censorship challenges since it first appeared in 1993. Coming in at number 23 on the American Library Association's Top 100 Banned/Challenged Books: 2000–2009, Lowry's novel has been challenged for its depiction of the community's use of euthanasia and its regulation of sexuality. Lowry, who believes that it is "essential that all artistic exploration be unrestrained" (Hintz and Ostry 198), thinks that young people who read about her 12-year-old protagonist Jonas facing "moral dilemmas and acting heroically" may be "more inclined to back off from moral compromise in the adult world they'll eventually enter" (Hintz and Ostry 197). Writing *The Giver* while her mother was dying, Lowry began to consider "the importance for people to pass along their memories to the next generation" (*Reading Teacher* 308). Whatever concerns parents and community members might have about the troubling aspects of her dystopian novel, the author intended the book, which has been the winner of the Newbery Award and numerous other honors, to celebrate the power of memory and the need for self-determination.

Well-known young adult fiction writer Avi says that *The Giver* is "a brilliantly written defense of individualism" (173) and a critique of conformity of thought and action. Ironically, he adds, those who feel threatened by the book "are precisely the kind of people who would create the society portrayed in the book" (175). Lowry recognizes this, saying that one "huge" irony about *The Giver* is "that a book that depicts a society that has lost its literature is one of the most frequently challenged books in the U.S." (*Instructor* 72). It seems a shame that adults would challenge such a book, which, as Susan Lea says, is an ideal text "for fostering inquiry into racism, a colorblind stance, and social justice, as well as for raising question of self, identity, difference, and the other" (65).

The novel also encourages resistance to an oppressive status quo. Literary critic Don Latham points out that *The Giver* contradicts Roberta Trites' view that young adult literature teaches adolescents how to live within *existing* power structures, "suggesting instead that Jonas should be admired precisely *because* he resists the institutional structures of his community" (135). The novel, he says, "serves to reintegrate readers into the power structures of our own society while at the same time empowering them as potential agents of social change" (135). Lowry agrees. "[E]ach time a child opens a book," she says in her Newbery Award speech, "he pushes open the gate that separates him from Elsewhere. It gives him choices. It gives him freedom. Those are wonderfully unsafe things" ("Newbery" NP). She continues this subject in an article in *Reading Instructor*:

> Too many adults look back through rose-tinted glasses to a sunlit place of unmitigated happiness. Kids, on the other hand, know what it's really like; they understand the cruelties that children inflict on one another and the hypocrisies that adults practice. Literature for the young has to address these things, I think, or risk being dishonest. A surprising number of adults prefer the dishonest literature, that which pretends a pain-free past [72].

Like Chris Crutcher and Mildred Taylor, Lowry believes that writers for young adults should tell the truth, warts and all, about life and not hide the pain that children already know exists in the world.

Susan Stewart is less convinced that novel is as "unsafe" as Lowry believes it to be. *The Giver*, she says, "reifies several ideological foundations without providing a space to openly interrogate them" (23). "While it appears that Jonas's actions are quite radical," she adds, "they are actually very conservative. He simply reinforces one of our most persistent

Nine. "Simple moments of exquisite happiness"

fears—the loss of choice. His flight from his community is nothing less than a return to the humanist subject position many readers occupy where the individual takes precedence over the community..." (25). The text, she argues, "ultimately returns readers to the ideals liberal humanism proposes without actually examining them and does little to challenge some concepts that under close inspection are problematic" (32). "In *The Giver*," Stewart continues, "we are encouraged to critique Jonas's culture and not our own" (33). Carter Hanson disagrees, saying that while the novel endorses the values of liberal humanism, "it does not intend just to recuperate twentieth-century western individualism." Instead, its treatment of memory "indicates a forward utopian momentum" (56–7).

Perhaps the proper position is somewhere in between. Carrie Hintz makes the link between adolescence and dystopian novels like *The Giver*, saying that in them "political and social awakening is almost always combined with a depiction of the personal problems of adolescence" (255). They also serve a larger purpose, she says, becoming "a way of using the transition from adolescence to adulthood to focus on the need for political action and the exercise of political will within a democratic society" (255). This is clearly the case with Jonas, who must grow into his new role in the community (as do all adolescents), while at the same time coming to see that it will be up to him to change it. His society is not yet democratic, but he certainly does recognize the need for action to help save it.

However, the primary roadblock for Jonas in this quest, as is the case for many of the characters in both Chris Crutcher's and Robert Cormier's novels, is that "[i]nstead of finding the assistance of competent adults, the helpers they have are flawed, and at the critical moment, ineffectual" (111). Jonas, like Jerry in *The Chocolate War*, and T.J. in *Whale Talk*, is on his own. The adults in their lives, while often well-meaning, are unable (or sometimes unwilling) to help. Jonas, finally, has to make his escape (which will facilitate the healing of the community) by himself, accompanied only by a helpless infant.

Readers are first introduced to 12-year-old Jonas as he is about to attend an as-yet-unexplained ceremony, about which declares he is feeling "apprehensive" (4). It isn't clear exactly what the purpose of this ceremony is, but from the start of the novel, things in Jonas' world do not perfectly resemble our own. It is important to recognize that the story begins in December, as Barbara Lehman and Patricia Crook point out.

"Unsuitable" Books

Thus the narrative is circular, beginning and ending in December, with the beginning foreshadowing the ending (76). The month—evocative of celebrations and of endings (as well as beginnings)—also calls attention the growing number of differences between Jonas' world and our own. Still, whatever is about to happen and in what sort of world this is taking place only becomes clear over time.

Jonas has many of the standard concerns of young adolescents—friends, incipient romance, connections to his parents and siblings—but something seems a bit off. The world in which he lives, for example, is highly controlled and calm, right down to the ritual sharing of feelings in the evening and dream telling in the morning. No one yells, or expresses frustration, or tries to humiliate one another. Still, Jonas, even early on, has trouble fitting in. His seven-year-old sister Lily feelings were "always straightforward, fairly simple, usually easy to resolve" (7), but from the beginning of the novel, Jonas' feelings are more complicated and hard to put into words. This inability to speak clearly marks him as existing outside the prevailing ethos of his community (while at the same time marking him in our world as a fairly typical adolescent). Lehman and Crook say that throughout the novel "language becomes a tool for political control and manipulation, and means to conceal unpleasant truths, to allow adults to feel satisfied about themselves, and to ensure conformity" (74). Ironically, though, the language the community uses is actually "doublespeak and lies" (75), and ultimately, Jonas will be seen as right to call this use of language into question.

After Jonas' failed attempt to communicate in the family setting, he participates in his first private talk with his parents, and his mother tells him that the upcoming ceremony is the most important one for him, as he will begin receiving "preparation for adult life" (17). After the Ceremony of Twelve, she tells him, adults lose track of their age and concentrate on their work (17). This suggestion that both children and adults in this society have their roles chosen for them is the one of the early indications that Jonas' community functions differently than those of his readers and suggests the beginning of Lowry's satirical portrait of this "ideal" world. Don Latham says Lowry presents what appears to be a "perfect" adult-child relationship, where children are protected from internal and external harm. However, she suggests throughout the novel "that such overprotection stymies personal growth and impedes freedom" ("Childhood" 9).

Nine. "Simple moments of exquisite happiness"

At this point in the novel, readers learn that babies are born to surrogate mothers, that marriages are arranged between mutually compatible adults, that children spend their first year in a "Nurturing Center" and then are carefully placed in these families (one boy and one girl to each). The number of children born is carefully controlled, young people must volunteer at various work sites, jobs are carefully chosen, meals are sent from a common kitchen, only bikes are ridden for transportation, couples whose children are grown separate and live with other childless adults, and the elderly live out their prescribed number days in the House of the Old. Disobedient adults, the elderly, and deformed children are "released" from the community. Overall, it seems a planned and orderly life free of the usual chaos of family and romantic life.

There are troubles beneath the surface, though. The first complication comes into Jonas' life when his father brings home a baby from the Nurturing Center. Looking at the child Gabriel's eyes, he sees a certain "depth ... as if one were looking into the clear water of the river, down to the bottom, where things might lurk which hadn't been discovered yet" (21). Jonas is "self-conscious," as he is afraid he may look this way as well (21). These clear and depth-filled eyes will later mark characters of significant insight—and importance to the plot—but right now they just make Jonas uncomfortable. This difference (among many to be revealed) between Jonas and his community continues, when he notices that he sees differently, that an apple "changed" when he looks at it (24). It isn't exactly clear what Jonas sees at this point (or what his community members do not see), but it is enough to set him apart from the others. As becomes evident later, though, being different is what marks Jonas both as a critic of his society and as its eventual leader.

The novel continues to move between a realistic adolescent novel of development and work of dystopian science fiction. As a typical adolescent, Jonas begins having sexual feelings, which in his community are called "stirrings," which he describes as the "wanting" that runs through him (36). Unlike in our world, however, all sexually mature members of the community take pills to stop these feelings. One might image that would-be censors would approve of such a world, where all teenage sexuality is chemically repressed and discussed only in the blandest terms. Perhaps what rankles them about this novel, though, is that Lowry hints that his repression of sexuality might be a bad thing. Eventually Jonas' decision to leave the community to save it is prompted by his stopping the pills and allowing his "stirrings" to lead him to make emotionally-motivated choices. For the time being, though, he dutifully takes his medicine.

The first significant challenge in Jonas' life concerns his future career. Jonas initially worries that he will be given a wrong assignment, that he won't fit in. However, he consoles himself by remembering that his community "was so meticulously ordered, the choices so carefully made" (48). At the ceremony, the 12-year-olds are thanked for their childhood (56), and, eventually, they are given their assignments. Jonas is initially passed over in the assignments but after several tense moments, he is given the role of Receiver of Memory at the end. The community begins to chant his name, which causes him to feel "gratitude and pride" but also fear. He also has no idea what his new job entails: "He did not know what he was to become. Or what would become of him" (64). At first, Jonas is concerned that things will change with his friend Asher (66), but it soon becomes obvious that he will have bigger problems.

His instructions for his job as Receiver of Memory give him new freedoms and raise deep concerns. In his new role, he is allowed to ask questions, to be rude, and to lie (68), which have been forbidden until now. In a world like ours, we would say he is given permission to no longer be a child, but in this world, these same restrictions appear to apply to adults as well. He immediately worries that others might have been given this same permission, and then realizes that he would have no way of knowing who is telling the truth (71). This is an essentially adult dilemma—once you understand that the world is not an truthful place, and that you have the capacity to lie, it becomes necessary to determine new and more complex ways of discerning the truth. Still, in Jonas' world, people act as children all their lives, and it appears that only Jonas has been given the excruciating task of trying to tell truth from falsehood and having to decide when it might be appropriate to lie.

The next day, he meets The Giver, whose job it is to pass on the collective memories of the community to Jonas. The Giver tells him what he knows: "There's all that goes beyond—that is Elsewhere—and all that goes back, and back, and back. I received all of those, when I was selected. And here in this room all alone, I re-experience these again and again. It is how wisdom comes. And how we shape our future" (78).

Nine. "Simple moments of exquisite happiness"

Because memories, experiences of both joy and sorrow, war and love, have been deemed too confusing for this world, The Giver holds onto those memories and uses them to guide the community in making wise decisions. The Giver tells Jonas, however, that he has "honor" not power (84). Carter Hanson says Lowry "makes memory both the source of potential transformative change and of the novel's final moment of possible utopian realization" (46). Jonas and The Giver are both transformed by these memories, and, eventually, will use them to change their world.

The process of receiving memories is sometimes an unpleasant one. Almost immediately, learning about his community's lost past creates complications for Jonas. He begins to dream about a sled and snow and a place that was "welcoming" (88), and he longs to live in such a place, so unlike the colorless, weather-free world in which he resides. He also begins to feel separate from the other children, who could never understand what he is experiencing (89), and he starts to question the "sameness" of his world. The Giver tells Jonas that the community gained many things (stability, security, lack of conflict) but also had to give things up (color, desire, differences). Jonas exclaims "fiercely" that they shouldn't have (95). Lowry agrees. "The loss of music, art, and literature," she says, "was the truly dystopian element in *The Giver* for me" (198).

As he continues to receive memories, both good and bad, Jonas finds himself "irrationally angry" at his classmates, whose lives "had none of the vibrancy his own was taking on," and he is angry at himself that he can't share it with them (99). The Giver tells him that people have chosen a life "so orderly, so predictable—so painless" (103) and explains that he will have to embody the memories for the community (104). After he experiences profound physical and psychological pain, he feels "desperately lonely" that he can't share this (110), and he doesn't want to go back to his sessions with The Giver. He sees his community living "ordinary lives free from anguish" because he has been chosen to bear their burdens. Latham says that "through his training, Jonas begins to move beyond the innocence typically associated with childhood. In his world, however, he is moving not just beyond the innocence associated with a particular stage of life, but beyond the 'innocence' of his entire community. Jonas's reaction is like that of many adolescents as they being to mature—he wants to recover his lost innocence" ("Childhood" 9).

Jonas does want to recover his "innocence" before receiving memories, but he also knows that he has "experienced countless bits of happiness, things he had never known of before" (121). For example, he experiences love for the first time when The Giver gives him a memory of Christmas in a family (125). He is prompted by this memory to ask his surrogate parents if they love him, and they answer that that is an inappropriate question, as they have very little understanding of complex emotions without memories (or sexual feelings for that matter). They ask him if he understands why this kind of question is irrelevant in their world, and he lies to them and tells them he does. This is his first lie to his parents (127) and represents his movement away from them and their world. When Jonas looks at Gabriel, he realizes that he could have love in his life, and the next day he stops taking the pills for the stirrings (129). He now knows that he can't go back to the old world and that the "feelings" his family shared weren't didn't have the depth of his. His family and other members of the community "analyzed with endless talk" (131).

Jonas has lost his sense of security, and although he understands that he loves his friends, he can't share that love with them because they can't feel it. He also believes at this point that he can't change anything (135). However, The Giver begins to realize that Jonas has to leave in order to force the community to experience memories, and The Giver has to stay and help them cope with the disturbing flood of images they will experience (145). At this point, it seems clear that Jonas has been designated as the community's hero and is destined to open their world up (although indirectly, since he won't be there) to variety and emotion. Thus Jonas appears at this point to be a kind of Moses, leading his people into the promised land but unable to go there himself.

Jonas and The Giver create an orderly plan for Jonas's escape, but those plans change quickly, initiated by Jonas's discovery of the true meaning of release as he witnesses his father's euthanizing of a smaller of two twin infants. At the sight, Jonas feels "a ripping sensation inside himself, the feeling of terrible pain clawing its way forward to emerge in a cry" (151), and he determines to prevent future release at all costs. The Giver, however, reminds Jonas that the people in their community can't help what they do. "They know nothing," he stresses (153), calling Jonas to feel compassion for those he had just condemned. When Gabriel, who has never been a docile-enough child, is scheduled for release in the morning, Jonas knows that he must leave (with the baby)

Nine. "Simple moments of exquisite happiness"

immediately. With Gabriel in a child carrier behind his bicycle, Jonas leaves his secure world, realizing that "the orderly disciplined life he had always knows would continue again, without him. The life where nothing was ever unexpected. Or inconvenient. Or unusual. The life without color, pain, or past" (165). As that passage moves forward, readers can see that while Jonas might miss the "orderly disciplined life," he also must move away from a life with no inconveniences, with nothing unexpected or painful. On the run, not quite sure where he's heading, Jonas directly experiences fear, hunger, cold, for the first time, but he also is notices color, birds, wind, and feels "simple moments of exquisite happiness" (171). Of course Lowry is saying here that one cannot have one without the other; hunger and cold are matched by birds and wind, and pain by happiness. This passage has much to say to would-be censors: while we might like to keep our children's world free of pain and fear, we are also depriving them of the "exquisite happiness" that comes with a fuller experience of life.

At the end of the novel, Jonas seems to be heading to a hill, where he finds the sled of his dreams (apparently waiting for him) and heads downward, where he hears singing. Also, he thinks he hears music from the place he left, but he thinks that "perhaps it was only an echo" (179). In her Newbery Award speech, Lowry said that there isn't a "right" ending or interpretation of the ending. "There's a right one for each of us, and it depends on our own beliefs, our own hopes" ("Newbery" NP). Latham suggests a slightly more muted reading of the ending:

> The novel ultimately suggests that, while Jonas has resisted and escaped the power structures of his own dystopian community, he is moving toward integration into the power structures of another kind of community, one more hopeful and more positive, but constituted by power structures nonetheless. The novel thus shows that resistance to power structures is possible and even productive [150].

Jonas can and did resist his community's power over him, but he has acquiesced in another potential power structure waiting for him at the bottom of the hill. In another article on the novel, he puts it somewhat more hopefully: "The richness and ambiguity of the final scene are appropriate parallels to the richness and ambiguity of Jonas' character—and indeed, the richness and ambiguity of all children" ("Childhood" 9). We're never quite sure what happens to Jonas, just as we are never sure, when we are adolescents, how we will turn out. Hintz comments on this duality, saying that *The Giver* "ends with the heroism of the adolescent, but also a bittersweet note of personal sacrifice" ("Monica Hughes" 263). As with the transition from adolescence to adulthood, there is both gain and loss at the end of the novel. Hanson says that Jonas' final journey is "through and beyond memory" and that "whatever utopian hope resides in the ending, it is memory, the novel's one real agent of change, which makes this possible" (58). Without memory, there is no hope.

There has been some criticism of the novel's conclusion, though. Stewart says that even though Lowry wants readers to "figure out for themselves" how the novel ends, she "expunges that choice" by writing *Messenger* as a sequel that explores Jonas' life after going Elsewhere (30).[1] Levy says, "Read as a work of dystopian fiction, *The Giver* seems complete. Read as a bildungsroman, however, the novel's ending seems abortive" (56). He calls the book an "ambiguous dystopia" in the tradition of *Brave New World* because elements of Jonas' world are positive and says that the novel never completes the bildungsroman cycle, letting Jonas enjoy his success or establish himself in a new world (51). Lowry's position on her ambiguous ending is this:

> Young people handle dystopia every day: in their lives, their dysfunctional families, their violence-ridden schools. They watch dystopian television and movies about the real world where firearms bring about explosive conclusions to conflict. Yes, I think they need to see some hope for such a world. I can't imagine writing a book that doesn't have a hopeful ending [199].

Lowry—like Paterson, Crutcher, Hinton, Blume, and each of the writers in this study—believes that young people are capable of handling difficult truths about the world in which they live (and embracing equally challenging imagined worlds), but she does think that some hope needs to be offered, especially at the end for "simple moments" of happiness. Jonas, wherever he ends up, is exhilarated about his ride downhill and thrilled about what might await him when he arrives. He has also provided his former community with a richer and fuller life and given his readers a truer sense of the complexity of this (actual) world in which we live.

CHAPTER TEN

"Don't you two be strangers!"
M.E. Kerr's Deliver Us from Evie *(1994)*

[There is] a need to see one's face reflected in the pages of a book and thus to find the corollary comfort that derives from the knowledge that one is not alone in a vast universe, that there are others 'like me'"—Michael Cart and Christine Jenkins, *The Heart Has Its Reasons*, 1

M.E. Kerr's road to writing young adult fiction has been a long (and somewhat circuitous) one. She was born Marijane Meaker in 1927, and her first published work featured a young adult male protagonist in a short story for *Ladies Home Journal* (13) and was written under the pseudonym Laura Winston. She made her living during the 1950s and 60s writing mysteries and non-fiction about lesbian relationships under the pen names Vin Packer and Ann Aldrich. She finally began young adult novels as M.E. Kerr in 1972 with *Dinky Hocker Shoots Smack*!, and she hasn't looked back. She won the Margaret A. Edwards Award, presented by the American Library Association and *School Library Journal* in 1983. She also came out publicly as a lesbian in 1994, in a preface to *Hearing Us Out: Voices from the Gay and Lesbian Community*, the same year her YA novel, *Deliver Us from Evie*, featuring a lesbian main character, Evie Parr, came out as well.[1]

Her relatively late start writing for young adults is not the only thing that sets her apart from her fellow YA writers. As Alleen Pace Nilsen says in her book-length study, unlike some young adult writers, Kerr never taught high school; unlike many others, she never had children of her own, and unlike S.E. Hinton, she wrote her young adult novels twenty to thirty years after she was a young adult (*Presenting* 12).

"Unsuitable" Books

Also opposed to most YA authors, especially those writing before the 1990s, Kerr tries in many of her books "to normalize homosexuality by dropping in one or more non-threatening references, often presented through the viewpoint of a minor character or in the form of a joke or a smart remark designed to make readers smile at the same time they question cultural prejudices" ("Awakening" 504). Even when she's not writing about gay and lesbian characters, Kerr has "always identified with the outcast" (*Presenting* 134). Nilsen adds that much of young adult fiction today, which features "intriguing stories about what it means to be different from the majority, whether through sexual orientation, ethnic identification, socio-economic status, physical condition, or intellectual ability," owes a great deal of credit to M.E. Kerr (*Presenting* 158).

In spite of the ways in which she's helped to open doors for fiction about gay and lesbian teens, her openness has created tension in her family and with those who seek to censor YA fiction. She writes in her introduction to *Hearing Us Out* that although her mother eventually "came to terms" with her being a lesbian and even with the word (which she hated), she made Kerr promise that she would never "bring any of them to this house" because she "couldn't hold my head up" in her small town of Auburn, New York (Foreword ix). Kerr writes, sadly: "So formed by what others thought, so in thrall to convention and conformity, both my parents missed the chance to know my warm and loving friends—as well as to know me better" (Foreword ix). Her novels are, in part, a way to prevent such alienation from happening in other families.

Consequently, Kerr brings much of the pain and loss (and warmth outside her family) she experienced into her novels about both gay and straight characters. Patricia Sweeney, writing in 1978, long before *Evie* (and Kerr) came out, says that Kerr's characters "succeed in realizing the person shut up inside of them ... and even for some of the apparent failures, there is hope. At least they have become aware of the possibility of change and they have gained insight into their own identity" (37). This applies to her young protagonists as well as to the adults in their lives. However, Sweeny says, this progress toward understanding "cannot always be measured in a straight line" (38). It usually takes adults an especially long time to come to terms with the differences that the young adult characters exhibit and frequently display proudly. The bottom line, as Sweeney puts it, is that Kerr provides readers with "a wonderful relish for the variety in human nature" (42). Whether she's writing about

Ten. "Don't you two be strangers!"

dwarfism, obesity, or homosexuality, Kerr displays her characteristic sympathetic humor and compassion.

Two of her novels, *Night Kites* (1986) and *Deliver Us from Evie* (1994), focus primarily on homosexuality. Both, as Nilsen says, are valuable because they "discuss stereotypes and illustrate that homosexuals are individuals; some fit cultural expectations and some do not" (148). In these books, she argues, "families experience instances, if not intervals, of frustration and fear that usually lead to the beginning of acceptance, at least by some family members" (149). While *Night Kites* focuses on the grim story of an adult gay man, an uncle to the protagonist, who dies of AIDS, *Evie* concentrates on the 18-year-old title character and her initially troubled and eventually accepting family. As Nilsen says, Kerr doesn't just write about lesbianism in this novel, she "also touches on the challenge of running a small family farm, on the complications of friendships that cross socioeconomic and religious lines, and, more importantly, on family dynamics when one or more players pull out of a carefully structured pyramid" (47). Yes, this is story with a lesbian main character, but it is also the story of young love (both straight and gay), religious fanaticism, and a struggling family farm. Evie is unique (at least for YA literature in 1994) in that the main character is as comfortable with her sexuality as she is with fixing a tractor. As Spring says, "Evie has no trouble coming to terms with her homosexuality. Instead of depicting her as a troubled victim, most of her scenes in the novel illustrate her (very capably) involved with work on the family farm" (46–7).

Clearly, many readers have loved the book. It has received starred reviews or "best" placements in *School Library Journal, English Journal, Booklist, Horn Book, Voice of Youth Advocates (Voya), Publishers Weekly,* and the *New York Times Book Review* ("Awakening" 495). *Deliver Us from Evie* also represents a personal breakthrough for Kerr, coinciding as it does with Kerr's coming out as a lesbian. "Suddenly her ability to depict those who experience oppression with such empathy made much more sense to both critics and readers," says Thompson (282). However, this is not just a "problem novel," Thompson points out. "[I]t is an excellent young adult novel that engages the sympathy of heterosexual readers and leads them toward empathy, introduces a surprisingly sophisticated analysis of the relationship between gender and sexuality, and provides some effective lessons on reading for young readers" (283). Thus, *Evie* is not just a story about lesbians—it is also a story about families, about gender, and about economics. It even teaches young readers to regard a first-person narrator with some suspicion.

This doesn't mean that it has been smooth sailing for Kerr and other writers who treat GBLTQ issues. *In the Heart Has Its Reasons*, Cart and Jenkins report that in 2006, challenges to books with GBLTQ content were on the rise, citing bills in the Alabama and Oklahoma state legislature (which failed, fortunately) to eliminate or restrict access to young adult books with homosexual themes in school and public libraries (xvi). Although the number of books with GLBTQ content has risen since the early 70s, from one book a year to 12 titles per year in the early 2000, "a certain specter of fear has haunted this field since its beginning and has often impeded open discussion" (Cart xvii). Even though in *Evie* "the focus is not on the physical relationship between the young lovers, but instead on the emotional challenges faced by the protagonists and their parents and siblings as they seek to come to terms with this new situation in their families" ("Awakening" 499), the novel has been subject to many challenges, including in 2009, when, as Library Director Michael Tyree outlines in a report to the American Library Association in July of that year, community members in West Bend, Wisconsin, petitioned to have 33 YA novels with GLBTQ content removed from the library removed from the library, or transferred to the adult section, using as "evidence" a list of 83 works that included *Evie*. While ultimately they didn't succeed, they did manage, in the process, to have two Library Board members removed. Eventually, the Board voted to retain their acquisition policies, and all books remained on the shelves ("West Bend Community Memorial Library"), but this serves as an exemplar of the special challenges that YA literature with GLBTQ content faces.[2]

There has also been some critical concern about the ways in which YA fiction depicts homosexuality. In an essay focusing on fiction about gay young men, Thomas Crisp says that "any book that seeks to educate readers about homophobia and intolerance by presenting a world in which homophobia and intolerance are 'the norm' on some level, ultimately reinforces these as inevitabilities" (344). These books can both distort and reaffirm stereotypes and prejudices, even while attempting to combat them. "[I]t is important to remain cognizant of the ways in which authors and publishers work to create—and readers attempt to confront, embrace, or reject—depictions that feel 'affirmatively' queer," Crisp says

Ten. "Don't you two be strangers!"

(346). Although *Evie* does chronicle stereotypes and prejudice, it could be argued that it just as equally presents a character who is "affirmatively queer." It also follows the narrator, who is at first reluctant to admit his sister's sexuality, as he becomes his sister's strongest supporter. Michele Abate says that while the novel's appearance indicates that "changing societal circumstances have made it possible for young adult authors to address the issue of homosexuality more openly and realistically," there still are remnants in the novel revealing that "negative postwar attitudes continue to circulate amidst more progressive present thinking" (34). These attitudes, however, are often balanced with Evie's family's growing levels of tolerance and, eventually, acceptance.

The story is told in the first-person voice of her younger brother, Parr Burrman, the 15-year-old son of a farmer, and brother to Doug as well as Evie. It opens on Parr's first day of a new high school, where students are teasing him about his "other brother" Evie (1). Parr doesn't mention the comments when he gets home. Abate says having Parr narrate the story is a wise choice, as many readers will "share much of the ignorance, ambivalence, and possibly even prejudice about same-sex love that Parr both feels himself and hears from others," and then they will see "the young man's deep love for his sister and his steady education about homosexuality lead him, and, by extension, the book's readership" to empathize with Evie (242). Also, by keeping readers "out of Evie's head," she says, "Kerr manages to avoid reflecting one other very familiar experience: the shame and self-hatred, the internalized homophobia, that we all know and that is still part of any gay and lesbian self" (292). Thus, what readers mostly see is Parr's growing acceptance and awareness and not Evie's possible fear and frustration.

Very early in the novel, Parr wonders how a woman as feminine as his mother could have given birth to a daughter as masculine as Evie (3). That fall, he says, his mother was trying to change Evie into a traditional woman, "but it was like trying to change the direction of the wind" (4). From the beginning, Kerr establishes that Evie's masculinity is natural and unchangeable. Evie's father always supports her, and their mother blames him for how Evie has turned out, not being willing, at this point, to accept that Evie is (and will remain) a lesbian. Parr says, "She only listened to my father. Listened to him, walked like him, talked like him, told jokes like him" (6). Jenkins says that in Evie Kerr has created "one of the few portrayals of queer gay characters" (324). Indeed,

"Unsuitable" Books

Evie seems to be both comfortable with her sexuality and with her butch appearance and manner.

Shortly after, Patsy Duff comes on the scene. She is the daughter of the richest man in town, headstrong, feminine, and lesbian. When her mother says that Patsy is a nice girl and comments that she'd like to "get something going between you two," Evie mistakenly thinks she means between her and Patsy. However, she actually is talking about Patsy and Parr, who says he'd "never get to first base with her kind" (12). Parr means someone as wealthy, but the implication—of both his comment and Evie's "mistake"—is that Evie's "kind" are girls, not boys. Interestingly, here Kerr introduces a sub plot about financial and social class conflicts between the small-farming Parrs and the farm, bank, and (virtually) town-owning Duffs. Neither Parr nor Evie stand a chance with Patsy unless she is willing to violate both traditional sexual mores and/or financial barriers.

At this point, readers are starting to realize that there is something different about Evie, which Parr doesn't quite understand and her mother is unwilling to acknowledge, but all that has been explicitly stated is that Evie likes to wear "boys" clothes and work as a farmer. The delay seems intentional, to allow readers to slowing come to a realization about Evie's sexuality while they are building a relationship with her. Furthering the tension, Evie shows Parr a poem ostensibly about going to China (but actually about her attraction to the exotic continent that is Patsy), and Parr begins to think that "something was going on with her that was just bursting to come out" (25). Like many adolescents—gay and straight—journal/poetry writing is often the way difficult truths are indirectly revealed. Soon after she reads Parr the poem, Evie gets a postcard from Patsy that says that she's visiting a friend, but she "wishes you were her." Not one to accept an unconventional idea quickly, Parr becomes more suspicious about Patsy and Evie's relationship. Amusingly, Parr says that although his father likes travel shows on TV that no one in their family had ever been outside of the United States (30). It will soon turn out, though, that at least one family member (an uncle) has been "outside" all his life.

When Evie goes to a concert with Patsy, Parr begins to think more about their relationship, although he isn't quite clear *what* to think about it. "What I got was this blurred picture of Evie and Patsy with a crush on each other," Parr comments: "It was blurred because that sort of thing

Ten. "Don't you two be strangers!"

was never clear to me, and I wasn't even sure what that sort of thing really meant" (30). Like many adolescents, he isn't clear about the details of homosexuality, much as he is inexperienced with heterosexuality. As he tries to puzzle it out, Parr remembers his father's cousin Joe, who his father called "Cousin Josephine" because he lived with a man (37). Suddenly, the joking about Joe doesn't seem quite as funny with the possibility that Evie might actually be his "other brother," as the students said on Parr's first day of class.

After the concert, Patsy's father becomes suspicious of their relationship and tries to stop Evie from seeing his daughter. Evie declares that Mr. Duff will never control Patsy "because she's got a will like the river" (41). This gets Parr thinking about nature and fate, and, although he's not at all religious, he likes the idea that there might be "an invisible force behind life, something you couldn't see turning you down this road and that, changing your destiny and you" (42). He is attracted to the idea that certain aspects of love and attraction can't be changed by coercion or willpower because of his own attraction to a new girl, Angel.

When he meets Angel in church, where he goes only to please his mother, feels as though he'd "been turned down a new path by whatever that force was that I almost believed in" (43). At this point, readers can see that Evie's homosexuality, like Parr's heterosexuality, are part of their nature, not a matter of personal (and changeable) choice. This is a clear deviation from that GLBTQ books that came before the 1990s discussed by Kirk Fuoss, which often showed homosexuality "as a discrete, isolatable behavior that need not be assimilated as an enduring aspect of identity" (166). Through Parr's growing awareness, readers come to see that her sexuality is a permanent and essential part of her nature.

While she clearly shows Evie's natural attraction to women, Kerr is also skillful in this presentation and avoids the all-too-common YA device of having an adult character lecture young people about the innate elements of sexuality. Parr comes to this conclusion on his own (with some help from Evie). Both his mother and father are little help (although his father is more accepting), and they are actually "relieved and happy" that Parr has found a girlfriend (59)—in other words, that's he's found a socially-acceptable choice (unlike his sister).

As both the Evie/Patsy and Parr/Angel relationships are heating up, Cord, a local famer with his eye on Evie as a potential wife, talks to the siblings' mother about Evie and Patsy's friendship. He says they make a "strange pair," although he means (at this point) just because of Patsy's money—and the Burrman's lack of it. At this point, although she has some suspicions about the "women's music" concert they went to, their mother is still publicly denying that the relationship is anything but a friendship (52). Even with this meager encouragement, Cord is content to keep trying to win Evie to his side. Both Cord and Mrs. Burrman want desperately to believe that Evie is just going through a phase, that eventually she will turn "normal," marry (Cord), settle down, and run the farm.

When Mr. Duff shows up unexpectedly at the farm to complain again about the young women's relationship, Parr and his mother are forced to have a talk about Evie. She tells him that she hopes there's nothing going on with Patsy and Evie, and they talk around the subject of her lesbianism. His mother says she doesn't like the word "dyke" but doesn't offer a substitute, saying that it will be hard for Evie, as her masculine appearance and stubbornness won't allow her (unlike Patsy) to "pass herself off as something else. It isn't in her nature" (65). Parr says it is a "relief to tell the truth: to admit that my sister's way wasn't going to be fixed by a turtleneck sweater or a skirt. She was deep-down different" (66). When his mother finally uses the word "lesbian," Parr says his "stomach did a flip at the harsh sound of that word" (66). His mother asks him not to tell his father, and says that she hopes that Evie has "the name without the game. It's hard enough to look that way, but it's awful to look it and actually be it…. Then you're a stereotype. You're what everybody's always thought one of those women was like" (66–7). Parr says he's a stereotype of a farm boy, but his mother counters that the difference is "you're not against the law, Parr. And the church doesn't call you a sinner" (67). Parr opines that something is wrong with the law, then, and his mother insists that it's "not a wholesome thing to be," especially if you look the part (67). Thompson says that Evie's mother and brother's conversation about her lesbianism and butch appearance shows "just how overdetermined the construction of 'Evie' is; she is constructed in and through an ideology that continues to demand an explanation for the existence of homosexuality" (294). The two families, the church, the town all attempt to explain—and thus explain away—Evie's behavior.

Pasty's relationship with Evie is paralleled neatly with Parr's with Angel. As Parr is trying to woo her, he steals a line from Evie's journal, and tells Angel she's "like some new color I've never seen" (74). He admits to stealing looks at her journal when she leaves it downstairs, but he justifies it by thinking that she left it out for the family to see. "It must have been hard for Evie to try and keep it all inside," he thinks, "I couldn't have" (74). In this passage, readers can see that Parr's romantic and sexual feelings for Angel are similar to Evie's for Patsy; they even describe it with the same kind of language. Also, it becomes clear that keeping her love a secret, something Parr and Angel don't have to do, is "hard," to say the least. At this moment young love is young love, whether with boys and girls or girls and girls, but two girls can only confess their feelings in journals and when they are alone.

Before they are completely public about their relationship, Patsy gives Evie an ID bracelet and some k.d. lang tapes (another veiled hint, like the women's music concert they attend) for Valentine's Day (84). When questioned, Evie admits that she has a post office box where she's been receiving letters from Patsy, who is away at school. She comes out to her mother and says that Patsy didn't make her this way, she's just never met anyone "like me" before. She then makes the very good point that Parr never "did anything" to compel Angel to love him, and neither did Patsy. Unable finally to ignore Evie's sexuality, her mother comes back to her earlier argument that if she's a lesbian that she ought to dress more femininely, be more "presentable" (85). Evie says, "Some of us look it, Mother! I know you so-called normal people would like it better if we looked as much like all of you as possible, but some of us don't, can't, and never will! And some others of us go for the ones who don't, can't, and never will" (86). Her mother starts to cry, and Evie tells her to save her tears, that Patsy loves her for who she is (86). Abate says that Evie's comments about her appearance and identity "constitute what can be seen as a 're-queering' of the butch figure." In doing so, Abate argues, "Evie demonstrates that the butch stereotype is not merely a leftover legacy from the 1950s but an important lived form of contemporary lesbian gender identity and sexual expression" (243). Evie's insistence on her lesbianism and her butch appearance, taken with Patsy's hyperfeminine persona, shows young readers there are a variety of ways to be a lesbian, to "look it"—or not.[3]

In spite of her coming out to her mother, Evie's public persona is less confrontational. She even goes to church with Cord, who is still around and still not taking her relationship with Patsy seriously yet. At church, Cord, who is growing frustrated at Evie's reluctance, says, "Deliver us from Evie" as a lame joke. Evie nudges him in the ribs, "her face flushed for a moment" (91), showing that the pitiful joke may have hit the mark and expressed some of the truth of their situation. Abate says that Cord clearly "needs to be delivered from his desire for a woman who clearly will not reciprocate his affection," but the phrase is even more complicated. When it is read as "deliver us from evil," Abate argues, it appears on the surface (and in Cord's mind) to indicate that homosexuality is evil, yet clearly this is not the end of the novel; rather, "it seeks to deliver us from the evil of homophobic prejudice" (287–88). This seems a bit optimistic: the novel does end with a reconciliation of sorts between immediate family members, but most of the community prejudice remains intact (at least as far as readers can tell).

Shortly after the scene in church, Cord and Parr drink beer and talk about Evie and Patsy, which are very much on both of their minds—although for different reasons. They agree that it's Patsy's fault, and Cord opines that two women together is "not serious enough to be a sin," while male homosexuality is the real sin (101). Again, both Cord and Parr feel the need to make Patsy and Evie's relationship both temporary and trivial in order to contain it. Dismissive conversation is not enough, though. Cord makes a sign with Evie and Patsy's name in it, and, slightly drunk, Parr agrees to put it up on the local statue. Cord believes if Patsy's father knows about the affair that he will send his daughter off, and Cord then can help Evie "get past this stage she's in" (103). Parr justifies his action by saying that Evie has let him down by threatening to leave the farm and therefore leave him with all the responsibility (106). This ill-conceived plan fails (of course), although it does lead to Patsy leaving the farm for good (and, although it isn't clear to readers yet, to meet up with Patsy).

Before Evie leaves, she and her mother talk again, and Mrs. Burrman offers the somewhat desperate interpretation that Patsy might be lesbian because her mother is an alcoholic. Evie treats that comment as ridiculous, but her mother doesn't stop there. She offers next that Evie's father is responsible for making her so masculine, because he needed her help on the farm. Evie denies this as well, saying that she was always the way she was: "I came out of the womb ready to handle tools. I knew how to change a tire when I was six, and when I was ten I could fix anything broken. You couldn't have learned it if Dad had spent an hour every day of the week instructing you!" (112). Although she's said it many times so far, apparently her mother needs to hear—once again—that fixing tractors did not make her daughter a lesbian. No one is at "fault," she is saying, and nothing needs to be fixed.

After they discover that Evie has left, Eve's mother and father finally talk, and he says his cousin Bob was "more of a fluke." Pointing out that every family has one, he, jokingly tells his wife that they even had a rooster on the farm who had no interest in hens (129–30). Mom is still upset, though, and Parr vows to keep secret his role in the note on the statue (131). Cord eventually steps up and takes the blame for the sign, and Parr's father nevertheless goes back to work with him. His father is "first and last" a farmer, Parr says, "and whatever was in between there wasn't time for" (143). Evie calls home from New York City, and her mother still tries to fix her, saying there are doctors who could help or that it could be a "phase" (145). At this point, her mother's comments seem merely desperate. In the course of the conversation, Evie tells Parr to "get on with your life, and I'll get on with mine" (146). This applies to her brother *and* her mother.

Parr does just that and "gets on" with his relationship with Angel. Because of her family's fundamentalism, Angel has some trouble at first with Evie's lesbianism, but later in the novel she and Parr talk about it again, and she says, "What if it was a world where males and females weren't allowed to love each other, and we felt like we do? I couldn't change. Could you?" (148-9). It looks as if things are going to go smoothly with their relationship, but when Parr is put in charge of taking care of Angel by her father, and he gets her home late, (in part because of bad weather, but mostly because she wanted to stay and make out in the dance parking lot), she is prohibited from seeing him. She goes along with her father's decision (and world view), and she tells him, "I wasn't the one in charge, or driving the car. Maybe I didn't know better, but you should have. You're the boy" (170). In another capitulation to the fundamentalist values of her family, she also concludes that she was wrong to accept Evie's sexuality, and she breaks up with him. Here, Parr is the victim of gender stereotyping, not Evie, and this suggests to readers that no one is immune from the harm caused by forcing people into rigid categories.

A flood comes and destroys their house (which might be seen by Angel's parents as divine retribution, although they, too, have suffered from floods in the past, in spite of their goodness). This flood doesn't completely destroy the family, however; they are able to survive because a neighbor has willed them his hogs (which were brought to higher ground), and he has died. Parr thinks that life is "about trade-offs. A levee breaking would ease some lands, but drown others. A good neighbor's death would save our necks. A flood with all its hard lessons would soften our ways of looking at things" (175). They also learn that nothing is going to be around forever.

Shortly after the flood, Evie returns for a final visit, having taken a trip to Paris with Patsy, and before settling in New York with her. After welcoming Evie warmly, her mother, surprisingly, also tells her to say hi to Patsy, shouting after her as she's leaving, "Don't you two be strangers!" (177). Jenkins argues that this scene indicates that the tension between straight families and their queer children is resolved in *Evie*. "It appears that *Evie* and Patsy will be able to be both queer and family," she says (325). I think the stress needs to be on *appears*, though. It seems somewhat implausible that Evie's mother will have completely reconciled the contradictory feelings she has about Evie and her relationship with Patsy. Still, she has invited them both back to the farm, which promises further easing of relations between them, which is far more realistic than an uncomplicated happy ending.. In addition, as I said earlier in this chapter, the responses of the rest of the town (especially Mr. Duff) are not included in this happy family reunion, and this shows Kerr's insight into the realities of life for gay and lesbian youth—your families might come to accept you, but your neighbors, likely as not, won't.

In their study of gay and lesbian fiction for young adults, Cart and Jenkins stress their "continued belief in the power of books to help teen readers understand themselves and others, to contribute to the mental health and well-being of GLBTQ youth, and to save lives—and perhaps even to change the world—by informing minds and nourishing spirits" (xviii). At the end of the novel, Cart says, "the reader realizes that mutual acceptance of personal differences is a viable but attainable goal, despite the emotional obstacles one must overcome to reach it" (Cart 103). Using the metaphor of knitting a sweater, Cart says that GBLTQ writing for teens has shown "a similarly slow, sometimes tedious and often incremental process plagued by more than a few dropped stitches along the way." However, he says, "progress has been made, especially in the area of queer consciousness and community" (165). Certainly, *Deliver Us*

Ten. "Don't you two be strangers!"

from Evie represents a step in the slow progression. Evie and Patsy are still alive and happy at the end of the novel (which was rarely the case in earlier works), and at least part of their extended family is becoming reconciled to their relationship. At least the situation isn't as dire as Fuoss picture in the same year *Evie* was published, where he compares the acceptance of a gay lifestyle by a character in a YA novel with the "appearance of a cough for a character in a soap opera: both tend to function as warning signals" of impending death (168). Nobody (except for a neighbor) dies in the novel, and no one is even injured as the result of Evie's homosexuality. The family farm is saved, Parr seems to have a clearer idea of where he's headed, and Evie and Patsy are on the way to New York. Tragic coughs seem altogether missing.

This doesn't mean that there isn't still progress to be made. Cart says that GLBTQ literature "needs to include more stories about young people whose homosexuality is simply a given and who are dealings with other issues and challenges—emotional intellectual, physical, social, developmental, etc. that are part of teens' lives" (166). This shift of the focus away from homosexuality and toward more "ordinary" aspects of teenage life begins in books like David Levithan's *Boy Meets Boy* (2003) and Levithan and John Green's co-authored novel *Will Grayson, Will Grayson* (2010), but the problem of representation of gay and lesbian teens in YA fiction is by no means happily resolved. Still, Kerr's *Deliver Us from Evie* has gone a long way toward showing a positive new direction. GBLT teens have become far less tragic, far funnier, and far more open, and their worlds much more peaceful—in part because of novels like this one.

CHAPTER ELEVEN

"Be the tree"
Trauma, Recovery and Voice in Laurie Halse Anderson's Speak (1999)

> We can no longer waste the ethical opportunities literature provides in the face of increasing teenage apathy, anger, and violence. The stakes are too high—Alsup, 162

> Some people are uncomfortable talking about rape. It makes them feel awkward or powerless, or ashamed. They often can't put their feelings about it into words. They find it easier to avoid the discussion. These are the kinds of people who try to remove *Speak* from the classroom—Laurie Halse Anderson, from her website

Coming in at number 60 on the American Library Association's Top 100 Banned/Challenged Books and frequently challenged for its depictions of sexual assault and suicide, Laurie Halse Anderson's *Speak* (1999) has also won a Printz Honor Book award and been selected as a National Book Award finalist. As is the case with all of the novels in this study, *Speak* has been challenged almost as often as it has been lauded. Also consistent with the novels by writers such as Kerr, Crutcher, and Alexie (just to name a few), Anderson's work touches a nerve with critics because of its brutal portrayal of the effect of sexual assault on the victim and it appeals to other readers because of the sophisticated (and often surprisingly funny) way it represents the realities of teenage life.

The novel tells the story of 14-year-old Melinda Sordino, who was raped at a party the summer before her freshman year of high school. Melinda, who is unable to speak about the attack, has been ostracized by her friends and taunted by her classmates, as her call to 911 after the rape led to the police being called to the party (resulting various minor disasters for the partygoers). Melinda's attacker, Andy (she calls him

Eleven. "Be the tree"

"The Beast"), is an attractive upperclassman, who has a long (but somewhat underground) history of sexual assault, and he continues his activities unchallenged through most of the school year. Melinda is befriended by a ditzy fellow freshman and by her equally scattered art teacher, who tries to draw her out with drawing. Eventually, she tells her story (first on the bathroom wall) and then at the end to her teacher. Her outing of Andy leads to another attack, which is first thwarted by Melinda (who finally speaks) and then, amusingly (given gender stereotypes), is broken up by the girls' lacrosse team.

Given the controversial subject matter (along with the irreverent attitude toward teachers and parents), it is no wonder that its use in classrooms has been frequently challenged. Still, many teachers continue to recommend it to students and teach it in their classes, in large part because it offers a narrative of healing and of empowerment, one that shows the realities (both the traumatic and the ridiculous) of high school life. Young readers love it as well, even those who (fortunately) don't share Melinda's traumatic experiences.

Still, Anderson struggled to create an authentic-seeming voice for her main character. Anderson tells interviewer Christine Hill that she woke up in the middle of the night hearing a "crying girl," who said she had a story to tell, and this was the genesis of Melinda (325). This anecdote, of course, is similar to the quasi-supernatural transmissions from characters that authors frequently mention, but it suggests that Anderson is simply recording what is being "said" by her young narrator. However, in the same interview she also reminds her readers that "anything told in the first person is unreliable" (323), which indicates that, regardless of how she first heard Melinda's voice, she knew that she must shape that voice to serve her thematic purposes. Mike Cadden says that all adolescent novels are "inherently ironic because the so-called adolescent voice is never—and can never be—truly authentic" (146). What they are instead, he says, is "a sophisticated representation of a lack of sophistication; it is an artful depiction of artlessness" (146). Anderson had to create a voice that seems both artless and (at least partially) aware. Like Parr in *Evie*, Melinda in *Speak* has to sound as if she knows a great deal while at the same time unconsciously revealing the limitations of her adolescent perspective.

This is, of course, true for all YA narratives, but it may be especially problematic for writers attempting to describe traumatic events faced by their characters. According to Barbara Tannert-Smith, the key question for the adolescent writer of narratives like *Speak* is "how such a traumatized state can be narratively represented" (400). Anderson does this, Tannert-Smith perceptively argues, by using "a nonlinear plot and disruptive temporality to emphasize Melinda's response to her traumatic experiences." These techniques allow Anderson to show "exactly how her protagonist experiences self-estrangement and a sense of shattered identity" (400). In other words, the fragmented and asynchronic narrative structure mimics Melinda's dislocated and shattered sense of self.

Another interesting critical reading comes from Don Latham, who says that Anderson's strategies for Melinda are "queer," in that they "are largely self-initiated and self-constructed, and her recovery occurs outside the context of professional intervention." She does not seek (and in fact passively rejects) therapy, and her healing comes primarily from her own roundabout methodology. Her therapeutic strategies, Latham adds, also "serve to question and undermine accepted norms, concerning gender and identity" (371). Thus, she moves toward healing in silence, alone, and without help from friends, parents, or educators (except, indirectly, from her art teacher).

Critical response to the novel has not been entirely positive, though. According to Lisa Detora, Melinda gets her life, voice, and identity back by buying and mastering the right consumer goods (29). *Speak* illustrates, Detora argues, "a *de facto* level of commodity fetishism in suburban adolescence and articulate[s] recovery from rape into a dynamic of consumerism" (34). Rather than gaining insight or equilibrium through psychological or interpersonal methods, Detora argues, Melinda instead buys her way back to happiness. The novel, she argues, offers no sustained critique of this commodity fetishism. I would agree that Melinda's parents seem to think that credit cards can buy happiness, but Melinda mocks the emptiness of such a world view. She also admires her art teacher, who is almost aggressive in his lack of personal materialism (even though he does carp about the lack of art supplies and funding for the arts in schools). In addition, she turns her back on her friend Heather's Martha Stewart and *Seventeen* magazine-inspired vision of popularity.

In one of the most compelling critiques of the novel, Chris McGee says that *Speak*'s narrative structure actually works against the traditional interpretation of the novel as an empowerment narrative (which, iron-

Eleven. "Be the tree"

ically, is what makes adults think it is worth recommending to teens) (174). Melinda's power, he says, comes as often from "*not* speaking about what happened" as from speaking about it (176). Indeed, she becomes increasingly silent as the novel progresses. He continues:

> Melinda's inability to name what has happened to her as well as her overall silence after the rape is not *purely* a psychological mechanism of repression, which is where many other young adult novels on the same subject might choose to stop. Her trouble with language, rather, is deeply connected to the power around her, particularly the power expressed by the many adults in her life [178].

Melinda seems to recognize that adults want her to speak, he argues, and keeping silent increases her autonomy and sense of self control. McGee applauds this direction the novel seems to be taking. Finally, though, he says he is "disappointed by the turn the book makes at the end" (181)—when Melinda finally speaks. The bottom line for McGee is that although *Speak* is willing to explore the "complexities of power that operate on a teenager," it, unfortunately, "seems at times less concerned with Melinda's healing than it does her simply getting over her moping" (186). McGee believes the novel would have provided a stronger message about coping with trauma if Melinda had kept her silence to the end.

One wonders, though, what Melinda would have been like had she remained unable (or unwilling, in McGee's formulation) to speak. Perhaps the bathroom stall communication would have been sufficient to start a reaction that eventually would land her attacker Andy (the "Beast") at the very least, without a date for the prom. It is also possible that the novel would have taken a much darker turn, suggesting that Melinda's self-absorbed parents are ultimately unable to help her (given their own troubled relationship) and that teachers are beyond the pale when it comes to offering useful guidance and support for teens. It would also hint that confronting one's accuser has no real therapeutic value and, given the general fecklessness of adults, will not lead to any meaningful punishment. It could go further to indicate that perhaps Melinda's version of the attack is flawed as well, motivated by adolescent self-absorption or even psychosis.

This is, of course, not the novel that Laurie Anderson wrote; instead, she suggests that Melinda's parents, while flawed, are groping toward an effective way to care for their troubled daughter. Her actual novel shows teachers as both sadistic and sympathetic (as does Crutcher) and a school system that appears to be more focused on mascots than on the physical safety and mental stability of its students. It condemns teenagers as narcissistic and inadvertently (and sometimes purposely) cruel, but it also allows them opportunities—which they eventually take—to be empathetic and altruistic. Ultimately, the novel demonstrates both the power of silence and the power of speaking, writing, and creating art.

The book opens with Melinda's first morning of high school (much as *Evie* does). She reports that she has "seven new notebooks, a skirt I hate, and a stomachache" (3). Nothing is indicated about her recent assault, and it appears that, given her worries about having "the wrong hair, the wrong clothes, the wrong attitude" and no one to sit with, her situation resembles that of many first year high school students (4). Even her referring to herself as "Outcast" (4) could be seen as adolescent hyperbole or melodrama. Still, her comment "Nobody really wants to hear what you have to say" (9) suggests a deeper issue. Like Parr, she tells no one about her horrible day—or the reasons behind it.

Melinda's first encounter with a teacher is with her art teacher Mr. Freeman, who tells students that art is "the only class that will teach you how to survive" (10). Although she is scornful of Mr. Freeman throughout much of the novel (he has problems of his own), his assignment of a year-long project "to make your object say something, express an emotion, speak to every person who looks at it" (12) will prove initially frustrating but eventually therapeutic for her. The novel may be far less sympathetic to other teachers (a bully known as "Mr. Neck" and the scattered English teacher called "Hairwoman"), but Mr. Freeman, with his appropriate name, is complex and ultimately necessary for her survival. Mr. Freeman tells her that "fear is a great place to begin art" (31), and so Melinda begins to draw her tree (which is what she chooses in a blind drawing as her subject). It will start with fear, move to frustration, and eventually emerge as personal expression and a kind of liberation.

Melinda's parents are initially absent most of the time, and prone to sarcasm or frustration when they are there. The family communicates mostly through notes on the kitchen counter about what supplies or food is needed and when they will be home. "What else is there to say?" (14), Melinda asks. Still, she comments early in the novel that her mother "loves doing the things that other people are afraid of" in her job as a department store manager (15). This suggests that her mother, at least in her career, is a relatively brave and confident woman, which may serve

Eleven. "Be the tree"

to inspire Melinda's later actions. Her parents also don't offer any religious or moral guidance that might help her through her trials. The "closest we came," she says, "to worship is the Trinity of Visa, MasterCard, and American Express" (29), she says. In their attempts to provide a picture-perfect lifestyle for themselves and their daughter, they have instead created a world that is only very superficially successful.

Melinda imagines that her parents, who are clearly in an unhappy marriage, would have already been divorced it if hadn't been for her (and she is probably right). She also says that they probably think she's a disappointment, as she has no special talents and is, like them, "an ordinary drone dressed in secrets and lies." Like Jerry in *The Chocolate War*, Melinda has little confidence in her parents' ability to conduct their lives with joy and grace, let alone help her to do the same. She wonders why her family can't just admit they've "failed family living, sell the house, split up the money, and get on with our lives" (70). This failed family seems to reflect all the things that Melinda is failing: classes, telling her story, pulling her life together. Still, Melinda's parents do try, in various ineffective ways, to reach out to her several times in the novel, with no success, in large part because they are so absorbed in their own, individual unhappiness.

Since she believes she will find no help from her parents, Melinda decides she needs a friend, but not one she really cares about, "just a pseudo-friend, disposable friend. Friend as accessory. Just so I don't feel and look so stupid" (22). She finds that friend in Heather, who is annoying perky and maniacally focused on high school success. While Heather has many goals for her ninth-grade year, and encourages Melinda to find some herself, Melinda says that her only goal is "to take a nap" (24). This friendship is doomed from the start, and eventually Heather "breaks up" with her, saying that Melinda is too depressed (and therefore hindering her popularity). Even her "pseudo-friend" has rejected Melinda's continuing passivity and sadness.

Because she comes to feel that high school leaves her exposed in a hostile environment, she seeks a place to hide, a shabby abandoned janitor's closet that "has no purpose, no name." She says that it is "the perfect place for me" (26). Melinda, who feels aimless, unnoticed, and unattractive, believes that only a nameless, purposeless, relentlessly ugly place with provide her with a safe space. She decorates the closet with a poster of Maya Angelou (who was herself raped as a child, although

Melinda doesn't mention this), and she tries to cover up the moldy smell with potpourri. While hiding out in the closet helps her feel safe and provides a "quiet place that helps me hold these thoughts inside my head where no one can hear them" (51), it soon becomes clear that she needs to break out of the closet of her silence.

Not surprisingly, Melinda's isolation and depression worsens. She can't stop biting her lips: "It looks like my mouth belongs to someone else, someone I don't even know" (17). At this point, Melinda is disassociated from her body, as she separated herself from the experience of the rape as it was happening. Crying after an insult by a group of decoration-obsessed girls known as the "Marthas," Melinda says that she washes her "face in the sink until there is nothing left of it, no eyes, no nose, no mouth. A slick nothing" (45). Not only does she fail to recognize herself in the mirror, she feels herself fading away to nothing. Shortly after this, she reports that it is getting harder and harder to talk, which she acknowledges:

> I know my head isn't screwed on straight. I want to leave, transfer, warp myself to another galaxy. I want to confess everything, hand over the guilt and mistake and anger to someone else. There is a beast in my gut, I can hear it scraping away at the inside of my ribs. Even if I dump the memory, it will stay with me, staining me [51].

In fact, at Career Day, Melinda confesses that she worries more "about making it out of ninth grade alive" (53) than she does about her future career. Readers should be able to see here that Melinda is moving toward a possible suicide.

In the midst of her turmoil, Melinda's family attempts a Thanksgiving dinner that turns into a disaster (and ends with her mother leaving to go to work and her father ordering pizza). She says her mother's always futile attempt to cook Thanksgiving dinner is "Kodak logic. Only in film commercials does stuff like that work" (58). Once again, Melinda's parents think that if they can only create a simulacrum of a happy family, all will be well with their daughter. Still, out of the bones from the turkey (which they couldn't eat) comes a sculpture that represents her first successful attempt at making her tree project conform to her feelings. Mr. Freeman tells her that her sculpture "has meaning. Pain" (65). Even though the family Thanksgiving dinner didn't work out as planned, some insight has come out of it.

Melinda also understands, at some level, that reconnecting with

Eleven. "Be the tree"

her family (even only nostalgically) will be necessary for her recovery. Her pleasant memories of childhood are some of the only pleasant aspects of the novel. For example, when she is cutting an apple in biology class, she is cast back to a memory of picking apples with her parents, when the "sun warmed my hair, and wind pushed my mother into my father's arms, and all the apple-picking parents and children smiled for a long, long minute" (66). That she can recall a pleasant time for their family is key to reconstructing both Melinda's past and her present, and the apple tree memory becomes inspiration for the tree that Melinda is creating in art class. This nostalgia recurs when she makes a snow angel. She remembers a time when her family lived in a smaller house, when her mom was there when she came from work, when her dad liked his job, and when she "believed in Santa Claus" (71). Melinda longs for parents who are happier and a self who can find something in which to believe. At one point, Melinda wishes she were in fifth grade again, when she was "old enough to play outside without Mom, too young to go off the block" (99). That sense of adventure combined with security is something that is seriously lacking in her current life. The last time she was outside, she was raped.

These pleasant memories from childhood lead to her recalling the night she was raped, when she comes home to an empty house. Her parents are out in separate cars until 2 a.m. and don't return until sunup, which means that they aren't there for her when she comes home and that they are busily undermining the family with extramarital affairs (72). As her increasingly painful flashbacks of the rape continue, they start to affect her viscerally. When she sees blood after cutting herself stuffing promotional calendars into envelopes for her father, she sees Andy's face. Her father mentions that she might need professional help when he sees the blood (74), but he says it in such an angry way that it does no good. When dissecting a frog in biology class, the flayed corpse also brings back memories of the rape. Melinda says she "can feel the cut, smell the dirt, leaves in my hair" (81). As painful as these memories seem, they are also crucial in her eventual journey toward health and happiness.

She initially responds to these images and the pain she feels by cutting her wrist with a paper clip. She even calls this a "pitiful" suicide attempt. "If a suicide attempt is a cry for help" she says sardonically, "then what is this? A whimper, a peep?" (87). This may be all Melinda can handle, right now, a peep, although it will soon prompt her to find

"Unsuitable" Books

her voice. Jennifer Miskec and Chris McGee say that "Melinda's quick and sole experience with cutting in the novel challenges the old clichés with a keen awareness and dismissal of the outdated medical language that connects cutting with suicide" (167). Thus, Melinda is using the paper clip to release the pain, not as a baby step toward killing herself, and Anderson is perceptively outlining this for her readers.

Thus, this experience with cutting doesn't really amount to a suicide attempt, but it does seem to wake Melinda up, and she acknowledges that she should probably tell someone about the rape, "let it out" (99). At this moment, it appears Melinda is on the path to healing—or at least she has identified the trailhead. She also begins to identify with Hester Prynne, the much-put-upon heroine from Hawthorne's *The Scarlet Letter*, which she is reading in English class. She thinks that she and Hester would "get along," as they are both kind of quiet. "I can see us," she says, "living in the woods, her wearing that A, me with an S maybe, S for silent, for stupid, for scared. S for silly. For shame" (101). This doesn't seem to be a positive identification, but, as Tannert-Smith points out, "Melinda, like her sister outcast Hester ... is going to be given her own A for Art" (407). Perhaps also like Hester, by accepting both what happened to her and how people choose to see it (as well as turning it into something creative) she can find a kind of contentment.

Indeed, art is going to be Melinda's means of self-integration. As she struggles to make her tree speak for her, she learns about Cubism, which she determines is about "seeing beyond what is on the surface. Moving both eyes and a nose to the side of the face. Dicing bodies and tables and guitars as if they were celery sticks, and rearranging them so that you have to really see them to see them. Amazing" (119). As Latham puts it, Melinda's growth "is not toward any sort of 'integrated' self but rather toward an acceptance of the performative nature and inherent fluidity of identity" (375). At a department store trying on clothes, she says that her "face becomes a Picasso sketch, my body slicing into dissecting cubes" (124). Melinda's identity, Latham continues, "as reflected in her narrative, is multiply refracted, revealing the inconsistencies in her performances, and through these fissures we glimpse the other story that Melinda must tell in order to construct a new identity" (380). It is actually therapeutic for Melinda and instructive for readers that she identifies with Picasso's vision of fragmented reality. As Mr. Freeman puts it, "When people don't express themselves, they die one piece at a

Eleven. "Be the tree"

time" (122). By turning herself into art, albeit in a "dissected" way, Melinda is able to avoid the living death of Mr. Freeman's warning.

This fragmented identity first reveals itself in the world when her lab partner, friend, and possible romantic interest David Petrakis invites her to a party after a basketball game. She says no but realizes that she may have a kind of multiple personality disorder, where "two Melindas fight every step of the way," with one having a tantrum and the other watching from the sidelines (132). Here, Melinda is becoming aware that she must no longer watch her life go by, that she must participate in order to integrate, and David may be one of the people who help her do this. Like Junior-Arnold in the next chapter, it may take a geeky (but brilliant) friend to help put her together again.

David helps in a concrete way by encouraging her to speak in class. She writes a report on the Suffragettes for her history class, but she refuses to present her work to the class. Her bullying teacher, Mr. Neck, tries to force her to do so, rather than trying to understand why she might need to be silent. Although Melinda makes the somewhat spurious point that her silence represents solidarity with the women she has researched, David makes the very important argument that "you can't speak up for your right to be silent. That's letting the bad guys win" (159). Of course, he doesn't yet know about the rape, but his comment is appropriate in that context as well. Until she talks about the rape, the "bad guy" will continue to prey on other young women. Internalizing this sense of responsibility likely leads her to her later actions.

Her drawing is also helping her, making her "closet seem smaller" (152) and, perhaps, less necessary. Mr. Freeman tells her to "breathe life into her tree: "Make it bend—trees are flexible, so they don't snap. Scar it, give it a twisted branch—perfect trees don't' exist. Nothing is perfect. Flaws are interesting. Be the tree" (153). This injunction to "be the tree" leads her to look more at trees and other greenery around her, as well as encouraging her to "blossom" in other ways. She notices that her family's yard is a "mess," unlike her neighbors' "magazine-cover yards with flowers that match their shutters and expensive white rocks that border fresh mounds of mulch" (165). She asks her father to buy her some flower seeds (168) and thinks that the new calluses on her hands might help her win at tennis. "It would be the only glory of a really sucky year if I could beat someone at something," she thinks (170). Without a doubt, Melinda needs some sort of victory this year.

"Unsuitable" Books

Shortly after her working on the lawn, Melinda tells her friend Rachel, who is dating Andy, about what he did to her. Rachel doesn't believe her, in part because she's a ninth grader and he's a handsome, popular upperclassman. After this setback, she puts his name on the girls' bathroom stall along with a warning to stay away from him (175), showing that she intends to keep speaking (and writing) about what happened to her. When she begins to find responses on the bathroom stall from other girls who have been assaulted by Andy, she is vindicated (186). She also stands up to Heather (who is back in her life because she needs her), telling her in no uncertain terms that she won't help her with the prom decorations nor let her redecorate her room (179). "The time has come to arm-wrestle some demons," she thinks (180).

At this point, Melinda decides to go back to the place where she was raped. She acknowledges that she has survived and that it might be possible to clear away all the "dirt" of the past year and find a "small, clean part of me" (188) that she will be able to nourish. As a result of this new resolve, she is prepared emotionally for her confrontation with Andy, who, angered by the truths she has been telling about him, tries to attack her in her closet at school. She puts a shard of glass to his throat, so HE can't speak, and then she tells him "no" (195). By silencing Andy (both with the glass and with her "no"), she is now able to speak. The fact that she is rescued by girls also shows the need for women to work together to end sexual assault.

After this dramatic moment, Melinda and her art tree both begin to grow (196–98), and she starts talking to Mr. Freeman as well. "Let me tell you about it," she says, out loud this time (198). As Latham says, "By performing and transforming her trauma, Melinda succeeds in recovering her ability to speak the truth of her experience and ultimately to re-create her identity" (380). Melinda needed to re-experience what happened to her and change the outcome in order to heal, but she must also "transform" that experience into art. Tannert-Smith agrees, saying that in order to "master her trauma" Melinda must recreate it "in a reconstructed aesthetic space of her making" (408). Melinda must become the tree; she must learn to prune off the dead or dying branches and grow new leaves. She must also leave the closet of her silence and move toward a clean, well-lighted place—both at school and at home.

In spite of McGee's argument that Melinda has more power when she doesn't speak and Detora's claim that the novel fails to offer a sufficient critique of commodity capitalism, I believe instead that this novel shows a sardonic, intelligent, ultimately resourceful young woman who is able, through her words (*AND* her silences) and her actions to overcome a traumatic event in her life. She confronts her accuser, seeks help from her friends and a teacher, and even seems to forgive her parents for their inattention and self-absorption. While of course we wouldn't want young people to have to experience such a violent act in real life, surely there is much to be gained from their reading about how to cope with violence if it happens to them or to those around them. The harshest indictment in the novel remains with the attacker but also with those fellow students who ostracize Melinda and the teachers who are incapable or even unwilling to do anything to alleviate her suffering. It would be a pity to prevent young readers from having the opportunity to learn both from Melinda's struggle to speak and from the insensitivity of her classmates and friends. Restricting access to this book in classrooms and libraries silences Melinda permanently; allowing students to read about her experience, and perhaps identify with them, gives voice to all sorts of trauma they might have experienced. Teachers and librarians, parents and community members, need to speak out as well.

Chapter Twelve

"A beautiful and ugly thing"
Sherman Alexie's Absolutely True Diary *(2007)*

> Censorship is the child of fear, and the father of ignorance. Our children cannot afford to have the truth of the world withheld from them. They need us to be brave enough to give them great books so that they can grow into the strong women and men that we need them to be—Interview with Sherman Alexie, Kirsten Reach, NP

Winner of the National Book Award for Young People's Literature, Sherman Alexie's 2007 novel *The Absolutely True Diary of a Part-Time Indian*, which tells the story of Arnold/Junior Spirit (a 14-year-old Spokane Indian living in on the reservation in Wellpinit, Washington),[1] has drawn accolades from the School Library Journal and the Young Adult Library Services Association and has won literary prizes in California and Boston. In spite of its acclaim, this hard-hitting, often painful story of Arnold/Junior's life has also been the subject of much controversy. The American Library Association places *Diary* high on its list of Frequently Challenged books of the 21st Century. Having made the top five in 2012, 2011, and 2010, the novel has been challenged for offensive language, racism, sexually explicit scenes, for being unsuited for its intended age level, as well as for its "religious viewpoint," and violence. The only common categories it *wasn't* cited in (at least in these years): were "homosexuality," "occult themes," and "anti-family." Obviously, the book has managed to move the hearts of many *and* to offend a wide variety of readers. (Of course, one uses "readers" cautiously, as a good number of Alexie's critics haven't actually *read* the book.)

Twelve. "A beautiful and ugly thing"

A few details from censorship cases will give a sense of how complex the battles have been. According to the American Library Association website, *Diary* was banned in Richland, Washington, and in Dade County, Georgia. In 2013 in Richland, which is in the same relatively-conservative Eastern Washington where Alexie grew up, the school board voted to remove the book from district reading lists and then reversed their decision (after all members of the board finally read the book). In an equally-conservative northwestern Georgia community, the book was removed from library shelves and required reading lists in 2011 for vulgarity, racism, and anti–Christian content. Ironically, the book had been the community's choice for the "One Book Many Voices" in the nearby city of Rome, Georgia, three years earlier, and young people were encouraged to read, write about, and discuss it. The book has also been banned in Stockton, Missouri in 2010 and variety of other places (americanlibrariesmagazine.org). It is clear that the novel has managed to provoke both praise—and ire, although for the most part the censorship attempts have failed (or been withdrawn).

Alexie is vocal in his criticism of would-be censors such as these. In an interview with Ed Winstead in *Guernica*, he said, "Censorship in any form punishes curiosity" (NP). Speaking to the National Coalition Against Censorship, he said that the problem with censorship "isn't that one parent doesn't want their kid to read the book. The problem is they want to control what every kid reads." He is equally articulate about the need for books such as his that tell the truth about reservation life. "I know that there are kids who need these books," he told Kirsten Reach, "and I know there are kids like me, who aren't frightened by these books, but dream of them" (NP). He tells Reach that he wishes that when he was "young and growing up on the reservation that there was a book like mine about alcoholism, death, destruction, violence, and yes, masturbation, because that's real life" (NP). In a video available on the America Booksellers Foundation for Free Expression website, he speaks more generally about the value of literature in young people's lives. Contemporary young adult literature, he says, "surprises people, and scares some, because it's an accurate reflection of the way that today's teenagers talk and think, and the issues that they're dealing with. Our books have to be honest in order to connect to the teen reader today. American teens are desperate for responsible, trustworthy adults to talk to about some of these issues. Sometimes they can only find the answer that they're seeking—the moral answer, moral guidance—in books." Sounding very much like Chris Crutcher, Alexie argues that honesty in young adult writing is more important, both morally and practically, than appealing to adults who naively wish for a protected and innocent world for their adolescents.

In an interview with James Mellis, Alexie says that he hopes this book will reach kids on the reservation, but also "poor kids of any variety who feel trapped by circumstance, by culture, by low expectations. I'm hoping it helps them get out" (183). When he was writing the book, he says that he took some of the original profanity out, but his editor Jennifer Hunt asked him to put it back, which pleased him. Teenagers curse, he tells interviewers Tanita Davis and Sarah Stevenson, and they "worry about sex and drugs and booze and violence" (188). He does acknowledge in that interview, however, that there isn't much a book like his (or any book) can do to "combat the epidemic of alcoholism in the Indian world." Nevertheless, he adds, "it's really a matter of this one book reaching particular kids, who will find sobriety, inspiration, and love in the words, and let them change their lives" (190). Obviously, Alexie believes he has a mission to reach both Native and non–Native children who feel trapped by the violence, alcoholism, and limited expectations of their worlds.

While most literary critics (and young readers) have loved the novel, there has been critical controversy as well, with some Native writers challenging what they believe to be Arnold/Junior's assimilation into white society. In an interview with Nelson, Alexie argues that Native scholars (in particular) who argue that Indigenous authors should write to strengthen Native communities represent "a kind of fundamentalism about Indian identity, and what 'Indian' can be and mean, that damages Indians" (40). In a fascinating discussion of this issue, Christopher Taylor analyzes a debate in Native American literary studies, which he says has become "polarized between theorists favoring an inward-facing nationalism and those insisting on an outward-facing cosmopolitanism" (26). Taylor suggests instead an approach "that sees North America as a field of overlapping sovereignties represents the best method of connecting Native American literary texts to the cultural context from which they emerge" (27). The goal, he argues, "must be to develop a vision of North American cultural history that maintains the national histories of Native peoples without imagining that these national histories are

Twelve. "A beautiful and ugly thing"

entirely insular" (32). Alexie does just that here—create a picture of Indian life that reflects the internal realities of the reservation and moves his main character outside of that "insular" world.

It is important to mention that Taylor uses Alexie's novel *Reservation Blues* as his example, saying that "the reservation remains a safe place to which characters can return for emotional and spiritual (though not economic) solace, and there is no hint that any character feels any inclination toward assimilating to white culture" (41). This may be only partially true for *Diary*, a later novel, as Arnold/Junior does find the reservation an often-terrifying place, at least outside of his family home, and he thinks about blending his identity with a broader, non–Native one when he goes off the reservation for high school. It may be possible to see this novel as representing an evolution in Alexie's thinking about identity and community. Taylor agrees, arguing that Native American writers must adopt "an approach that allows not just for the collision of colonizer and colonized but for the negotiation of Euroamerican, African American, Spokane, and Flathead cultures in one text" (42). Arnold/Junior's journey in *Diary* shows just such a trajectory toward "overlapping sovereignties," or, as the narrator puts it, membership in all sorts of "tribes," only some of which are Native American.

Other critics see the novel's purposes and effects on readers in a positive light. In her book on postcolonial readings of children's fiction (written before *Diary* was published but still relevant), Clare Bradford says that texts written by indigenous writers "are much less likely than non–Indigenous producers to fall back on the myths and stereotypes that inform Western modes of thought." They offer Indigenous children "experiences of narrative subjectivity by proceeding from the norms of minority cultures" and help non–Indigenous children appreciate cultural differences and realize "that many ideologies that they thought to be natural and universal are culturally constructed" (12). These books, Bradford claims, have messages both for Native and non–Native children. *Diary* can be seen as one of those works that allow Native young people to identify with the protagonist and non–Native adolescents to become aware of cultural differences.

There is no question that Alexie attempts (and I believe succeeds) in *Diary* to reach both kinds of readers, as well as attempting to reconcile the categories of Native identity Taylor articulates—nationalism and cosmopolitanism. Alexie, Daniel Grassian says, is "determined to remain fiercely independent, without catering to any specific group, except in his desire to help his audience think about issues he writes about, even if his positions on those issues are radical, disturbing, and confrontational" (14). Quentin Youngberg comments that Alexie's writing "embodies an attempt to break out of representations that feed American culture's fanciful stereotypes of the Indian. Given the intensified consumption of Native literature by non–Native audiences, this project of representing other realities of contemporary Native American's experience is necessary in order to disrupt the tendency for outside audiences to essentialize cultures other than their own" (56). Agreeing with Bradford, Youngberg says that the value of the novel lies in its ability to represent Native experiences in ways that encourage outsiders to develop more complex readings of that culture.

It is also possible to see *Diary* as representing an evolution as well in Alexie's thinking about Native culture and its representation. The novel, Dawn Thompson says, tries to "address some of the criticisms made of his earlier work, in that it does emphasize the importance of family, the value of elders as living repositories of cultural teachings, and the beauty of and connection to the land" (68). However, this novel, Thompson continues, "marks a specific point in Alexie's attempt to work out his own place among Native American writers, and the process is not yet complete" (73). Although they are not unanimous in their view of Alexie's success in straddling both worlds, critics do acknowledge that his work has value for a diverse group of young readers.

Cleverly and amusingly Illustrated throughout by Ellen Forney,[2] *Diary* begins with Arnold/Junior Spirit first days of high school on the reservation. Known as Junior on the reservation and Arnold when he eventually changes to the all-white school, Arnold is, in the words of his creator, "a mouthy little bastard" (Mellis interview 184). Both "sad but hilarious" (Thompson 65), the novel is told through Arnold/Junior's perspective, which positions non-indigenous readers "as outsiders to the culture of the rez" and addressing them "as an interested but uninformed audience," according to Clare Bradford and Rafaella Baccollini (47). After first outlining the differences between the two communities, "the novel then traces the process whereby Junior/Arnold revises his internalized sense of inferiority and achieves the agency which will enable him to progress beyond the boundaries imposed on him by the cultural expectations of both the rez and the mainstream society," Brad-

Twelve. "A beautiful and ugly thing"

ford and Baccollini say (46). Still, as the novel begins, Arnold/Junior clearly has nowhere to go but up. An outsider even on the reservation, which is already on the margins of white society, Arnold/Junior nearly died as a child because of hydrocephaly, and describes himself as having too many teeth, too big of a head, too skinny a body, with glasses and a stutter, who belongs to the "Black Eye of the Month Club" (4).[3] He's ugly, sickly, and bullied, and yet he already describes himself with the wry humor that later will save him.

After Arnold/Junior first introduces his physical self to his readers, he then tells them that (like Jess Aarons in *Bridge to Terabithia*) he likes to draw because words are "too unpredictable [and] too limited" (5). He says he feels "important with a pen in my hand," and he expresses the hope that he might become a famous (and rich) artist (6). "I think the world is a series of broken dams and floods," he says, "and my cartoons are tiny little lifeboats" (6). Arnold certainly needs a lifeboat, as his life on the reservation is filled with poverty, hunger, alcoholism, and abuse from his peers. However, he says he can't blame his parents "because my mother and father are the twin suns around which I orbit and my world would EXPLODE without them" (11). From the very beginning, Alexie establishes that Arnold/Junior is both alienated from and drawn toward his life on the reservation—and that he likely will be drawn away from that life as well. The novel has all the makings of a *Bildungsroman*, albeit one that is darkly comic as well as inspiring.

In many ways, the first-person, confessional writing style is similar to Judy Blume's (and to the voice of Parr in *Deliver Us from Evie*), but the problems in this adolescent novel are much more severe than Blume's girls, who mostly worry about getting their periods and breasts, and sometimes about God and their parents' divorces. It may resemble most closely Blume's *Tiger Eyes*, and the poverty and violence of this world is also similar to *The Outsiders*. Unlike S.E. Hinton's novel, though, the poor characters on the reservation are not made to seem like Romantic outlaws. "Poverty doesn't give you strength or teach you lessons about perseverance," Arnold/Junior says. "Poverty only teaches you how to be poor" (13). Still, unlike his best friend Rowdy's family situation, Arnold/Junior has never been abused or beaten by his parents (16). It is true that there is violence in the book (which the censors point out), but there is also the warmth and caring of family.

Like Melinda in *Speak*, he has two friends—one he must move beyond and one who will help him with the current crises in his life. Arnold/Junior's relationship with Rowdy, his childhood riend on the reservation, is both hilarious and filled with pathos. Rowdy has protected Arnold/Junior all his life (17), and he is "a big, goofy dreamer" who pretends he lives inside of comic books because of the harshness of his actual life (23). Arnold/Junior says that Rowdy may be more important to him than his family (24), which seems similar to Louise Bradshaw's relationship to Call in *Jacob Have I Loved*. This closeness between the two boys creates a certain amount of anxiety in both their minds, however, and Arnold/Junior feels compelled to clearly establish his heterosexuality, especially since he's also frail and likes school (noted characteristics of sissies). "Don't get me wrong," he says. "I like girls and their curves. And I really like women and their curvier curves" (25). It seems here that Alexie may be deliberately complicating the stereotype of the weak, dreamy, artistic loner by making him resolutely heterosexual, and, as will become clear later in the novel, athletically gifted.

The conflict that instigates his move away from the reservation (and toward his broader education) comes when Arnold/Junior, angry at finding out his math textbook was used by his mother decades before, flings the book and hits his teacher, Mr. P., in the head. This is a scene reminiscent of the one in *Roll of Thunder*, when Cassie Logan refuses to take a book handed down (and down and down) from white children to end up finally in the segregated black school. Instead of having him arrested or expelled (he is suspended), Mr. P. comes to Arnold/Junior's house, surprisingly, to apologize for what white teachers tried to do to Indian children in the past: "We were supposed to make you give up being Indian," he says. "We were trying to kill Indian culture" (35). This introduces readers to the very real practice on Indian reservations of denying Indian children their traditional clothing, language, and cultural practices. Mr. P. has made progress, though, and, in addition to apologizing for a whole system of racism, encourages Arnold/Junior to leave the reservation and go to the white high school in Reardan, Washington.

This is similar to Jess Aaron being encouraged by his music teacher to continue his drawing in *Bridge*—and to see it as a way out of his limiting life in rural Virginia. However, Mr. P.'s earlier behavior also reminds readers of the sometimes unsavory (or even grim) view of teachers reflected in *The Chocolate War*, where students were victims of their

Twelve. "A beautiful and ugly thing"

teachers' ambition or even sadism. It also is a sad commentary on reservation schools that Arnold/Junior must leave in order to succeed academically. Still, Mr. P. does recognize something determined and special about Arnold/Junior. "You have been fighting since you were born," Mr. P. says. "You fought off those seizures. You fought off all the drunks and drug addicts. You kept your hope. And now, you have to take your hope and go somewhere where other people have hope" (43). As with all heroes in *Bildungsromanen*, Arnold/Junior must leave home in order to learn and grow, but Alexie complicates the trope with some of the darker aspects of American history.

Arnold/Junior takes Mr. P.'s advice to heart, and, surprisingly to him, his parents easily agree that he should go to the off-reservation predominantly white school. He realizes that his "parents love me so much that they want to help me." His parents may both be "drunks" (his father still drinks and his mother is in recovery), "but they don't want their kids to be drunks" (46). Arnold/Junior's parents recognize what Mr. P. knows—that unless he leaves the reservation he will never be able to progress beyond the lives of his parents. This may be in part what caused some of the objections to the novel—both the depiction of parents as helpless (and alcoholic) but also the clear suggestion that leaving home is Arnold/Junior's best option. Many traditional parents are made uncomfortable by books that encourage their children to stray too far from the nest.

Rowdy doesn't take Arnold/Junior's desire to leave the reservation school well, though, and they have a fight (the only approved way of showing emotion for homophobic young men). Afterward, Arnold/Junior wants to tell Rowdy that he "love[s] him like crazy but boys didn't say such thing to other boys" (48-9). Concerns about how one's sexuality will be perceived arise, much as they did for the male narrator of *Deliver Us from Evie*. Lying on the ground after the fight, Arnold/Junior realizes "that my best friend had become my worst enemy" (53). Later on, when he's out of school for Thanksgiving, Arnold/Junior takes a picture of himself and Rowdy as super heroes to his house, and Rowdy's father says he's "kind of gay." Arnold/Junior wants tell him, "I was trying to fix my broken friendship with Rowdy, and that I missed him, and if that was gay, then okay, I was the gayest dude in the world," but he doesn't say anything (103). Still, this is progress—of a sort. Arnold/Junior is willing to admit, even to Rowdy's violent and homophobic father, that his relationship with Rowdy matters to him. He also admits (at least to himself) that he doesn't mind being thought of as "gay" for expressing these feelings. All this conversation about "gayness" ought to have caught the attention of censors, but this, strangely enough, was not one of the reasons cited for challenges.

In spite of the inevitable break with his friend caused by leaving the reservation school, Arnold/Junior continues in his plan to attend Reardan. As his father drops him off on the first day, Arnold/Junior thinks about turning around and going back to the reservation, but he stays put. "You can't just betray your tribe and then change your mind ten minutes later," he thinks. "I was on a one-way bridge. There was no way to turn around, even if I wanted to" (55). At this moment, Arnold/Junior realizes the seriousness of what he's done and the inevitable difficulty arising from his choices. The first of these will be that he will now be surrounded by people who consider themselves superior to him. When his father tells him that white people aren't better than they are, Arnold is certain that he's wrong: "He was the loser Indian father of a loser Indian son living in a world built for winners," he thinks, as at the same time he realizes how much his father loves him (55). Clearly, Arnold/Junior is going to have to love his family and yet leave them if he's going to survive, and he is entering a world (he thinks) where no one will respect or care for him.

The first day of school, Arnold/Junior decides to go by "Arnold" at school (in part because his soon-to-be love interest, Penelope, makes fun of the name "Junior"—a common enough name on the reservation but unfamiliar in white Reardon). "I felt like two different people inside of one body," he tells the reader. "No, I felt like a magician slicing myself in half, with Junior living on the north side of the Spokane River and Arnold living on the south" (61). Like Julie/Miyax, the Inuit girl in *Julie of the Wolves*, Arnold/Junior has a dual identity and dual names but this is felt more as a loss than a gain for Arnold/Junior, at least at first. On the road to Reardan every day, he says he becomes "something less than Indian," and once he arrives at the school, he becomes "something less than less than less than Indian (83). Going to school where he is a minority of one unmoors him almost completely from his community. Although his family has typically stayed in one place and is "absolutely tribal," his mother and father have "lost two kids to the outside world" (89). His sister, who suffers from depression and nurses an unfulfilled

Twelve. "A beautiful and ugly thing"

desire to write romance novels, has married outside the tribe and left the reservation as well. This "tribal" family has given up two of its members in the hopes of saving them.

Arnold/Junior's time spent at Reardan is not without benefits, though. His new, white, genius friend Gordy teaches him how to read literature carefully and critically (95), and he tells him that his cartoons are serious. "If you're good at it, and you love it, and it helps you navigate the river of the world, then it can't be wrong" (95), Gordy encourages him. Arnold/Junior says that Gordy "not only tutored me and challenged me, but he made me realize that hard work—that act of finishing, of completing, of accomplishing a task—is joyous" (98). This realization is vital; Arnold/Junior has found a society (albeit a limited one) that appreciates art and culture and intelligence; he has made his first inroads into a new tribe—one of intellectuals. Clare Bradford says that Gordy "undercuts Arnold's tendency to succumb to discourses of hopelessness and victimhood" through his encouragement of Arnold/Junior's intellect and talent ("Reading Indigeneity" 337). Like Melinda in *Speak,* Arnold/Junior needs a friend who is smart and iconoclastic enough to help him move forward.

As Arnold/Junior continues to understand the white students at Reardan, he comes to realize that their lives have problems as well. His new "almost" girlfriend Penelope is bulimic, and many of the Reardan kids are neglected by their parents. Noticing this, he comes to appreciate his parents even more. "Sure, my dad has a drinking problem and my mom can be a little eccentric, but they make sacrifices for me," he says. "They worry about me. They talk to me. And best of all, they listen to me" (153). He starts to understand that everyone has pain and seeks ways of making it go away. Penelope "gorges on her pain and then throws it up and flushes it away," he says. "My dad drinks his pain away" (107). Reardan and Wellpinit start to seem not that far apart. This message about the unhealthy ways in which people from all sorts of communities—rich and poor, white and non-white—try to eliminate suffering is a valuable one for young readers and one which censors threaten to take away.

Fortunately for Arnold/Junior, he can work out his frustrations on paper, in conversations with Gordy and Penelope, and, eventually, on the basketball court. He also realizes that in this new world he has something else to offer, other than his intelligence and skills in basketball: he

"Unsuitable" Books

is different. "What was my secret?" he says. " I looked and talked and dreamed and waked differently than anybody else" (110). Arnold/Junior is "an exciting addition to the Reardan gene pool" (111). He's also perceived as slightly dangerous. Penelope, he thinks, is "bored of being the prettiest, smartest, and most popular girl in the world." She wants to "get a little smudged," and Arnold/Junior is that smudge (110). To put it another way, Penelope is "all white on white on white, like the most perfect kind of vanilla dessert cake you've ever seen." Arnold/Junior wants to "be her chocolate topping" (114). More importantly, though, Arnold/Junior realizes that they aren't really all that different. Penelope, like him, has big dreams, and neither Indian boys nor girls from small towns weren't supposed to "dream big." Instead, they were "supposed to be happy with our limitations." Neither he nor Penelope are happy with that outcome, they want "to fly" (112). Arnold has found another tribe: one of kids who dream big.

There are certain harsh realities to confront, however, one of which is financial. Arnold/Junior doesn't have the money that the other kids have for new clothes, school pictures, and meals out. When he goes to the dance with Penelope, he doesn't have money for food afterward or a ride home, but Roger, ironically the boy with whom he fought on the first day of school, is kind enough to give him enough cash to get him through the night. "If you let people into your life a little bit, they can be pretty damn amazing" (129), he thinks. Roger's unselfish and modest action shows Arnold/Junior that even privileged white kids can be kind and generous. He also learns that the reservation doesn't have a lock on community and sharing.

The contradictions and ironies of his new life are clarified by the following incident. Missing Rowdy, Arnold/Junior sends him an email message, and Rowdy returns picture of his ass. Although this is in part insulting, it also reminds him that "Rowdy could be so crazy-funny-disgusting," unlike most of the Reardan kids, who spent so much time worrying "about grades and spots and THEIR FUTURES that they sometimes acted like prepressed middle-aged business dudes with cell phones stuck in their small intestines" (130–31). In trying to explain the picture, Arnold/Junior tells Gordy that Rowdy hates him for going to school at Reardan. "[S]ome Indians think you have to act white to make your life better," he says. "Some Indians think you become white if you try to make your life better, if you become successful" (131). Gordy tells him

Twelve. "A beautiful and ugly thing"

they have a "tribe of two," and then Arnold wants to hug Gordy but doesn't because Gordy tells him not to get "sentimental." "Yep," Arnold/Junior thinks, "even the weird boys are afraid of their emotions" (132). Two strands of the narrative are joined here: the anxiety of close male friendship and the further extension of the tribal metaphor. Unfortunately, those who would ban this book for what they consider vulgar scenes such as this one miss the important message.

Although he never expected to succeed in this way (especially at a white school), Arnold/Junior makes the varsity basketball team, and their first game is on the reservation against Wellpinit High School. "It was like something out of Shakespeare," Arnold/Junior tells the reader (142). The people in the bleachers call out, "Arnold sucks!" and he notices that they weren't calling him by his "rez name" but by his "Reardan name" (143). His new identity has turned into an epithet. After insulting him verbally, they turn their backs on him. "It was a fricking awesome display of contempt" (144), he comments. Not surprisingly, Arnold/Junior starts to cry, and the coach tells him, "If you care about something enough, it's going to make you cry. But you have to use it. Use your tears. Use your pain. Use your fear. Get mad, Arnold, get mad" (144). The game goes from bad to worse, and Arnold/Junior ends up in the hospital with a concussion, which is especially dangerous because of his hydrocephaly. The coach spends the night with him, and he quotes Vince Lombardi: "The quality of a man's life is in direct proportion to his commitment to excellence, regardless of his chosen field of endeavor" (148). This coach sounds very much like the gruff but supportive coaches in Chris Crutcher's many novels, who teach their young students the importance of playing with integrity and honor.

To make matters worse, shortly after the basketball debacle, Arnold/Junior's father spends all the Christmas money on getting drunk, but he saves five dollars in his shoe. Arnold/Junior thinks about how much that money meant to his father, how drunk he could have gotten on it. The fact that he saves it (and that he spent all the rest of the Christmas money) is "a beautiful and ugly thing" (151) in Arnold's mind. This sums up complications of reservation life and the doubled life that Arnold/Junior lives. As he says, "Indians are screwed up, but we're really close to each other" (153); nevertheless, they still harm each other (and themselves) in a myriad of ways.

Only his grandmother, who hangs onto "that old-time Indian spirit" and approaches each new person and experience with "openness and curiosity and lack of judgment" (155), is a completely positive figure in his life. When she is killed by a drunk driver, her last act is "a call for forgiveness, love, and tolerance" for the driver (157), which is, once again, a beautiful and ugly thing. Ironically, given that she was killed by a drunk driver, his grandmother was one of the only Indians in the tribe who didn't drink alcohol. "Drinking would shut down my seeing and my hearing and my feeling," she says. "Why would I want to be in the world if I couldn't touch the world with all my senses intact?" (158). In what seems almost like a cosmic joke, a rich white man shows up at her wake with a ceremonial outfit he thinks belongs to Junior's grandmother, but it turns out to be from a completely different tribe. This causes the whole group at the wake to laugh. "When it comes to death, we know that laughter and tears are pretty much the same thing," Junior thinks (166).

In spite of this brief and humorous moment, Junior is depressed after the loss of his grandmother. Reading *Medea*, he sees the quote "What greater grief than the loss of one's native land?" and he thinks, "Well, of course, man. We Indians have LOST EVERYTHING. We lost our native land, we lost our languages we lost our songs and dances. We lost each other. We only know how to lose and be lost" (173). At this point, Arnold, Junior feels that he has lost everything: his grandmother, his sense of belonging in Wellpinit, and even his sense of self. Still, as Bradford points out, Euripides "provides Arnold with a way of thinking about his experience and that of his community" that offers solace and a sense of a wider commonality of suffering ("Reading Indigeniety" 338). Through his absorption of non-Native literature, Arnold/Junior has found a way to put his experience into a larger context.

Also, he comes to realize that he has the support of his new friends in Reardon. Gordy and his classmates defend him against a bullying teacher, who makes fun of him for missing class because of the deaths in his family (a family friend has also died). He tells teacher, "I used to think the world was broken down by tribes," I said. "By black and white. By Indian and white. But I know that isn't true. The world is only broken into two tribes. The people who are assholes and the people who are not" (176). Once again, Arnold/Junior is formulating the world into wider kinds of tribes. These sorts of determined and rebellious students and bullying teachers appear frequently in Crutcher as well as in Anderson's novel, *Speak*. After this incident, Arnold is inspired to begin making

Twelve. "A beautiful and ugly thing"

a list of things that make him "feel joy" and drawing things that make him angry. "Writing and rewriting, drawing and redrawing, and rethinking and revising and reediting" becomes his "grieving ceremony" (178). This is similar to Melinda's ongoing art project in *Speak* and Jess's drawings in *Bridge*.

Along with his newfound sense of camaraderie with his fellow students, Arnold/Junior discovers that he is actually a good basketball player. He believes this is because on the reservation he wasn't expected to be good, but at Reardan his coach and the other plays expected him to excel, and he did (180). The season culminates in another game against his home team, with Arnold/Junior as the star player. Asked by a reporter about how he feels to be playing his hometown team again, he is initially reluctant to tell him, as revealing his emotions to outsiders makes him feel exposed. Eventually, he tells him that he will "never quit playing hard. And I don't just mean in basketball. I'm never going to quit living life this hard, you know? I'm never going to surrender to anybody. Never, ever, ever" (186). During the game, his coach tells him he can stand up to Rowdy and help the team win. Arnold/Junior comments: "Do you understand how amazing it is to hear that from an adult? Do you know how amazing it is to hear that from anybody? It's one of the simplest sentences in the world, just four words, but they're the four hugest words when they're put together" (189). Until Mr. P. encouraged him to leave Wellpinit, no one other than his parents had ever believed he could achieve anything, and now he has his coach, his friend, Gordy, and Penelope confident that he can achieve anything he wants.

Of course, the Reardan team wins, but after the game he realizes that the victory is hollow, that the Wellpinit team is David and Reardan is Goliath (although a Goliath that wins). He realizes that, unlike the reservation kids, "all of the seniors on our team were going to college. All of the guys on our team had their own cars. All of the guys on our team had iPods and cell phones and PSPs and three pairs of blue jeans and ten shirts and mothers and fathers who went to church and had good jobs" (195). Arnold/Junior is "suddenly ashamed of my anger, my rage, and my pain" and goes to the bathroom, throws up, and then cries (196), needing to purge himself of his guilt and sorrow. After he recovers, he emails Rowdy, who tells him Wellpinit will beat them next year, and Arnold/Junior will "cry like the little faggot you are" (198). Surprisingly, Arnold/Junior takes this as a positive sign. "I was a happy faggot" (199), he says. At this point, Arnold/Junior seems so confident in his multi-faceted identity that he doesn't care what he's called. He can be Rowdy's best friend, Reardon's star basketball player, and a "faggot" for expressing his emotions all at once; he can also associate with Penelope and Gordy and also feel connected to his family back on the reservation. He can mourn the loss of loved ones and look forward to the future as well.

Toward the end of novel, Arnold/Junior becomes more philosophical about life on the reservation. Quoting Tolstoy, who said that all unhappy families are unhappy in their own ways, he says: "Well, I hate to argue with a Russian genius, but Tolstoy didn't know Indians. And he didn't know that all Indian families are unhappy for the same exact reasons: the fricking booze" (200). As Bradford and Baccollini put it, "The novel's narration, at once confiding and entertaining, gradually shifts from such descriptions of the rez's dysfunctional relationships and practices to more nuanced accounts of the circumstance which have contributed to the poverty and hopelessness of its inhabitants" (47). Arnold/Junior is coming to understand the role alcohol has played in the lives of Native peoples on the reservations, the way that it has destroyed lives and families and, most importantly, community life. Still, this realization also means that he can, by avoiding alcohol himself, carve out a different kind of life than the one he has known. This seems like a message that would be important for young people to absorb, painful as it might be.

Along with his growing understanding of reservation life and his relation to it, he also starts to come to terms with the death of his sister, who suffocates with her husband while passed out drunk in their burning trailer. At first he blames himself, thinking that his desire to "spend my life with white people" (211) led to her leave the reservation. However, he soon comes to realize that "it was courageous of her to leave the basement and move to Montana. She went searching for her dreams, and she didn't find them, but she made the attempt. And I was making the attempt, too. And maybe it would kill me, too, but I knew that staying on the rez would have killed me, too" (217). In the Davis and Stevenson interview, Alexie says that Arnold, "by leaving the rez, is escaping a slow-motion death trap." Still, he wants his readers to know that a "small white 'mainstream' town can be a kind of death trap, too .... Metaphorically speaking, we all grow up on reservations, don't we?" (189). Although this could imply that we are all trapped, Arnold/Junior comes

Twelve. "A beautiful and ugly thing"

to realize that while he "might be a lonely Indian boy, but I was not alone in my loneliness. There were millions of other Americans who had left their birthplace sin search of a dream" (217). After this important realization, he lists the "tribes" he belongs to, including, cartoonists, chronic masturbators, poverty, and beloved sons (217). Alexie seems here to be telling his readers that they all belong to "tribes," some of which they are proud to claim and others they wish no one knew about. This mention of masturbation probably caused the challenge based on sexual explicitness, but this seems a small-minded interpretation of much bigger idea represented here.

In the last scene in the novel, Arnold/Junior and Rowdy climb a huge tree they had climbed as kids. From the top they can see their "entire world," which is "at that moment, was green and golden, and perfect" (226). Thinking about returning to Reardan, missing his "semi-girlfriend," thinking about Gordy coming to visit over the summer break, Arnold/Junior, feels "hopeful and silly about the future" (227). In a final one-on-one basketball game, Rowdy tells his friend that he's "an old time nomad....You're going to keep moving all over the world in search of food and water and grazing land. That's pretty cool" (230). Arnold/Junior is both "old-time nomad," identified with the nomadic lifestyle of many indigenous peoples, and part of a larger tribe that includes his family and Rowdy, Gordy and his white girlfriend, all the cartoonists and writers (and chronic masturbators) in the world. He is truly part-time Indian and part-time melting pot American. Arnold/Junior is moving out into the wide, wide world, but he is also taking important parts of his Native heritage with him. The tree suggests that he remains rooted, while at the same time being nomadic. Young readers could do much worse than having Arnold/Junior's inclusive, adventurous world view.

Most importantly, though, Arnold/Junior has reached this place of relative comfort because of the concrete actions he takes (with the help of his parents and grandmother) to change his life. He has had to abandon everything familiar and make himself vulnerable to shame and isolation. This may be the most important lesson for young people, both on and off the reservation, of this novel: change is painful and absolutely necessary. As Adrienne Kertzer says, "[P]aying attention to the radical potential of *The Absolutely True Diary of a Part-Time Indian* requires that readers not only to listen to Junior's story, but also choose to live their lives differently. To do otherwise, to remain exactly the same, means that we have not paid attention" (72). If readers are shocked by the violence (and, perhaps, by the dark humor), this is a small price to pay for the painful wisdom that comes with it. The only absolutely true shame comes when young readers are prevented—by well-meaning (one hopes) but misguided adults—from reading such a powerful story.

CONCLUSION

Challenges Ahead

> Instances of book censorship represent the tensions of society writ small, a struggle for political, social, and/or cultural power waged in the limited arena of the pages of a book—Jenkins, 452

> Censorship—in the classroom, in the library, at the school board level—will make forgetters of us all—YA Novelist Jane Yolen, quoted in Boyd and Bailey, 658

As Lee Burress points out in in his aptly-titled *Battle of the Books*, censorship was infrequent in U.S. Schools before World War II (xiii); however, larger numbers of graduates and the increasing diversity of the student body, as well as the introduction of non-canonical materials into the curriculum, "have created new tensions in what had been an essentially white, middle-class institution" (xiv). More high-school graduates usually mean a better paid and more satisfied work force. Diversity is clearly a good thing: students from multi-ethnic backgrounds are increasingly experiencing (at least in theory) equal education and opportunity. Variety in the curriculum is also valuable: students are now, more than they ever were in the past, able to see their experiences reflected in literature. However, these apparent advances are not without complexities and imperatives for further action, many of which can be seen in censorship challenges.

Burress notes, for example, that books by American authors and writers of color featuring non-white characters are disproportionately challenged, compared to all books published (xix). This suggests that at least one part of the motivation for censors is their discomfort with works that treat characters and situations that (they believe) deviate from the mainstream—whether in terms of race, income, gender, or sexuality. Thus, students are denied the opportunity to read, think, and discuss freely ideas that will enhance their emotional and intellectual development. The larger effect, though, is that our democratic values

Conclusion

will be obscured if we accede to these limitations on the representation of a full and complete picture of the United States, warts and all.

In order to illuminate the multivariate aspects of this issue, teachers Fenice Boyd and Nancy Bailey use a number of provocative metaphors to show the variety of effects censorship has on students and teachers. "[C]ensors," they say, "evoke barriers to free thought and speech when they block knowledge acquisition, intellectual development, as well as creative and critical thinking" (655). Book challenges, they continue, also "act like a patina, a layer of corrosion that effectively seals beneath itself the wealth of our nation—the values and ideas that we live by in a democratic society" (657). In addition, they evoke the metaphor of a "very tenuous and dangerous tightrope" that teachers walk. As they put it, "[T]eaching is not for the faint-hearted. The job at its best requires careful balance and skillful decision making" (658). The bottom line is that "[w]hen censorship is practiced the professionalism of teachers—who were hired due to their knowledge, skills, dispositions, and expertise—is placed at risk" (660). So, book banning limits access to knowledge, undermines democracy by concealing flaws in need of correction, and forces teachers to cope with fear and uncertainty in their working lives. Put this way, it is difficult to see what, if any, benefits arise from censorship.

Boyd and Bailey also reiterate Burgess's point about diversity. "If books are challenged and disappear from the curriculum," they ask, provocatively, "who will teach students to think about and question the status quo when what passes as the norm is privilege for one group at the expense of another, or when denigration of people from diverse backgrounds is so routine that many do not even see it?" (657). Books such as the ones discussed in this study expose students to the injurious effects of racism, economic inequality, homophobia, and violence, and, through skillful manipulation of sympathetic narrators and characters, allow young adults to empathize with their struggles and, one might hope, to do something to change their worlds. As President Obama pointed out at the end of 2013, income inequality is undermining our democracy, and removing works that encourage students to question economic, racial, and sexual difference risks making injustice at best invisible, at worst acceptable.

Susan Ohanian, award-winning freelance writer, opponent of high-stakes testing, and former teacher, says in her foreword to *At the School-*

house Gates (which summarizes the harrowing story contained in her book of two teachers' struggle with censorship) that "[t]he long term damage of book banning is spiritual and it runs too deep to tabulate" (xi). Being a teacher, she says, "means being able to make choices and helping students learn how to do the same," and censors deny teachers the ability to do the most important part of their job (xii). The hard truth about schools, she continues, is that, regardless what we might claim, they have never been "bastions of intellectual freedom .... Free speech and inquiry have not been valued in K-12 schools except as rights reserved, at least nominally, for adults" (xvii). As a number censorship battles (and court cases) have proven, constitutional rights are all-too-often abandoned at the (locked and metal-detected) school doors. Instead of being a place where students can use their own minds to make choices, evaluate their world, and grow intellectually, schools are in danger of becoming (if they haven't already) places devoted to "inculcating (in that word's root sense, of grinding in with the heel) information and skills into docile vessels/vassals" (xviii). The question for teachers, librarians, parents, and concerned citizens is whether we really want the next generation of America's leaders to be "docile vassals" or independent, critical thinkers and active members of society.

The two teachers who tell their stories in *At the Schoolhouse Gates*, Gloria Pipkin and Releah Lent, were both involved with censorship cases that eventually made it into the court system (and who, even though they were excellent, award-winning teachers, eventually decided to leave the classroom). They share Ohanian's belief about the origin of censorship in schools. "The conflict arises," they say, "when a minority of parents, those who view kids as rebellious creatures in need of heavy-handed discipline to mold them into productive citizens, are frightened of allowing their children the freedom we feel is essential in schools." These parents, they argue, "want to limit knowledge to safe topics and sanitized textbooks that remove all the bodily fluids and the mistakes, messiness, and mayhem that characterize the human condition" (217). The problem with this position, though, is that children and adolescents have been "excluded from political discourse and participation" and get no voice in this process of sanitizing what they are allowed to read. Pipkin and Lent continue: "The rights children are accorded exist only at the discretion of adults, who are increasingly prone to treating them like intellectual incompetents but punishing them as adults when they

Conclusion

err" (219). Young people, then, are between a rock and a hard place: would-be censors want to deny them the right to learn how to make their own decisions (including mistakes) and then blame them when they fail to choose wisely.

So, what is to be done? Pipkin and Lent offer a number of solutions. To those who fear free choice of reading materials by students and their parents, they reply that "diversity ought to be sought and accommodated rather than avoided and squelched" (208). Teachers, certainly, could lead this charge by embracing provocative and diverse literature and making it available in their classrooms. This is only part of the problem, however. They are also concerned about the emphasis on high-stakes standardized testing, which they say "deprives students of the opportunity to ask their own questions, pursue their own projects, dig deeper into topics that interest them, rattle cages, tilt at windmills, question authority, rock boats, challenge oppression, create art, and do all the other things that make us fully and freely human." They ask: "What better way to ensure a docile, malleable population than to keep students so busy with reductive skill building that no real questions ever arise?" (210). Indeed, if students have less and less choice about what they can read in school libraries, in teachers' classroom collections, and in class—and if they spend the bulk of their school day preparing for tests—then we are guaranteed that "docile, malleable population" that some believe might work best in the low-wage jobs available in the service sector. However, it does nothing to combat the problems of poverty, the national debt, or legislative gridlock, and it inhibits the scientific and other intellectual discoveries that an inquiring, free-thinking society needs to grow and change.

The bottom line for Pipkin and Lent is that it will take a "revolution" on the part of parents and students, and teachers who "are willing to risk everything; until they refuse to bend to the desires of those whose motives are not in the best interest of children, then there will be little hope of significant change, and our story will be retold with different characters and settings" (211). Standing up to censors is by no means easy, especially in our politically-polarized times. It is my hope that this book will inspire at least some teachers to "risk everything" and encourage their students to read widely, provocatively, and questioningly. I also intend it as ammunition for those who defend against censorship in classrooms, libraries, and communities, allowing them to defend with confidence these books, which offer young adult readers all the messiness of life, combined with a large dose of hope.

I see the challenges ahead being two-fold: one, the emphasis on high-stakes testing, if continued, will lead (especially in underperforming schools) toward even more removals of young adult novels from the language arts classroom and curriculum. This will mean that often urban, predominantly-minority students will become less and less likely to see their own experiences reflected in literature, as they are called upon to study grammar (which has been proven to be ineffective in improving writing skills) and to read excerpts from "classic" (and therefore safe) in textbooks. Two, if teachers' self-censorship continues to be the dirty little secret of middle and high schools, the effect will be that many valuable works aren't challenged because they are never brought into the classroom. Students with parents who, for a variety of reasons—lack of education, poverty, fear—do not encourage their children to read widely, will never know that books such as those by Chris Crutcher, Mildred Taylor, Laurie Anderson, Sherman Alexie, and David Levithan (among many others) exist. These books, of course, are the ones that most accurately reflect their personal situations and have the highest likelihood to reach them and lead them out of the restrictions of their lives.

The solutions are, of course, less easy to identify than the problems. Perhaps one thing that can be done is that institutions that train teachers can expose students to works that challenge (and have been challenged) and offer them ways to defend those works to their administrators and parents. This normalizes the work for future teachers, who may themselves come from homes or school systems where censorship was the norm. It also gives them the basis for creating justifications for the books available in their classroom libraries and those they require their own students to read. Also, those who are planning to work in education administration need to learn how effectively to deal with book challenges and how to support their teachers in those challenges. This could work to their advantage, as the best and brightest teachers will often gravitate to schools where they have the most freedom of choice in helping to design the curriculum.

Another idea is to follow the lead of librarians, who strenuously resist challenges to intellectual freedom. The website for the American Library Association offers a number of recourses for those facing chal-

Conclusion

lenges and suggestions for combatting those challenges. Banned Books Week, initiated by the ALA, can be a great place to start. Its focus on challenged materials can be a focus for discussions on censorship, and more importantly, an impetus to bring challenging books such as the ones in this study into the classroom.

A third suggestion would be for educators, librarians, and school board members to bring speakers on censorship into universities, schools, and the community. Many of the writers featured in this book are ardent champions of the First Amendment and will be happy to speak to classrooms, libraries, and community forums. They are articulate, well-known, and often charismatic speakers will do much to sway the hearts of would-be book banners. Chris Crutcher, Laurie Anderson, and Sherman Alexie and other YA writers have spoken many times on this topic, usually to wide and receptive audiences.

Most importantly, however, it is up to teachers, parents, and community leaders to be the best advocates of the wide and exciting range of young adult literature. They must be willing to go to the mat for these authors and even risk their jobs and, perhaps in some conservative communities, their reputations—and their friendships. It is incumbent upon us as adults who care about children to offer them all that literature has to offer: the inspiring, the shocking, and even, sometimes, the downright disgusting. All of the authors discussed here deal with these things—with skill, with compassion, and with insight. A child's experience will be poorer—and his adult life less thoughtful—without them.

Chapter Notes

Preface

1. While the Newbery Award has been seen as a benchmark of quality for adolescent fiction and as a defense against would-be censors, Kenneth Kidd problematizes the award. The medal, he says, stands for "the middlebrow culture of public schools and libraries" (169), rather than as a sign true literary quality and books that challenge the status quo. Books written by women, with "decidedly American settings and themes have been staples" since the 1940s, he argues (177). It wasn't until the 1950s that a book about African Americans won, he points out, and it was "a historical novel of assimilation written by a middle-class white woman" (179). Most winning books that address racism are "historical novels that give priority to the folk/vernacular and are set no later than the Depression" (180). In fact, after Mildred Taylor won the award in 1977 for *Roll of Thunder, Hear My Cry*, "the Medal did not go to another African American-authored book until 2001" (183). Finally, he says, no book "with lesbian/gay/bisexual content received Newbery recognition (not even Honor status)" (183). As useful as the Medal might seem for defending a book against a challenge, it might be wise for teachers and librarians to move beyond Medal winners in their selections, toward books that are truly challenging, and not just challenged.

Chapter One

1. An excellent summary of relevant First Amendment court cases can be found in Robert P. Doyle's *Banned Books* (2007), Herbert Foerstel's *Banned in the U.S.A.* (2002), and Joan DelFattore's *What Johnny Shouldn't Read* (1994). The cases most often cited as significant are (from Doyle): *Tinker v. Des Moines Independent Community School District* (1969), in which the Supreme Court said that the "First Amendment protects public school students' rights to express political and social views (185). The next is *Board of Education, Island Trees Union Free School District v. Pico* (1982), where the Court decided that school boards cannot remove books because of religious or political views (185). In *Hazelwood School District v. Kuhlmeier* (1988), the Court said that if the school board's actions are related to "legitimate pedagogical concerns" they may censor material (186). *Virgil. v. School Board of Columbia County* (1989) reinforced that position in the U.S. Circuit Court of Appeals (186). A more recent case, *John D. Ashcroft, Attorney General, et al. v. Free Speech Coalition, et al.* (191), however, supported free speech as the foundation of free thought.

Chapter Two

1. For a detailed discussion of possible reasons why *The Outsiders* has been so effectively canonized, see Tribunella. The

purpose of the novel, he says, is an "explicitly didactic one" (89), unlike *The Chocolate War*, which he says has been more often challenged because it "raises questions" and "provokes outrage" (97). He concludes his essay this way: "The novel itself works to encourage the reader to remain innocent and unknowing of its own limitations as a solution to the problems of social class, and as long as U.S. culture is invested in the image of children or young adults as innocent and unknowing, *The Outsiders* will continue to be an umproblematized and underachieving mainstay of the high school reading list" (100). As is clear from my argument, I disagree.

2. For a recent discussion of this issue, see Cart.

3. In an essay on socioeconomic status in the novel, M. Pearlman perceptively (and uniquely) comments that Hinton "capitalizes the "S" in "Socs" throughout the book while the "g" in greaser is invariably lower case" (NP).

Chapter Three

1. Blume's editor told Weidt that the punctuation of the title is deliberate: "There is no comma before God, and there is a period after Margaret. There is no comma before God because Judy felt very strongly that there was no distance between Margaret and God, and she wanted it in this kind of informal, rushed way, the way people talk, the way people think" (49). Interestingly, many of Blume's critics make this error in citing the title, which may indicate that they aren't paying close enough attention to the author's thematic and narrative purposes.

Chapter Four

1. In her 1973 Newbery Award acceptance speech, George describes her research trip to the Arctic with her then husband. In Barrow in 1970, George felt the "push and pull of two cultures" (339). She also discussed her the ways in which that trip taught her about the delicacy of the Arctic environment and the need to protect it: "The ecology of the Arctic is like a Chinese wooden puzzle"; she says, "each piece locks into the other, and if one is not right, the whole thing falls apart" (342). Clearly, much of the emotional resonance and scientific information in *Julie of the Wolves* came from this experience.

2. George completed two sequels to *Julie of the Wolves*: *Julie* (1994) and *Julie's Wolf Pack* (1997). In *Julie* the main character is still in Kangick with her father and stepmother (with whom she has reconciled), trying to combine the old ways with the new, and keep her wolves safe. She is also falling in love with Peter, although she refuses to marry him until she completes her education. The focus in *Julie's Wolf Pack*, as the title suggests, is much more on the behavior and struggles of various wolf packs (including members of her original pack) to survive, although Julie does play some part. At the end of the novel, Julie has become known as the "Jane Goodall" of the Arctic wolves, she marries Peter, and they settle down to life in the Arctic studying wolves. Although both novels are full of fascinating and accurate details of wolf behavior in the wild, the focus on Julie's growth and development is moved to the background. Also, George seems more determined in these books reconcile the old with the new, to find a place where Julie fits into her dual world.

3. Kenneth Kidd raises concerns about the "edubrow" culture (169) that is endorsed and encouraged by the Newbery Award, persuasively arguing that Newbery award winners have often avoided difficult societal issues by locating those issues in the past or in more exotic cultures. Certainly, setting *Julie* in the Arctic may make it vulnerable to

Chapter Five

1. The novel has a sequel, *Beyond the Chocolate War*, which was published in 1985. In it, Jerry returns to Monument (but not to Trinity), and the focus in on Obie, who has become increasingly disenchanted with Archie's rule. David Caroni commits suicide and Archie is humiliated, but the power structure remains in place, with Brother Leon continuing as head of the school and the Vigils turned over to a new generation, one, it is implied, that will be more ruthless, violent, and less intelligent Archie's. Neither the cynicism nor the bleakness of Cormier's world view is diminished or mitigated by the sequel.

Chapter Seven

1. Interestingly, *Athletic Shorts* is one of his few books to be challenged from the left, in particular for the use of what some perceived as racist language in "Telephone Man." Crutcher tells Gillis and Cole that this was the "only time [he] was devastated by the charges." He says that critics (many of whom hadn't read the story, or read it without the introduction explaining the language in the collection) didn't realize that the story was one of "racist redemption." Would-be banners also objected to the book's negative portrayal of Chinese-Americans. "I was appalled," he says, that the diversity committee who examined the book in a Grand Rapids, Michigan, dispute "thought it was more important to have a culturally balanced story (which is probably impossible to tell) than it was to have a good story" (51). What Crutcher learned from this experience was that he "could not trust the left with an agenda to be reasonable then

Kidd's critique, but many of the social and cultural conflicts remain clearly delineated.

I could trust the right with an agenda to be reasonable" (52).

2. Crutcher has written two new works since *Deadline*: *Angry Management* (2009) and *Period 8* (2013). *Angry* revisits several of his characters, including Sarah Byrnes (from *Staying Fat*), Montana West (from *Sledding Hill*), and Angus Bethune (from *Athletic Shorts*), and it features Mr. Nak (from *Ironman*) as a counselor back from retirement who is trying (with wise-cracking honesty) to help the children figure out their lives. *Period 8* is a young adult suspense novel, with what seems to me a rather melodramatic plot. However, Gillis and Cole correctly argue that *Period 8* gives readers "possibly the strongest adult character Crutcher has ever created" (157), and Crutcher agrees, saying that teacher Mr. Logsdon, while not modeled after himself, is "modeled after what I believe I've learned" (159). While enjoyable books, I nevertheless think they don't add much new information to the discussion here.

Chapter Eight

1. *The Road to Memphis* is part of a trilogy of novels, which chronicles the Logan family (which is loosely based on Taylor's own), beginning when Cassie is nine years old in *Roll of Thunder, Hear My Cry* (1976). The story picks up a year later in *Let the Circle Be Unbroken* (1981) and concludes several years later with *The Road to Memphis* (1990); Taylor has written about earlier periods in the Logan family and community in five shorter works: *Song of the Trees* (1975), *The Friendship* (1987), *Mississippi Bridge* (1990), *The Well* (1995), and *The Land* (2001). A planned final book, tentatively called *Logan*, has not yet been published. Her novel, *The Gold Cadillac* (1987), tells a story also based on her father's life but is set more in the North.

2. In *Circle*, Cassie's cousin Suzella, who is the child of a black father and a

white mother, comes to stay with them. She flirts with passing as white when a white boy shows an interest in her (assuming she is white). The Logan family is quick to warn her of the dangers if the boy discovers that she has been misleading him. In general, Suzella's presence is seen as threatening to the Logan family, and, after a humiliating (and potentially dangerous) confrontation with that boy and his friends, Suzella's father takes her back to New York. This story is interspersed with that of Jacey, who gets pregnant with a white man's child. Although Cassie is only 10 in this novel, her father is already talking to her about the need to avoid white men (154).

3. This issue of black people referring to whites by first names first appears in *The Friendship,* with tragic consequences, and is based on a true story related to Taylor by her family.

4. Stacey's comments echo an earlier conversation Cassie, her brothers, and Moe have about the upcoming war, and they decide that they may have no choice about going but also that they are unlikely to advance in the service (90–91). Moe is more positive about possible economic and social opportunities, but Cassie says that her Uncle Hammer only saw black soldiers "unloading ships and cleaning spittoons" in World War I (96). "Colored folks want to get killed so bad," she says, pointedly, "they can stay right here in Mississippi and do that" (96).

Chapter Nine

1. Since writing *The Giver,* Lowry has written three companion books with various degrees of connection to Jonas and Gabriel's stories. *Gathering Blue* creates a quasi-medieval dystopian society featuring main character Kira, who has magical embroidery powers, and whose father has escaped to a community where it appears that Jonas now lives. Like Jonas, Kira has partial responsibility for maintaining the history of the community, but she discovers that she is being controlled by the corrupt leadership. *Messenger* tells the story of Kira's friend Matty and also of her father as they struggle, along with Jonas, to keep their community together. *Son* provides the back story on Gabriel's mother, who is forced to be a birthmother at 14 and eventually escapes to Jonas' and Gabriel's community. In each of her novels, young adults are charged with initially resisting and eventually reshaping their communities. Lowry is also interested in how communities organize themselves, some more cooperatively and others more coercively, and in each of these novels she attends closely to the use of language and the power of naming. In part, these subsequent novels clarify what happens to Jonas in *The Giver,* which may satisfy some critics and readers alike.

Chapter Ten

1. After her coming out, Kerr tells Abate, some of her visits to schools and colleges have been cut back, and when she is asked why she did it says what she said to her parents when they asked her why she had to "announce it." "And I would say back to them, well you announce it all the time. You wear wedding rings. You have me and my brothers. Everybody looks at you and knows who you are. They don't know who I am, and I'm proud of who I am. So, that's why I announce it" (196).

2. In her detailed study, Christine Jenkins notes that almost 100 young adult novels with gay or lesbian content have appeared (as of 1997) since the first one in 1969 (John Donovan's *I'll Get There: It Had Better Be Worth the Trip*) (298). Between 1969 and 1992, Jenkins found that gay male characters outnumbered lesbian characters three to one. Nearly all lesbians were in coupled relationships, unlike gay males. In books

with female protagonists, the gay/lesbian secondary characters were equally likely to be male or female. With male protagonists, the secondary gay/lesbian characters were always male. The novels also moved from primary experiences of gay and lesbian characters to the gay and lesbian characters being secondary characters (301). Between 1993 and 1997, gay and lesbian characters of color have increased from 5 to 24 percent. The characters all continue to be middle class, the trend of making gay/lesbian characters secondary continues, and gay male characters continue to outnumber lesbian characters three to one. Jenkins says that *Evie* is a "breakthrough book," in that it has a male protagonist with a lesbian sister" (302), as, with the exception of the AIDS plot, little has changed in the subject matter of gay and lesbian fiction since 1969. She asks: "In a society with such volatile political and cultural attitudes toward gay men and lesbians, why is this literature so tenaciously conservative?" (305).

In the earliest YA novels from the 1940s and 50s she adds, "content was limited to angry epithets and the occasional shadowy character included to represent the oddities—or the dangers—of the larger adult world into which young people were moving" (307). In the 60s and 70s, homosexuality "was portrayed in a brief passage in the story of heterosexual development" (308). Shortly after "exceptional" gay people appear, but they are all male. (308). In 30 years of YA problem novels, gay and lesbian characters have been "beaten, shot, gay-bashed, drowned, sexually molested, kidnapped, framed on drug charges, or killed in car accidents. Others have been fired, received hate mail, or had their lockers, cars, or homes vandalized. Teens living with their families have been disinherited, cut out of family photos, sent to deprogrammers, or thrown out of the house; others leave voluntarily, for the sake of the family's good name" (309). There have also been "very few depictions of their lives within a wider gay/lesbian/queer community" (309). Only *Weetzie Bat* (1989) presents such a community (at least by 1998), although it is more "magical" than "realism" (311). YA literature that allows readers to empathize, not to pity, gay and lesbian teens, she says, "with rare exceptions ... has yet to be written" (315).

3. Much of Kerr's account of Mrs. Burrman's attitude toward Evie is mirrored by what Kerr reports her mother saying about not flaunting her sexuality, using the word "lesbian" to describe herself, or bringing women to their home in rural New York State, which she briefly recounts in her coming-out foreword to *Having Our Say*. Patsy's relationship with Evie also has clear parallels with Kerr's relationship in the 1950s with Patricia Highsmith, who dressed in a butch way and often embraced typically male activities as Evie does. The story of their often stormy relationship and the closeted world of 1950s lesbians can be found in Meaker's memoir of that time period, *Highsmith*.

Chapter Twelve

1. I have chosen to call the main character Arnold/Junior in each reference, to maintain a sense of his dual identity, which I believe is central to Alexie's message. I have decided to put "Arnold" first, as this seems to be his dominant identity by the end of the novel. Other critics have called him "Junior" when he's on the reservation and "Arnold" when he's in Reardan, but this seems needlessly confusing.

2. Forney's illustrations, which are represented as Arnold/Junior's drawings, Kertzer says, "play a major role in affecting the novel's tone simply because they minimize the violence and rage of Junior's narrative" (69). It is true that the illustrations do add humor to the bleak

representations of reservation life, but they certainly don't attempt to cover it up. However, they may make the book more palatable to younger readers (and their parents).

3. Every biography of Alexie and nearly every review of the novel mentions that Alexie suffered from the same health problems (such as hydrocephaly) as Arnold/Junior. His mother is a recovering alcoholic, and his father continued to drink all his life. He also lived on the Wellpinit reservation and attended Reardan High School. He dedicates his book to both places, which he calls his "hometowns." Still, the story transforms Alexie's actual autobiography into something more universal. These are—and are not—the worlds in which Alexie grew up. As his epigraph to the novel (which he and others attribute to Yeats) says, "There is another world, but it is in this one." Arnold/Junior lives exactly in that space between one world and another.

Bibliography

Abate, Michelle Ann. "Conversations with YA Novelist M. E. Kerr." *Children's Literature* 35 (2007): 191–97. Ebsco.

———. "From Cold War Lesbian Pulp to Contemporary Young Adult Novels: Vin Packer's *Spring Fire*, M.E. Kerr's *Deliver Us from Evie*, and Marijane Meaker's Fight against Fifties Homophobia." *Children's Literature Association Quarterly* 32 (2007): 231–51. Print.

Agee, Jane M. "Mothers and Daughters: Gender-role Socialization and Two Newbery Award Books." *Children's Literature in Education* 24 (1993): 165–83. Ebsco.

Alexie, Sherman. *The Absolutely True Diary of a Part-Time Indian*. Ellen Forney, Illus. New York: Little, Brown, 2007. Print.

Alsup, Janet. "Politicizing Young Adult Literature: Reading Anderson's *Speak* as a Critical Text." *Journal of Adolescent and Adult Literacy* 47 (2003): 158–66. Ebsco.

American Library Association. "Frequently Challenged Books of the 21st Century." October 8, 2012. ala.org/bbooks/frequentlychallengedbooks/top 10. Website.

Anderson, Laurie. *Speak*. New York: Penguin, 2001 (1999). Print.

———. http://madwomaninthissforest.com/. Website.

"Anti-Christian Charges Prompt Review of *Part-Time Indian*." *American Libraries Magazine*. October 8, 2013. americanlibrariesmagazine.org. Website.

Applebee, Arthur N. *Literature in the Secondary School: Studies of Curriculum and Instruction in the United States*. Urbana, IL: NCTE, 1993. Print.

———. *A Study of Book-Length Works Taught in High School English Courses*. Albany: Center for the Learning and Teaching of Literature, 1989. Print.

Appleyard, J.A. *Becoming a Reader: The Experience of Fiction from Childhood to Adulthood*. Cambridge: Cambridge University Press, 1990. Print.

Avi. "Lois Lowry's *The Giver*." In Karolides. 173–75.

Ballis, Stacey. "Forever … Again." In O'Connell. 101–12. Print.

Barker, Jani L. "Racial Identification and Audience in *Roll of Thunder, Hear My Cry* and *The Watsons Go to Birmingham—1963*." *Children's Literature in Education* 41 (2010): 118–45. Ebsco.

Beach, Richard. "Students' Resistance to Engagement with Multicultural Literature."

Beach, Richard, Deborah Appleman, Susan Hynds, and Jeffrey Wilhelm. *Teaching Literature to Adolescents*. Mahwah, NJ: Lawrence Erlbaum, 2006. Print.

Bengal, Rebecca. "Cover Girls." *Print* 62 (2008): 60–65. Ebsco.

Bhroin, Clara Ni. "Cynical or Compassionate? The Young Adult Novels of Robert Cormier." *Journal of Children's Literature Studies* 2 (2004): 23–32. Print.

Blume, Judy. *Are You There God? It's Me, Margaret*. New York: Random House. 1988 (1970). Print.

Bibliography

———. *Blubber*. New York: Random House, 1986 (1974). Print.

———. *Forever*. New York: Simon & Schuster, 1976 (1975). Print.

———. "Judy Blume Talks About Writing *Blubber*." *Blubber*. New York: Random House, 1986 (1974), NP. Print.

———. *Then Again, Maybe I Won't*. New York: Random House, 2003 (1976). Print.

———. *Tiger Eyes*. New York: Random House, 1981. Print.

Bosmajian, Hamida. "Mildred Taylor's Story of Cassie Logan: A Search for Law and Justice in a Racist Society." *Children's Literature* 24 (1996): 141–60. Ebsco.

Boyd, Fenice B., and Nancy M. Bailey. "Censorship in Three Metaphors." *Journal of Adolescent and Adult Literacy* 52 (2009): 653–61. Ebsco.

Bradford, Clare. "Reading Indigeneity: The Ethics of Interpretation and Representation." *Handbook of Research on Children's and Young Adult Literature*. Ed. Shelby A. Wolf, Karen Coats, Patricia Enciso, and Christine A. Jenkins. New York: Routledge, 2011. 331–42. Print.

———. *Unsettling Narratives: Postcolonial Readings of Children's Literature*. Waterloo, ON: Wilfrid Laurier University Press, 2007. Print.

Bradford, Clare, and Raffaella Baccolini. "Journeying Subjects: Spatiality and Identity in Children's Texts." *Contemporary Children's Literature and Film*. Ed. Kerry Mallan and Clare Bradford. New York: Palgrave Macmillan, 2011. 36–56. Print.

Brooks, Wanda, and Gregory Hampton. "Safe Discussions Rather Than First Hand Encounters: Adolescents Examine Racism Through One Historical Fiction Text." *Children's Literature in Education* 36 (2005): 83–98. Ebsco.

Burke, James. *The English Teacher's Companion*. New York: Heinemann, 2007. Print.

Burress, Lee. *Battle of the Books: Literary Censorship in the Public Schools, 1950–1985*. Metuchen, NJ: Scarecrow, 1989. Print.

Bushman, John H., and Kay Parks Haas. *Using Young Adult Literature in the Classroom*. 3rd ed. Upper Saddle River, NJ: Prentice-Hall, 2001. Print.

Cabot, Meg. "Cry, Linda, Cry." In O'Connell. 65–77. Print.

Cadden, Mike. "The Irony of Narration in the Young Adult Novel." *Children's Literature Association Quarterly* 25 (2000): 146–54. Ebsco.

Cairns, Sue Ann. "Power, Language, and Literacy in *The Great Gilly Hopkins*." *Children's Literature in Education* 39 (2008): 9–19. Ebsco.

Campbell, Patty. "*The Outsiders*, Fat Freddy, and Me." *Horn Book* 79 (2003): 177–83. Ebsco.

Cart, Michael. "Naming Names." *Booklist*. March 15, 2009. 53. Ebsco.

Cart, Michael, and Christine Jenkins. *The Heart Has Its Reasons: Young Adult Literature with Gay/Lesbian/Queer Content, 1969–2004*. Lanham, MD: Scarecrow, 2006.

Carter, Betty. "Eyes Wide Open." Interview with Chris Crutcher. *School Library Journal* 46 (2000): 42–45. Ebsco.

Chaston, Joel. "The Blue Tortoise Tattoo: The Quixotic Reader in *Jacob Have I Loved*." *The Image of the Child*. Battle Creek: Children's Literature Association, 1991: 100–06. Print.

———. "The Other Deaths in *Bridge to Terabithia*." *Children's Literature Association Quarterly* 16 (1991): 238–41. Print.

Chauncey, George. *Gay New York: Gender, Urban Culture, and the Making of the Gay Male World, 1890–1940*. New York: HarperCollins, 1994. Print.

Cormier, Robert. *Beyond the Chocolate War*. New York: Dell, 1986 (1985). Print.

———. *The Chocolate War*. New York: Dell, 1986 (1974). Print.

Crisp, Thomas. "From Romance to Magical Realism: Limits and Possibilities in Gay Adolescent Fiction." *Children's Literature in Education* 40 (2009): 333–48. Print.

Crowe, Chris. *More Than a Game: Sports Literature for Young Adults*. Lanham, MD: Scarecrow, 2004. Print.

———. *Presenting Mildred Taylor*. New York: Twayne, 1999.

———. "Running with, Not from, *Running Loose*." *Censored Books II: Critical Viewpoints, 1985–2000*. Ed. Nicholas J. Karolides. Lanham, MD: Scarecrow, 2002. 357–65. Print.

———. "A Tribute to Katherine Paterson." *World Literature Today* 82 (2008): 28–30. Print.

Crutcher, Chris. *Angry Management*. New York: Greenwillow, 2009. Print.

———. *Athletic Shorts*. New York: Greenwillow, 1991. Print.

———. *Chinese Handcuffs*. New York: Greenwillow, 1989. Print.

———. *The Crazy Horse Electric Game*. New York: Greenwillow, 1987. (Harper Tempest, 2003). Print.

———. *Deadline*. New York: Greenwillow, 2007. Print.

———. *Ironman*. New York: Greenwillow, 1995. Print.

———. *King of the Mild Frontier*. New York: Harper Collins, 2003. Print.

———. *Period 8*. New York: Greenwillow, 2013. E-book.

———. *Running Loose*. New York: Greenwillow, 1983. Print.

———. *Stotan!* New York: Greenwillow, 1986. Print.

———. *The Sledding Hill*. New York: Greenwillow, 2005. Print.

———. *Staying Fat for Sarah Byrnes*. New York: Greenwillow, 1993. Print.

———. *Whale Talk*. New York: HarperCollins, 2001. Print.

Cummins, June. "Where in America Are You, God? Judy Blume, Margaret Simon, and American National Identity." *The Oxford Handbook of Children's Literature*. Ed. Julia L. Mickenberg and Lynn Vallone. New York: Oxford, 2011. 351–69. Print.

Curry, Renee. "I Aint No FRIGGIN' LITTLE WIMP: The Girl 'I' Narrator in Contemporary Fiction." *The Girl: Constructions of The Girl in Contemporary Fiction by Women*. Ed. Ruth O. Saxton. New York: St. Martin's Press, 1998. Print.

Daly, Jay. *Presenting S. E. Hinton*. Boston: Twayne, 1989. Print.

Davis, James. "Censorship and the Young Adult Novel." *Reading Their World: The Young Adult Novel in the Classroom*. Ed. Virginia Monseau and Gary Salvner. Portsmouth, NH: Boynton/Cook, 1992: 168–82. Print.

Davis, Kyra. "Are You Available God? My Family Needs Counseling." In O'Connell. 187–98. Print.

Davis, Tanita, and Sarah Stevenson. "Sherman Alexie." *Conversations with Sherman Alexie*. Ed. Nancy J. Peterson. Jackson: University Press of Mississippi, 2009. 187–91. Print.

Davis, Terry. "A Healing Vision." *The English Journal* 85 (1996): 36–41. Print.

———. *Presenting Chris Crutcher*. New York: Twayne, 1997. Print.

Davis-Undiano, Robert Con. "Mildred D. Taylor and the Art of Making a Difference." *World Literature Today* 78 (2004): 11–13.

DelFattore, Joan. *What Johnny Shouldn't Read: Textbook Censorship in America*. New Haven: Yale University Press, 1992. Print.

Detora, Lisa. "Coming of Age in Suburbia: Consumer Goods and Identity Formation in Recent Young Adult Novels. *Modern Language Studies* 36 (2006): 24–35. Ebsco.

Doyle, Robert P. *Banned Books*. Chicago: American Library Association, 2007. Print.

Duke, Charles. "Judy Blume's *Tiger Eyes*: A Perspective on Fear and Death." *Censored Books II*. Ed. Nicholas Karolides. Lanham, MD: Scarecrow, 2002. 414–18. Print.

Bibliography

Enciso, Patricia E. "Negotiating the Meaning of Different: Talking Back to Multicultural Literature." *Reading Across Cultures: Teaching Literature in a Diverse Society*. Ed. Theresa Rogers and Anna O. Soter. New York: Teachers College Press, 1997. 13–41. Print.

Foerstel, Herbert N. *Banned in the U.S.A.: A Reference Guide to Book Censorship in Schools and Public Libraries*. New York: Greenwood, 2002. Print.

Fuoss, Kirk. "A Portrait of the Adolescent as a Young Gay: The Politics of Male Homosexuality in Young Adult Fiction." *Queer Words, Queer Images: Communication and the Construction of Homosexuality*. Ed. R. Jeffrey Ringer. New York: New York University Press, 1994. 159–74. Print.

George, Jean Craighead. *Julie*. New York: Harper Trophy. 1994 (1996). Print.

———. *Julie of the Wolves*. New York: Harper Trophy. 1972 (2003). Print.

———. *Julie's Wolf Pack*. New York. Harper Trophy. 1997 (1998). Print.

———. "Newbery Award Acceptance." *Horn Book* (1973): 337–51. Print.

———. "Summer and Children and Birds and Animals and Flowers and Trees and Bees and Books." *Horn Book*. http://www.hbook.com/2012/05/authors-illustrators/summer-and-children-and-birds-and-animals-and-flowers-and-trees-and-bees-and-books/. August 26, 2010. Website.

Gillis, Bryan, and Pam B. Cole. *Chris Crutcher: A Stotan for Young Adults*. Lanham, MD: Scarecrow, 2012. Print.

Goforth, Caroline. "The Role of the Island in *Jacob Have I Loved*." *Children's Literature Association Quarterly* 9 (1984): 176–8. Print.

Grassian, Daniel. *Understanding Sherman Alexie*. Columbia: University of South Carolina Press, 2005. Print.

Gross, Melissa. "*The Giver* and *Shade's Children*: Future Views of Child Abandonment and Murder." *Children's Literature in Education* 30 (1999): 103–17. Ebsco.

Hanson, Carter. "The Utopian Function of Memory in Lois Lowry's *The Giver*." *Extrapolation* 50 (2009): 45–60. Ebsco.

Harper, Mary Turner. "Merger and Metamorphosis in the Fiction of Mildred D. Taylor." *Children's Literature Association Quarterly* 13 (1988): 75–80. Print.

Head, Patricia. "Robert Cormier and the Postmodernist Possibilities of Young Adult Fiction." *Children's Literature Association Quarterly* 21 (1996): 28–33. Print.

Hendershot, Judy, and Jackie Peck. "An Interview with Lois Lowry, 1994 Newbery Medal Winner." *Reading Teacher* 48 (1994): 308–9. Ebsco.

Hill, Christine M. "Laurie Halse Anderson Speaks: An Interview." *VOYA* 23 (2000): 325. Ebsco.

Hinton, S. E. *The Outsiders*. New York: Viking, 1995 (1967). Print.

Hintz, Carrie. "Monica Hughes, Lois Lowry, and Young Adult Dystopias." *The Lion and the Unicorn* 26 (2002): 254–64. Ebsco.

Hintz, Carrie, and Elaine Ostry. "Interview with Lois Lowry, Author of *The Giver*." *Utopian and Dystopian Writing for Children and Young Adults*. Ed. Carrie Hintz and Elaine Ostry. New York: Routledge, 2003. 196–9. Print.

Hirsch, Susan M. "*Bridge to Terabithia*: Too Good to Miss." *Censored Books II: Critical Viewpoints, 1985–2000*. Ed. Nicholas J. Karolides. Lanham, MD: Scarecrow, 2002. 100–6. Print.

Hubler, Angela E. "Beyond the Image: Adolescent Girls, Reading, and Social Reality." *NWSA Journal* 12 (2000): 84–99. Ebsco.

Huse, Nancy. "Katherine Paterson's Ultimate Realism." *Children's Literature Association Quarterly* 9 (1984): 99–101. Print.

Inderbitzin, Michelle. "Outsiders and Justice Consciousness." *Contemporary Justice Review* 6 (2003): 357–62. Ebsco.

Bibliography

Iskander, Sylvia Patterson. "Readers, Realism and Robert Cormier." *Children's Literature* 15 (1987): 7–18. Ebsco.

Jenkins, Christine. "Censorship." *Handbook of Research on Children's and Young Adult Literature*. Ed. Shelby A. Wolf, Karen Coats, Patricia Enciso, and Christine A. Jenkins. New York: Routledge, 2011. 443–54. Print.

———. "From Queer to Gay and Back Again: Young Adult Novels with Gay/Lesbian/Queer Content, 1969–1997." *Library Quarterly* 68 (1998): 298–334. Project Muse.

Karolides, Nicholas. *Censored Books II*. Lanham, MD: Scarecrow, 2002. Print.

———. "Introduction." *Censored Books: Critical Viewpoints*. Metuchen, NJ: Scarecrow, 1993. xiii-xxvi. Print.

Kendrick, Beth. "The Mother of all Balancing Acts." In O'Connell. 199–206. Print.

Kenner, Julie. "Vitamin K, Judy Blume, and the Great Big Bruise." In O'Connell. 124- 35. Print.

Kerr, M.E. *Deliver Us from Evie*. New York: HarperCollins, 1995 (1994). Print.

———. "Foreword." *Hearing Us Out: Voices from the Gay and Lesbian Community*. Ed. Roger Sutton. New York: Little, Brown, 1994. viii-xv. Print.

Kertzer, Adrienne. "Not Exactly: Intertextual Identities and Risky Laughter in Sherman Alexie's *The Absolutely True Diary of a Part-Time Indian*." *Children's Literature* 40 (2012): 49–77. Print.

Kidd, Kenneth. "Prizing Children's Literature: The Case of Newbery Gold." *Children's Literature* 35 (2007): 166–90. Ebsco.

Krasner, Jonathan, and Joellyn Zollman. "*Are You There God?* Judaism and Jewishness in Judy Blume's Adolescent Fiction." *Shofar* 29 (2010): 22–47. Ebsco.

Kuznets, Lois R. "The Female Pastoral Journey in *Julie of the Wolves* and *A Wild Thing*." *Webs and Wardrobes:*

Humanist and Religious World Views in Children's Literature. Ed. Joseph O'Beirne Milner and Lucy Floyd Morcock Milner. Lanham, MD: University Press of America, 1987. 99–110. Print.

Latham, Don. "Childhood Under Siege: Lois Lowry's *Number the Stars* and *The Giver*." *The Lion and the Unicorn* 26 (2002): 1–15. Ebsco.

———. "Discipline and Its Discontents: A Foucauldian Reading of *The Giver*." *Children's Literature* 32 (2004): 134–51. Ebsco.

———. "Melinda's Closet: Trauma and the Queer Subtext of Laurie Halse Anderson's *Speak*." *Children's Literature Association Quarterly* 31 (2006): 369–82. Print.

Lea, Susan G. "Seeing Beyond Sameness: Using *The Giver* to Challenge Colorblind Ideology." *Children's Literature in Education* 37 (2006): 51–67. Ebsco.

Lehman, Barbara A., and Patricia R. Crook. "Doubletalk: A Literary Pairing of *The Giver* and *We are All in the Dumps with Jack and Guy*." *Children's Literature in Education* 29 (1998): 69–78. Ebsco.

L'Engle, Madeleine. "Do I Dare Disturb the Universe?" *Innocence and Experience: Essays and Conversations on Children's Literature*. Ed. Barbara Harrison and Gregory Maguire. New York: Lothrop, Lee & Shepard, 1987. 215–23. Print.

Levithan, David. *Boy Meets Boy*. New York: Knopf, 2005 (2003). Print.

Levithan, David, and John Green. *Will Grayson, Will Grayson*. New York: Dutton, 2010. Print.

Levy, Michael M. "Lois Lowry's *The Giver*: Interrupted Bildungsroman or Ambiguous Dystopia?" *Foundation* 70 (1997): 50-7. Ebsco.

Lickteig, Mary. "*Julie of the Wolves* and *Dogsong*: The Cultural Conflict Between the Inuits and the Dominant American Culture." *Cross Culturalisms in Children's Literature. Selected Papers*

Bibliography

from the International Conference of the Children's Literature Association. Ed. Susan R. Gannon and Ruth Anne Thompson. New York: Pace University Press, 1987. 83–86. Print.

Lowry, Lois. *Gathering Blue*. New York: Dell, 2002 (2000). Print.

_____. *The Giver*. New York: Dell, 2002 (1993). Print.

_____. "Lois Lowry." *Instructor* 117 (1999). 72. Ebsco.

_____. *Messenger*. New York: Houghton Mifflin, 2012 (2006). Print.

_____. "Newbery Medal Acceptance." *Horn Book* 70 (1994). NP. Ebsco.

_____. *Son*. New York: Houghton Mifflin, 2012. Print.

MacCann, Donnarae. "The Family Chronicles of Mildred D. Taylor and Mary E Mebane." *Journal of African Children's & Youth Literature* 3 (1991): 93–104. Ebsco.

MacLeod, Anne Scott. *American Childhood: Essays on Children's Literature of the Nineteenth and Twentieth Centuries*. Athens: University of Georgia Press, 1994. Print.

Malone, Michael. "Tough Puppies." *The Nation*. March 8, 1986. 276–80. Ebsco.

Manning, Jimmie, Jacqueline McNally, and Stephanie Verst. "Questioning the Self, Questioning Others, Questioning Relationships: A Qualitative Inquiry into the Pedagogical Value of Judy Blume." *MP* 1 (2007): 7–15. Ebsco.

Martin, Michelle H. "Exploring the Works of Mildred Taylor: An Approach to Teaching The Logan Family Novels." *Teaching and Learning Literature* 7 (1998): 5–13.

_____. "Let Freedom Ring: Land, Liberty, Literacy, and Lore in Mildred Taylor's Logan Family Novels." *The Oxford Handbook of Children's Literature*. Ed. Julia L. Mickenberg and Lynn Vallone. New York: Oxford, 2011. 371–88. Print.

_____. "Periods, Parody, and Polyphony: Fifty Years of Menstrual Education Through Fiction and Film." *Children's Literature Association Quarterly* 22 (1997): 21–29. Print.

McCafferty, Megan. "Then. Now. Forever…" In O'Connell. 1–15. Print.

McGee, Chris. "Why Won't Melinda Just Talk about What Happened? *Speak* and the Confessional Voice." *Children's Literature Association Quarterly* 34 (2009): 172–87. Print.

Meaker, Marijane. *Highsmith: A Romance of the 1950s*. San Francisco: Cleis, 2003. Print.

Mellis, James. "Interview with Sherman Alexie." *Conversations with Sherman Alexie*. Ed. Nancy J. Peterson. Jackson: University Press of Mississippi, 2009. 180–86. Print.

Misheff, Sue. "Beneath the Web and Over the Stream: The Search for Safe Places in *Charlotte's Web* and *Bridge to Terabithia*." *Children's Literature in Education* 29 (1998): 131–41. Ebsco.

Miskec, Jennifer, and Chris McGee. "My Scars Tell a Story: Self-Mutilation in Young Adult Literature." *Children's Literature Association Quarterly* 32 (2007): 163–78. Print.

Moore, Opal, and Donnarae MacCann. "The Ignoble Savage: Amerind Images in the Mainstream Mind." *Children's Literature Association Quarterly* 13 (Spring 1988): 26–30. Print.

National Council of Teachers of English. "Guideline on the Students' Right to Read." http://www.ncte.org/positions/statements/righttoreadguideline. August 26, 2011. Website.

Nelson, Joshua B. "'Humor is My Green Card': A Conversation with Sherman Alexie." *World Literature Today* (2010) 84: 38–43. Print.

Nikolajeva, Maria. "Toward a Genuine Narrative Voice." *Bookbird* 42 (2004): 13–18. Ebsco.

Nilsen, Alleen Pace. "M.E. Kerr: Awakening Her Readers." *Para*Doxa* 2 (1996): 494–505. Print.

———. *Presenting M.E. Kerr*. New York: Twayne, 1997. Print.

Noll, Elizabeth. "The Ripple Effect of Censorship: Silencing in the Classroom." *English Journal* 83 (1994): 59–64. Ebsco.

O'Connell, Jennifer, ed. *Everything I Needed to Know About Being a Girl I Learned from Judy Blume*. New York: Pocket, 2007. Print.

Ohanian, Susan. "Foreword." *At the Schoolhouse Gate: Lessons in Intellectual Freedom*. Portsmouth, NH: Heinemann, 2002. i-xviii. Print.

Oneal, Zibby. "'They Tell You to Do Your Own Thing, But They Don't Mean It': Censorship and *The Chocolate War*." *Censored Books: Critical Viewpoints*. Ed. N. J. Karolides, L. Burress and J. M. Kean. Metuchen, NJ: Scarecrow, 1993. 179–90. Print.

Patterson, Katherine. *Bridge to Terabithia*. New York: HarperCollins, 1996 (1977). Print.

———. "Fighting the Long Defeat." *World Literature Today* 82 (2008): 19–24. Ebsco.

———. *The Great Gilly Hopkins*. New York: HarperCollins, 1987 (1978). Print.

———. *The Invisible Child*. New York: Dutton, 2001. Print.

———. *Jacob Have I Loved*. New York: HarperCollins, 1990 (1980). Print.

———. "Up from Elsie Dinsmore." *Gates of Excellence*. New York: Dutton, 1981. 99–108. Print.

———. "Where Is Terabithia?" *Children's Literature Association Quarterly* 9 (1984): 153–57. Print.

Pearlman, M. "The Role of Socioeconomic Status in Adolescent Literature." *Adolescence* 30 (1995): 223–31. Ebsco.

Pipkin, Gloria, ReLeah Cossett Lent. *At the Schoolhouse Gate: Lessons in Intellectual Freedom*. Portsmouth, NH: Heinemann, 2002. Book.

Quarles, Heather, and Suzanne M. Wolfe. "A Conversation with Katherine Paterson." *Image* 13 (1996): 49–63. Ebsco.

Reach, Kirsten. "Sherman Alexie and Laurie Halse Anderson Address Censorship." October 8, 2013. mhpbooks.com/Sherman-alexie-and-laurie-halse-anderson-address-censsorhip/. Website.

"Richland Schools Rescind Ban of Sherman Alexie Novel." *American Libraries Magazine*. October 8, 2013. americanlibrariesmagazine.org. Website.

Rogers, Theresa, and Anna O. Soter. *Reading Across Cultures: Teaching Literature in a Diverse Society*. New York: Teachers College, 1997. 69–94. Print.

Russell, Connie. "In Defense of *Gilly*." *Censored Books II: Critical Viewpoints, 1985-2000*. Ed. Nicholas J. Karolides. Lanham, MD: Scarecrow, 2002. 182–6. Print.

Scales, Pat. "Mildred Taylor: Keeper of Stories." *Language Arts* 80 (2003): 240–44. Proquest.

———. *Teaching Banned Books*. Chicago: American Library Association. 2001. Print.

Schmidt, Gary. *Katherine Paterson*. New York: Twayne, 1994. Print.

Schwartz, Shelia. *Teaching Adolescent Literature: A Humanistic Approach*. Rochelle Park, NJ: Hayden, 1979. Print.

Semonche, John E. *Censoring Sex: A Historical Journey through American Media*. Lanham, MD: Rowman & Littlefield, 2007. Print.

"Sherman Alexie Talks to NCAS's the Write Stuff About Being Banned." National Coalition Against Censorship. ncacblog.wordpress.com. October 8, 2013. Website.

Sherrill, Anne. "Julie-Miyax: The Emergence of Dual Identity in *Julie of the Wolves* and *Julie*." Ed. Nicholas Karolides. *Censored Books II: Critical Viewpoints, 1985-2000*. Lanham, MD: Scarecrow, 2002. 269–78. Print.

Siegel, R.A. "Are You There, God? It's Me, Me, ME! Judy Blume's Self Absorbed Narrators." *The Lion and the Unicorn* 2 (1978): 72–77. Ebsco.

Bibliography

Smedman, M. Sarah. "Out of the Depths to Joy: Spirit/Soul in Juvenile Novels." *Triumphs of the Spirit in Children's Literature*. Ed. Francelia Butler and Richard Rotert. Hamden, CT: Library Professional Publishers, 1986. 181–97. Print.

———. "Springs of Hope: Recovery of Primordial Time in 'Mythic' Novels of Young Readers." *Children's Literature* 16 (188): 91–107. Ebsco.

Smith, Karen Patricia. "A Chronicle of Family Honor: Balancing Rage and Triumph in The Novels of Mildred D. Taylor." *African-American Voices in Young Adult Literature: Tradition, Transition, Transformation*. Ed. Patricia Smith. Metuchen, NJ: Scarecrow, 1994. 247–76.

———. "Literary Pilgrimage to the Gates of Excellence." *Bookbird* 36 (1988): 6–10. Print.

Sommers, Joseph. "Are You There, Reader? It's Me, Margaret: A Reconsideration of Judy Blume's Prose as Sororal Dialogism." *Children's Literature Association Quarterly* 33 (2008): 258–79. Print.

Spring, Albert. *M.E. Kerr*. New York: Rosen, 2006. Print.

Stewart, Susan Louse. "A Return to Normal: Lois Lowry's *The Giver*." *The Lion and the Unicorn* 31 (2007): 21–35. Ebsco.

Stott, Jon C. "Jean George's Arctic Pastoral: A Reading of *Julie of the Wolves*." *Children's Literature: The Great Excluded*. Vol. 3. Ed. Francelia Butler and Bennett A. Brockman. Storrs, CT: Children's Literature Association, 1974: 131–9. Print.

Sullivan, Faith. "Protecting Them from What? In Praise of *Blubber*." *Censored Books II*. Ed. Nicholas Karolides. Lanham, MD: Scarecrow, 2002. 80–86. Print.

Sweeney, Patricia Runk. "Self-Discovery and Rediscovery in the Novels of M.E. Kerr." *The Lion and the Unicorn* 2 (1978): 37–43. Ebsco.

Tannert-Smith, Barbara. "'Like Falling Up into a Storybook': Trauma and Intertextual Repetition in Laurie Halse Anderson's *Speak*." *Children's Literature Association Quarterly* 35 (2010): 395–414. Ebsco.

Tarr, C. Anita. "The Absence of Moral Agency in Robert Cormier's *The Chocolate War*." *Children's Literature* 30 (2002): 96–124. Ebsco.

Taylor, Christopher. "North America as Contact Zone: Native American Literary Nationalism and the Cross-Cultural Dilemma." *Studies in American Indian Literatures* 22 (2010): 26–44. Print.

Taylor, Mildred. *The Friendship*. New York: Dial, 1987. Print.

———. *The Gold Cadillac*. New York: Dial, 1987. Print.

———. *The Land*. New York: Dial, 2001. Print.

———. *Let the Circle Be Unbroken*. New York: Puffin, 1991 (1981). Print.

———. *Mississippi Bridge*. New York: Dial, 1990. Print.

———. "My Life as a Writer." *World Literature Today* 78 (2004): 7–10. Ebsco.

———. "Newbery Award Acceptance." *The Horn Book* 53 (1977): 401–09. Ebsco.

———. *The Road to Memphis*. New York: Puffin, 1992 (1990). Print.

———. *Roll of Thunder, Hear My Cry*. New York: Puffin, 1991 (1976). Print.

———. *Song of the Trees*. New York: Dial, 1975. Print.

———. *The Well*. New York: Dial, 1995. Print.

Thompson, Dawn. "Educational Decisions: 'Traplines' in *The Absolutely True Diary of a Part-Time Indian*." *Knowing Their Place? Identity and Space in Children's Literature*. Ed. Terri Doughty and Dawn Thompson. Newcastle upon Tyne: Cambridge Scholars, 2011. 63–79. Print.

———. "Prussic Acid with a Twist: *The Well of Loneliness*, M.E. Kerr, and

Bibliography

Young Adult Readers." *Children's Literature Association Quarterly* 31 (2006): 282–99. Print.

"Top 100 Banned/Challenged Books: 200–2009." American Library Association. http://www.ala.org/advocacy/banned/frequentlychallenged/challengedbydecade/2000_2009. Sept. 6, 2012. Website.

Totaro, Rebecca Carol Noel. "Suffering in Utopia: Testing the Limits in Young Adult Novels." *Utopian and Dystopian Writing for Children and Young Adults.* Ed. Carrie Hintz and Elie Ostry. New York: Routledge, 2003. 127–38. Print.

Tribunella, Eric. "Institutionalizing *The Outsiders*: YA Literature, Social Class, and the American Faith in Education." *Children's Literature in Education* 38 (2007): 87–101. Ebsco.

Trites, Roberta Seelinger. *Disturbing the Universe: Power and Repression in Adolescent Literature.* Iowa City: University of Iowa Press, 2000. Print.

———. *Waking Sleeping Beauty.* Iowa City: Iowa University Press, 1997. Print.

Tyree, Michael. "West Bend Community Memorial Library." American Library Association Conference. July 13, 2009. Ebsco.

Van Horne, Geneva. "*Julie of the Wolves* by Jean Craighead George." *Censored Books: Critical Viewpoints.* Ed. N. J. Karolides, L. Burress and J. M. Kean. Metuchen, NJ: Scarecrow, 1993. 338–42. Print.

Veglahn, Nancy. "The Bland Face of Evil in the Novels of Robert Cormier." *The Lion and the Unicorn* 12 (1988): 12–18. Ebsco.

Washick, James. "Terabithian Shadow: Death and Narnian Theology in Paterson's *Bridge to Terabithia.*" *The Lamp-Post* 23 (1999): 3–7. Ebsco.

Weidt, Maryann. *Presenting Judy Blume.* Boston: Twayne, 1990. Print.

Winstead, Ed. "Sherman Alexie: The Value of Subverting Authority." *Guernica.* October 5, 2012. gurenicamag.com. October 8, 2013. Website.

Yoshida, Junko. "The Quest for Masculinity in *The Chocolate War*: Changing Conceptions of Masculinity in the 1970s." *Children's Literature* 26 (1998): 105–22. Ebsco.

Youngberg, Quentin. "Interpenetrations: Re-encoding the Queer Indian in Sherman Alexie's *The Business of Fancydancing.*" *Studies in American Indian Literatures* 20 (2008): 55–75. Print.

Index

The Absolutely True Diary of a Part-Time Indian 2, 150–66
African American 69, 91, 101, 108, 110, 153, 173 *preface*n1
alcoholism 134, 151–52, 155, 157, 162, 164
Alexie, Sherman 2, 138, 150–66, 171–72, 177*ch*12*n*, 178*ch*12*n*3; *The Absolutely True Diary of a Part-Time Indian* 2, 150–66; Native American 45, 150, 152–56, 158, 160–62, 164–65
American Library Association 2, 7, 24, 38, 47, 80, 115, 125, 128, 138, 150, 151, 171
Anderson, Laurie Halse 2, 16, 138–49, 162, 171–72; *Speak* 2, 70, 138–49, 155, 159, 162–63
Angry Management 89, 175*ch*7*n*1
Are You There God? It's Me, Margaret 1, 20, 27–31, 37, 174*ch*3*n*1
art 19, 61–62, 64–66, 121, 142, 145, 146–48, 155–56, 159, 163, 165, 170
Athletic Shorts 2, 80, 89–92, 175*ch*7*n*1–2

banned and challenged books 1–3, 7, 15, 24, 32, 34, 38, 47, 57, 67, 80–82, 88–89, 101, 115–16, 138–39, 150, 159, 167–68, 171–72, 174*ch*2*n*1, 175*ch*7*n*2
Beach, Richard 9, 102
bildungsroman 27, 44, 124, 155, 157
Blubber 24, 32–34, 36
Blume, Judy 1, 16, 24–37, 155; *Are You There God? It's Me, Margaret* 1, 20, 27–31, 37, 174*ch*3*n*1; *Blubber* 24, 32–34, 36; *Forever* 34–36; *Then Again, Maybe I Won't* 29, 31–32, 36; *Tiger Eyes* 1, 36–37
Boy Meets Boy 137
Bradford, Claire 48, 153–54, 159, 162, 164
Bridge to Terabithia 2, 57, 60–67, 72, 75, 95, 155–56, 163
bullying 32–33, 37, 51, 53, 56, 84, 94, 97, 98, 142, 147, 162

Cadden, Mike 50, 139
Cart, Michael 47, 51, 125, 128, 136–37, 174*ch*2*n*2
Chinese Handcuffs 88–89, 93
The Chocolate War 2, 19, 47–56, 117, 143, 156, 174*ch*2*n*1, 175*ch*5*n*1

Christianity 29, 57–58, 60, 68, 96, 151
coaches 80–81, 83–84, 86–89, 92–95, 98, 161, 163
community members' role: in censorship 1, 6, 9, 11, 39, 128, 149, 151, 172; in literature 61, 73–74, 97, 101, 106–9, 113, 115–24, 134, 153, 158, 160, 162, 164, 175*ch*8*n*1
Cormier, Robert 2, 36–37, 47–56, 58, 117, 175*ch*6*n*1; *The Chocolate War* 2, 19, 47–56, 117, 143, 156, 174*ch*2*n*1, 175*ch*5*n*1
court cases 11, 173*ch*1*n*1
The Crazy Horse Electric Game 87–88
Crowe, Chris 72, 83, 85, 101, 113–14
Crutcher, Chris 2, 5, 26, 36–37, 50, 58, 80–99, 101, 116–17, 124, 138, 141, 152, 161–62, 171–72, 175*n*1–2; *Angry Management* 89, 175*ch*7*n*1; *Athletic Shorts* 2, 80, 89–92, 175*ch*7*n*1–2; *Chinese Handcuffs* 88–89, 93; *The Crazy Horse Electric Game* 87–88; *Deadline* 97–98, 175*ch*7*n*1; *Ironman* 2, 80, 93–94, 175*ch*7*n*1; *King of the Mild Frontier* 80, 89–90, 92, 94; *Period 8* 175*ch*7*n*1; *Running Loose* 2, 80–86, 88, 91, 93, 98; *The Sledding Hill* 95–97, 175*ch*7*n*1; *Staying Fat for Sarah Byrnes* 2, 80, 92–93, 175 *ch*7*n*1; *Stotan!* 86–87; *Whale Talk* 2, 80–81, 94–95, 117

Davis, James 7, 9–10, 13
Davis, Terry 81, 86–89, 93, 95
Deadline 97–98, 175*ch*7*n*1
DelFattore, Joan 7, 173*ch*1*n*1
Deliver Us from Evie 2, 125–37, 155, 157
disrespect 37, 61, 67, 80, 96, 98
Doyle, Herbert 11, 173*ch*1*n*1
dystopia 2, 115, 117, 119, 121, 123–24, 176*ch*9*n*1

First Amendment 11, 172, 173*ch*1*n*1,
Foerstal, Herbert 5, 10, 11, 47, 56, 173*ch*1*n*1
food 31, 40, 42, 105, 119, 142, 144, 160, 165
Forever 34–36
friendship 28, 31, 36, 41, 59–60, 62, 66, 77–78, 79, 85, 105–6, 118, 122, 127, 138, 140, 143, 147, 149, 155, 157, 159, 161–66, 172

gender 18–19, 23, 44–46, 55, 62, 73–75, 104–5, 107, 127–28, 133, 135, 139–40, 167

Index

George, Jean Craighead 1, 28, 37, 38–46, 174ch4n1–2; Inuit culture 38–41, 43–45, 158; *Julie of the Wolves* 1, 28, 38–46, 158, 174ch4n1–2
The Giver 2, 115–24, 176ch9n1
The Great Gilly Hopkins 2, 57, 67–72

Hinton, S.E. 1, 15–23, 36, 124–25, 155, 174ch2n3; *The Outsiders* 1, 15–23, 155, 173–74ch2n1
Hintz, Carrie 115, 117, 123; with Elaine Ostry 115
homosexuality 89, 96, 126–29, 131–32, 134, 137, 150ch10n2

identity 15, 19, 28–29, 39–41, 48, 50, 62, 74, 104, 116, 126, 131, 133, 140, 146–48, 152–53, 158, 161, 164, 177ch12n1
Ironman 2, 80, 93–94, 175ch7n1

Jacob Have I Loved 2, 57, 72–79, 156
Jenkins, Christine 176–77ch9n2
Julie of the Wolves 1, 28, 38–46, 158, 174ch4n1–2

Kerr, M.E. 2, 125–37; *Deliver Us from Evie* 2, 125–37, 155, 157; lesbian 2, 125–27, 129–30, 132–37, 173prefacen1, 176–77ch10n2–3
Kidd, Kenneth 173prefacen1, 174–75ch4n3
King of the Mild Frontier 80, 89–90, 92, 94
Kuznets, Lois 44–45

Latham, Don 116, 118, 121, 123, 140, 146, 148
lesbianism 2, 125–27, 129–30, 132–37, 173prefacen1, 176–77ch10n2–3
Levithan, David 16, 137, 171; *Boy Meets Boy* 137
librarians' role: in censorship 1, 6–8, 10–11, 13, 47, 58, 149, 169, 171–72, 173; in literature 96–97
Lickteig, Mary 39, 41, 43
Lowry, Lois 2, 115–24, 176ch9n1; *The Giver* 2, 115–24, 176ch9n1

Martin, Michelle 28, 81, 102, 114
masturbation 151, 165
McGee, Chris 140–41, 146, 148
menstrual period 27, 28, 30, 31, 155

Native American 45, 150, 152–56, 158, 160–62, 164–65
Newbery Award 2, 46, 57, 101, 115–16, 123, 173prefacen1, 174ch4n1, 174ch4n3
Nilsen, Alleen Pace 125–127

obesity 32, 68, 71, 92, 90, 95, 106, 127
occult themes 61, 67, 150
offensive language 1, 7, 15, 24, 26, 37, 57, 61, 67, 80, 82, 84, 91, 98, 150
The Outsiders 1, 15–23, 155, 173–74ch2n1

parents' role: in censorship 1, 3, 5, 7–10, 11–14, 23–25, 34, 39, 48–49, 60, 67, 73, 80, 100, 114–15, 139, 149, 151, 169–72; in literature 17, 31–32, 35–36, 52, 64–65, 76–77, 81–90, 93–98, 105, 118, 122, 128, 135, 140–45, 149, 155, 157, 159, 163, 165
Paterson, Katherine 2, 5, 51, 57–79; *Bridge to Terabithia* 2, 57, 60–67, 72, 75, 95, 155–56, 163; *The Great Gilly Hopkins* 2, 57, 67–72; *Jacob Have I Loved* 2, 57, 72–79, 156
Period 8 175ch7n1

racism 3, 7, 10, 37, 89–91, 100–6, 108–9, 113–14, 116, 150–51, 156, 168, 173prefacen1
The Road to Memphis 2, 100–14, 175ch8n1
Running Loose 2, 80–86, 88, 91, 93, 98

Scales, Pat 25, 32, 100–1
Schmidt, Gary 59, 62, 66, 72, 74, 79
Schwartz, Sheila 3, 9
sexism 7, 10, 104
sexual assault 42, 110, 138–39, 142, 148
sexuality 1, 3, 6, 7, 8, 28, 34–37, 42, 44, 52–53, 55, 57, 62, 72, 80, 98, 107–110, 115, 119, 122, 133, 138–39, 150, 152, 156–57, 165, 167
The Sledding Hill 95–97, 175ch7n1
social class 15, 17, 19, 21, 32, 63, 65, 130, 174ch2n1
Speak 2, 70, 138–49, 155, 159, 162–63
sports 62–63, 83–85
Staying Fat for Sarah Byrnes 2, 80, 92–93, 175ch7n1
Stotan! 86–87
"The Students Right to Read" 9
suicide 89, 138, 144–46, 175ch5n1

Taylor, Mildred 2, 26, 58, 100–14, 116, 171, 173ch8n1; *The Road to Memphis* 2, 100–14, 175ch8n1
teachers' role: in censorship 1, 5–14, 26, 37–39, 46–48, 56, 58, 67, 98, 139, 149, 168–72; in literature 32, 53, 63, 65, 68–69, 80–81, 87–88, 92, 96–97, 139–42, 147, 156–57, 162, 175ch7n1
Then Again, Maybe I Won't 29, 31–32, 36
Thompson, Dawn 127, 132, 154
Tiger Eyes 1, 36–37
Tribunella, Eric 15, 17–18, 20, 22, 173ch2n1
Trites, Roberta 25, 28, 48, 53–55, 82, 85, 92–94, 116

violence 15, 17, 23, 93, 100, 124, 138, 149–52, 155, 166, 168

Weidt, Maryann 24–27, 31–32, 34–36, 174ch3n1
Whale Talk 2, 80, 81, 94–95, 117

www.ingramcontent.com/pod-product-compliance
Lightning Source LLC
Chambersburg PA
CBHW032101300426
44116CB00007B/844